VOGEL'S
CROSS REFERENCE AND INDEX
TO THE CONTENTS OF
LUTHER'S WORKS

A Cross Reference between the American Edition
and the St. Louis, Weimar
and Erlangen Editions of Luther's Works

Heinrich J. Vogel

Northwestern Publishing House
Milwaukee, Wisconsin

Library of Congress Card 82-63053
Northwestern Publishing House
3624 W. North Ave., Milwaukee, WI 53208-0902
© 1983 by Northwestern Publishing House, All rights reserved
Published 1983
Printed in the United States of America
ISBN 0-8100-0168-3

CONTENTS

The two indexes above were compiled with computer assistance by John Hartwig, c.r.m., while a senior at Wisconsin Lutheran Seminary, Mequon, Wisconsin. In these indexes L indicates a letter and S a sermon by Luther.

PREFACE

Most references to Luther's works are made to either the Weimar edition (WA), the St. Louis edition (St.L.), or the Erlangen edition (E). Since the completion of the American edition, which is only a selection of Luther's works, the question often arises whether a given reference to the Weimar, St. Louis, or Erlangen editions was included in the American edition, and if so, where.

The purpose of this cross reference is to facilitate finding such references in the American edition. In Part I all of Luther's works included in the American edition are located in the St. Louis, the Weimar, and the Erlangen edition, so that the German or Latin original may be easily found. In Part II, Part III, and Part IV these works are listed in the sequence in which they occur in the St. Louis, the Weimar, and the Erlangen editions respectively, so that references to them may be easily located in the American edition.

In all four parts of this cross reference all works included in the American edition are given in the sequence in which they occur in these four editions. Thus if a reference is not found in the listing of the St. Louis, the Weimar, or the Erlangen edition, it obviously was not included in the American edition.

It is hoped that this compilation of cross references will prove useful to students of Luther's works by enabling them to find the English translation of Luther's German and Latin writings whenever the work in question was included in the American edition.

References to the American edition are made to volume and page.

References to the St. Louis edition are made to volume and column.

References to the Weimar edition are made to volume and page.

References to the German Bible in the Weimar edition are prefixed with *DB*.

References to Luther's letters in the Weimar edition are prefixed with *Br*.

References to the Table Talk in the Weimar edition are prefixed with *TR*.

References to the Erlangen edition are made to the first edition of Luther's German writings unless otherwise designated.

References to Luther's Latin exegetical writings in the Erlangen edition are prefixed with *ex*.

References to Luther's various Latin writings in the Erlangen edition are prefixed with *var*.

3

References to Luther's Latin commentary on Galatians are prefixed with *gal.*

In a few instances where the item was not included in the first edition of the Erlangen edition the reference to the second edition is made and designated with the prefix E_2.

Throughout the cross reference the serial numbers assigned to Luther's Works by Kurt Aland in his *Hilfsbuch zum Lutherstudium* are listed in the left margin. This should facilitate locating the various items in some of the other editions of Luther's selected works to which references are sometimes made.

PART 1

Where works included in the American edition may be found in the St. Louis, the Weimar, and the Erlangen editions

American Edition	St. Louis Edition	Weimar Edition	Erlangen Edition
1, 1-359	1, 1-437	42, 1-263	ex 1, 1-2, 116
2, 1-399	1, 436-921	42, 264-549	ex 2, 116-3, 276
3, 1-365	1, 920-1369	42, 550-673 43, 1-137	ex 3, 277-5, 67
4, 1-409	1, 1368-1765 2, 1-123	43, 137-430	ex 5, 67-6, 243
5, 1-386	2, 122-609	43, 430-695	ex 6, 243-7, 354
6, 1-407	2, 608-1159	44, 1-304	ex 8, 1-9, 162
7, 1-377	2, 1158-1655	44, 304-581	ex 9, 162-10, 313
8, 1-333	2, 1654-2091	44, 581-825	ex 10, 313-11, 325
9, 1-311	3, 1370-1639	14, 489-744	ex 13, 1-351
10, 1-464	(4, 1-1913 — later works on the Psalms)	3, 11-519	
11, 1-553		3, 519-652 4, 1-414	
12, 1-136	5, 74-237	40^{II}, 193-212 45, 205-250	ex 18, 8-127 39, 4-61
12, 139-144	5, 1332-1339	31^{I}, 580-586	
12, 145-194	5, 254-307	51, 267-295 17^{I}, 228-243	39, 61-105 39, 106-122
12, 197-410	5, 340-619	40^{II}, 472-610 315-470	ex 18, 130-260 ex 19, 10-154
13, 1-37	5, 656-695	8, 4-35	39, 178-220
13, 39-72	5, 696-731	31^{I}, 189-218	39, 224-265
13, 73-141	5, 732-799	40^{III}, 484-594	ex 18, 264-334
13, 143-224	5, 800-887	51, 200-264	39, 265-364
13, 225-348	5, 922-1055	41, 79-239	40, 38-192
13, 349-387	5, 1056-1097	31^{I}, 393-426	40, 192-240
13, 389-420	5, 1098-1131	19, 297-336	40, 240-280
14, 1-39	5, 1132-1173	31^{I}, 223-257	40, 290-328
14, 41-106	5, 1174-1251	31^{I}, 65-182	41, 7-91
14, 107-135	5, 1302-1333	31^{I}, 430-456	41, 151-185
14, 137-205	4, 1634-1743	18, 479-530	37, 340-442
14, 207-277	5, 1-75	19, 552-615	38, 369-453

594   Psalms 1 and 2

172   Ecclesiastes

291   Song of Solomon

151   2 Samuel 23:1-7

306   Isaiah 1-39

306   Isaiah 40-66

294   Hosea

312   Joel

 22   Amos

539   Obadiah (1)

505   Micah (2)

529   Nahum

783   Zephaniah (1)

269   Haggai

449   Malachi

347   Jonah (from the Latin text) (2) 1525

348   Jonah (from the German text) (1) 1526

265   Habakkuk (from the Latin Text) (2) 1525

266   Habakkuk (from the German Text) (1) 1526

653   Zechariah (from the Latin text) 1526

654   Zechariah (from the German text) 1527

465   The Sermon on the Mount, Matthew 5, 6, 7

444   The Magnificat

316   John 1-4

318

324   John 6

324   John 7 and 8

328   John 14-16

334

646   Romans

229   Galatians 1-4 (1535)

American Edition	St. Louis Edition	Weimar Edition	Erlangen Edition
14, 279-349	4, 220-301	5, 19-74	ex 14, 1-89
15, 1-187	5, 1372-1579	20, 7-203	ex 21, 1-248
15, 189-264	5, 1580-1659	31^{II}, 586-769	ex 21, 267-368
15, 265-352	3, 1880-1973	54, 28-100	37, 1-104
16, 1-349	6, 8-471	31^{II}, 1-260	ex 22, 9-406
17, 1-416	6, 470-851	31^{II}, 261-585	ex 22, 406-23, 296
18, 1-76	6, 946-1029	13, 1-66	ex 24, 1-88
18, 77-123	6, 1414-1479	13, 88-122	ex 25, 55-125
18, 125-190	6, 1684-1773	13, 158-206	ex 25, 377-481
18, 191-204	14, 808-823	13, 215-223	ex 25, 507-527
18, 205-277	14, 978-983 14, 1178-1257	13, 299-343	ex 26, 149-233
18, 279-315	14, 1332-1373	13, 371-394	ex 27, 61-110
18, 317-364	14, 1604-1657	13, 480-509	ex 27, 61-110
18, 365-387	14, 1708-1733	13, 532-544	ex 27, 283-350
18, 389-419	14, 2158-2195	13, 675-703	ex 28, 287-323
19, 1-31	14, 912-943	13, 241-258	ex 26, 43-76
19, 33-104	14, 836-911	19, 185-251	41, 324-414
19, 105-148	14, 1506-1533	12, 424-448	ex 27, 169-220
19, 149-237	14, 1416-1507	19, 349-435	42, 1-108
20, 1-152	14, 1976-2159	13, 546-669	ex 28, 5-200
20, 153-347	14, 1768-1975	23, 485-664	42, 108-362
21, 1-294	7, 346-677	32, 299-544	43, 1-368
21, 295-358	7, 1372-1445	7, 538-604	45, 211-290
22, 1-530	7, 1538-2147	46, 538-789 47, 1-231	45, 294-47, 226
23, 1-197	7, 2192-2417	33, 1-314	47, 226-394
23, 198-422	8, 1-255	33, 314-675	48, 1-409
24, 1-422	8, 264-745	45, 465-733 46, 1-111	49, 1-392 50, 1-154
25, 1-528		56, 1-528	
26, 1-461	9, 16-601	40^{I}, 40-688	gal 1, 12-2, 286

American Edition	St. Louis Edition	Weimar Edition	Erlangen Edition
27, 1-144	9, 600-771	40^{II}, 1-184	gal 2, 286-3, 120
145-149	8-15	40^{I}, 33-36	
27, 151-410	8, 1352-1661	2, 445-618	gal 3, 126-483
28, 1-56	8, 1026-1085	12, 92-142	51, 169
28, 57-213	8, 1088-1273	36, 481-696	51, 70-275
28, 215-384		26, 4-120	
29, 1-90		25, 6-69	
29, 91-105		25, 69-78	
29, 107-241		57^{III}, 97-238	
30, 1-145	9, 958-1111	12, 259-399	51, 324-494
30, 147-199	9, 1342-1397	14, 14-74	52, 212-272
30, 201-215	9, 1742-1755	14, 75-91	52, 272-287
30, 217-327	9, 1398-1523	20, 599-801	
31, 3-16	18, 18-27	1, 224-228	var 1, 313-321
31, 17-33	18, 70-81	1, 233-238	var 1, 285-293
31, 35-70	18, 36-71	1, 353-374	var 1, 387-404
31, 71-76	14, 182-185	1, 378-379	63, 238-240
31, 77-252	18, 100-269	1, 529-628	var 2, 136-293
31, 253-292	15, 612-616	2, 6-26	var 2, 367-392
	568-569		
	571-587		
	617-625		
	539-547		
31, 293-306	10, 1262-1277	2, 145-152	var 2, 329-339
31, 307-325	18, 718-721	2, 158-161	var 3, 12-17
	15, 1162-1170	Br 1, 420-424	
31, 327-377	19, 986-1011	7, 1-38	27, 173-199
		7, 39-73	
31, 379-395	15, 1619-1631	7, 161-182	24, 150-164
32, 3-99	15, 1476-1565	7, 309-457	24, 52-150
32, 101-131	15, 1916-1935	7, 814-857	var 6, 5-23
32, 133-260	18, 1056-1201	8, 43-128	var 5, 397-521
32, 261-286	21, 687-709	18, 224-240	26, 313-337

American Edition	St. Louis Edition	Weimar Edition	Erlangen Edition
33, 3-295	18, 1668-1969	18, 600-787	var 7, 116-368
34, 3-61	16, 946-992	30^{II}, 268-356	24, 329-379
34, 63-104	16, 1666-1700	30^{III}, 331-388	25, 51-88
34, 105-132	19, 1436-1450	39^{I}, 44-62	var 4, 378-389
34, 133-144	19, 1462-1467	39^{I}, 175-180	var 4, 413-416
34, 145-196	19, 1450-1455	39^{I}, 82-126	var 4, 389-394
34, 197-229	10, 992-1019	50, 262-283	23, 251-201
34, 231-267	16, 1971-1994	50, 288-308	25, 146-175
34, 269-278	14, 376-381	50, 383-385	63, 353-355
34, 279-288	14, 432-437	50, 657-661	1, 67-72
			63, 401-406
34, 289-297	21, 2695-2698	9, 572-574	56, 2-5
34, 299-321	19, 1468-1473	39^{II}, 187-203	var 4, 452-455
34, 323-338	14, 438-449	54, 179-187	var 1, 15-24
34, 339-360	19, 1808-1817	54, 416-443	var 4, 480-492
34, 361-366	21, 3374-3377	54, 192-194	32, 425-430
35, 3-22	10, 1232-1245	2, 714-723	20, 179-193
35, 23-43	10, 2112-2127	2, 727-737	var 3, 394-410
35, 45-73	19, 426-449	2, 742-758	27, 25-50
35, 75-111	19, 1036-1067	6, 353-378	27, 139-173
35, 113-124	11, xxxviii-xlv	10^{I}, 8-18	7, 5-12
35, 125-153	19, 598-621	10^{II}, 72-92	28, 318-343
35, 155-174	3, 2-17	16, 363-393"U"	33, 3-21
35, 175-202	19, 968-985	30^{II}, 632-646	65, 102-123
35, 203-223	4, 124-136	38, 9-17, 69	37, 250-266
	4, 198-199		
35, 233-251	14, 2-17	DB 8, 10-32	63, 7-25
35, 251-253	14, 18-19	DB 10^{I}, 5-6	63, 25-27
35, 253-257	14, 20-25	DB 10^{I}, 99-105	63, 27-32

American Edition	St. Louis Edition	Weimar Edition	Erlangen Edition
35, 258-261	14, 26-29	DB 10^{II}, 7-10	63, 35-38
35, 261-263	14, 28-31	DB 10^{II}, 2-4	63, 38-40
35, 263-264	14, 30-33	DB 10^{II}, 104-106	63, 40-41
35, 265-273	14, 32-41	DB 11^{I}, 3-15	63, 42-52
35, 273-278	6, 4-9	DB 11^{I}, 17-25	63, 52-59
35, 279-282	14, 40-43	DB 11^{I}, 191-195	63, 59-62
35, 282-283	14, 44-45	DB 11^{I}, 393	63, 62-64
35, 284-293	14, 45-53	DB 11^{I}, 395-409	63, 64-74
35, 294-316	6, 896-917	DB 11^{II}, 3-49	41, 237-258
	6, 940-943	DB 11^{II}, 125-131	41, 294-324
35, 317-318	14, 54-55	DB 11^{II}, 183	63, 74-75
35, 318-319	14, 54-57	DB 11^{II}, 213-215	63, 75-77
35, 320-321	14, 56-59	DB 11^{II}, 227-229	63, 77-78
35, 321-322	14, 58-59	DB 11^{II}, 251-253	63, 79-80
35, 323-324	14, 60-61	DB 11^{II}, 259-261	63, 80-81
35, 324-325	14, 60-63	DB 11^{II}, 271	63, 82
35, 326	14, 62-63	DB 11^{II}, 289	63, 83
35, 327-328	14, 1421-1423	DB 11^{II}, 299-301	63, 84-85
35, 328-329	14, 64-65	DB 11^{II}, 311	63, 85-86
35, 329-330	14, 64-67	DB 11^{II}, 321	63, 86-87
35, 330-331	14, 66-67	DB 11^{II}, 329-331	63, 88-89
35, 332-333	14, 68-69	DB 11^{II}, 363-365	63, 89-90
35, 337-339	14, 68-71	DB 12, 5-7	63, 91-93
35, 340-344	14, 72-77	DB 12, 49-55	63, 93-98
35, 345-347	14, 76-77	DB 12, 109-111	63, 98-100
35, 347-349	14, 78-81	DB 12, 145-149	63, 100-102
35, 349-350	14, 80-81	DB 12, 291	63, 103-104
35, 350-352	14, 80-83	DB 12, 315-317	63, 104-106
35, 352-353	14, 82-85	DB 12, 417-419	63, 106-107
35, 353-354	14, 84-85	DB 12, 493	63, 107-108
35, 357-362	14, 84-91	DB 6, 2-10	63, 108-115
35, 363-365	14, 92-95	DB 6, 415-417	63, 116-119
35, 365-380	14, 94-109	DB 7, 2-27	63, 119-138

American Edition	St. Louis Edition	Weimar Edition	Erlangen Edition
35, 380-383	14, 110-113	DB 7, 82-87	63, 138-141
35, 383-384	14, 114-115	DB 7, 138-139	63, 142-143
35, 384	14, 114-115	DB 7, 172-173	63, 143-144
35, 385	14, 116-117	DB 7, 190-191	63, 144
35, 385	14, 116-117	DB 7, 210-211	63, 145
35, 386	14, 116-117	DB 7, 224-225	63, 145-146
35, 386-387	14, 118-119	DB 7, 238-239	63, 146-147
35, 387-388	14, 118-119	DB 7, 250-251	63, 147-148
35, 388	14, 120-121	DB 7, 258-259	63, 148-149
35, 389	14, 120-121	DB 7, 272-273	63, 149
35, 389-390	14, 122-123	DB 7, 284-285	63, 150
35, 390	14, 122-123	DB 7, 292-293	63, 150-151
35, 390-391	14, 122-125	DB 7, 298-299	63, 151-152
35, 391-392	14, 124-125	DB 7, 314-315	63, 152-153
35, 393	14, 126-127	DB 7, 326-327	63, 153-154
35, 394-395	14, 126-129	DB 7, 344-345	63, 154-155
35, 395-398	14, 128-131	DB 7, 384-387	63, 156-158
35, 398-399	14, 140-141	DB 7, 404	63, 169-170
35, 399-411	14, 130-139	DB 7, 406-421	63, 158-169
36, 3-126	19, 4-129	6, 497-573	var 5, 16-118
36, 127-230	19, 1068-1177	8, 482-563	28, 27-141
36, 231-267	20, 62-93	10^{II}, 11-41	28, 285-318
36, 269-305	19, 1304-1337	11, 431-456	28, 388-421
36, 307-328	19, 1198-1215	18, 22-36	29, 113-133
36, 329-361	20, 734-763	19, 482-523	29, 328-359
37, 3-150	20, 762-893	23, 64-283	20, 14-150
37, 151-372	20, 894-1105	26, 261-509	30, 151-373
38, 3-89	17, 1939-1943	30^{III}, 110-171	65, 88-91
38, 91-137	10, 2170-2209	30^{II}, 595-626	23, 162-207
38, 139-214	19, 1220-1285	38, 195-256	31, 307-377

American Edition	St. Louis Edition	Weimar Edition	Erlangen Edition
38, 215-233	19, 1286-1299	38, 262-272	31, 377-391
38, 235-277	10, 1168-1173	39^{II}, 3-30	var 4, 458-461
38, 279-319	20, 1764-1791	54, 141-167	32, 396-425
39, 3-22	19, 884-901	6, 63-75	27, 50-70
39, 23-47	19, 786-807	6, 157-169	var 4, 152-171
39, 49-104	18, 1002-1053	6, 285-324	27, 85-139
39, 105-115	18, 1250-1255	7, 262-265	27, 200-205
39, 117-135	18, 1256-1271	7, 271-283	27, 205-220
39, 137-224	18, 1270-1353	7, 621-688	27, 221-308
39, 225-238	18, 1352-1363	8, 247-254	27, 308-318
39, 239-299	19, 668-727	10^{II}, 105-158	28, 141-201
39, 301-314	10, 1538-1549	11, 408-416	22, 140-151
40, 3-44	10, 1554-1603	12, 169-196	var 6, 492-535
40, 45-49	16, 4-17	15, 210-221	53, 255-268
40, 61-71	15, 2047-2053	15, 391-397	53, 270-277
40, 73-223	20, 132-287	18, 62-125 18, 134-214	29, 134-297
40, 225-262	17, 2187-2225	26, 144-174	26, 254-294
40, 263-320	10, 1628-1687	26, 195-240	23, 1-70
40, 321-377	19, 902-957	30^{II}, 465-507 30^{III}, 584-588	31, 126-184
40, 379-394	20, 1664-1677	30^{III}, 518-527	31, 213-226
41, 3-178	16, 2144-2303	50, 509-653	25, 219-388

American Edition	St. Louis Edition	Weimar Edition	Erlangen Edition
41, 179-256	17, 1313-1381	51, 469-572	26, 1-75
41, 257-376	17, 1019-1132	54, 206-299	26, 108-228
42, 3-14	11, 574-583	2, 136-142	11, 144-152 var 3, 410-419
42, 15-81	7, 752-821	2, 80-130	21, 156-227 (45, 203-207)
42, 83-93	14, 1414-1421	2, 175-179	20, 290-294 var 3, 442-446
42, 95-115	10, 1984-2001	2, 685-697	21, 253-274 var 3, 453-473
42, 117-166	10, 1820-1917	6, 104-134	var 4, 84-135 (53, 31-34)
42, 167-177	12, 1354-1361	7, 692-697	17, 65-72
42, 179-186	10, 1732-1736	7, 784-791	54, 116-117 64, 294-296
43, 3-45	3, 1352-1361	10^{II}, 375-428	22, 3-32 (65, 266-268)
43, 47-55	10, 2002-2007	10^{II}, 322-326	22, 32-38 (53, 230)
43, 57-70	15, 1662-1672	10^{II}, 53-60	53, 119-129
43, 71-79	10, 1758-1761	Br 3, 138-140	197-201
43, 81-96	19, 1674-1685	15, 86-94	29, 102-113
43, 97-112	5, 1272-1283	15, 69-78	41, 115-128 (53, 233)
43, 113-138	10, 2008-2029	23, 339-379	22, 317-341 (53, 408)
43, 139-165	10, 1960-1981	23, 402-431	22, 294-316 (53, 408)
43, 167-177	10, 1712-1719	30^{II}, 700-710	23, 154-162
43, 179-186	10, 1776-1779	32, 547-548	64, 298-300
43, 187-211	10, 1394-1417	38, 358-375	23, 214-238
43, 213-241	20, 2194-2217	51, 585-625	32, 74-99
43, 243-250	10, 730-735	53, 205-208	23, 338-343
43, 251-288	17, 1396-1419	54, 389-411	26, 229-254 39, 221-223

American Edition	St. Louis Edition	Weimar Edition	Erlangen Edition
44, 3-14	10, 630-637	2, 166-171	16, 158-165 var 3, 446-452
44, 15-114	10, 1298-1389	6, 202-276	20, 193-290
44, 115-217	10, 266-351	6, 404-469	21, 274-360
44, 219-229	19, 808-815	7, 290-298	24, 202-209
44, 231-242	10, 1692-1701	7, 795-802	20, 301-308
44, 243-400	19, 1507-1665	8, 577-669	var 6, 234-376 53, 86-92
45, 3-9	10, 628-629	10^{II}, 265-266	20, 87-89 53, 156-157
45, 11-49	10, 598-628	10^{II}, 275-304	20, 57-87
45, 51-74	10, 360-373	8, 676-687	22, 43-59
45, 75-129	10, 374-417	11, 245-280	22, 59-105
45, 131-158	19, 1730-1745	12, 232-244	29, 16-33 (53, 162)
45, 159-176	10, 954-961	12, 11-15	22, 105-122
45, 176-194	10, 960-977	12, 18-30	22, 112-130 53, 196-197
45, 195-229	20, 1792-1821	11, 314-336	29, 45-74
45, 231-310	10, 914-937 10, 824-855	15, 293-313 17, 321-322 6, 36-60	22, 199-226 20, 89-122
45, 311-337	5, 1284-1303	15, 360-378	41, 128-150 (53, 281)
45, 339-378	10, 458-485	15, 27-53	22, 168-199
45, 379-393	10, 712-721	15, 163-169	53, 236-244

American Edition	St. Louis Edition	Weimar Edition	Erlangen Edition
46, 3-43	16, 45-71	8, 291-334	24, 257-286
46, 45-55	16, 71-77	18, 357-361	24, 287-294
46, 57-85	16, 77-99	18, 384-401	24, 294-319
46, 87-137	10, 488-531	19, 623-662	22, 244-290 53, 391-392
46, 139-154	19, 1689-1693	19, 287-293	29, 318-327
46, 155-205	20, 2108-2155	30^{II}, 107-148	31, 31-80
46, 207-258	20, 416-459	30^{II}, 517-588	20, 1-45
46, 259-320	10, 754-809	30^{III}, 205-248	23, 91-154
47, 3-55	16, 1624-1665	30^{III}, 276-320	25, 1-50
47, 57-98	20, 1828-1861	50, 312-337	31, 416-449
47, 99-119	20, 1610-1623	50, 468-477	32, 1-14
47, 121-306	20, 1860-2029	53, 417-552	32, 99-274
48, 3-5	21, 1-3	Br 1, 10-11	
48, 5-7	21, 5-7	Br 1, 18	
48, 8-11	21, 13-15	Br 1, 27-29	
48, 11-14	21, 19-22	Br 1, 33-36	
48, 14-16	21, 26-29	Br 1, 41-42	
48, 17-18	21, 35-36	Br 1, 50	
48, 18-19	21, 18-19	Br 1, 56	
48, 20-23	21, 38-41	Br 1, 57-59	
48, 23-26	18, 1972-1975	Br 1, 69-71	
48, 27-32	21, 49-52	Br 1, 72-73	
48, 32-36	21, 53-57	Br 1, 76-79	
48, 36-38	18, 16-19	Br 1, 88-89	
48, 39-41	18, 1974-1975	Br 1, 89-90	
48, 41-42	18, 1968-1971	Br 1, 98-99	
48, 42-43	21, 71-72	Br 1, 102-103	

99   16. Cardinal Albrecht, Archbishop of Mainz: Wittenberg, October 31, 1517

99   17. Elector Frederick: Wittenberg, about November 6, 1517

99   18. George Spalatin: Wittenberg, January 18, 1518

99   19. George Spalatin: Wittenberg, February 22, 1518

99   20. George Spalatin: Wittenberg, May 18, 1518

99   21. John von Staupitz: Wittenberg, May 30, 1518

99   22. George Spalatin: Wittenberg, August 8, 1518

99   23. George Spalatin: Wittenberg, August 28, 1518

99   24. George Spalatin: Wittenberg, August 31, 1518

99   25. George Spalatin: Wittenberg, September 2, 1518

99   26. George Spalatin: Augsburg, October 14, 1518

99   27. The Papal Legate, Cardinal Cajetan: Augsburg October 18, 1518

99   28. George Spalatin: Wittenberg, October 31, 1518

99   29. George Spalatin: Wittenberg, November 25, 1518

99   30. George Spalatin: Wittenberg, December 9, 1518

99   31. Elector Frederick: Altenburg, January 5 or 6, 1519

99   32. Pope Leo X: Altenburg, January 5 or 6, 1519

99   33. Elector Frederick: Wittenberg, between January 13 and 19, 1519

99   34. George Spalatin: Wittenberg, February 7, 1519

99   35. John von Staupitz: Wittenberg, February 20, 1519

99   36. George Spalatin: Wittenberg, March 13, 1519

99   37. Erasmus of Rotterdam: Wittenberg, March 28, 1519

99   38. Elector Frederick: Wittenberg, about May 15, 1519

99   39. George Spalatin: Wittenberg, May 22, 1519

99   40. Martin Glaser: Wittenberg, May 30, 1519

99   41. George Spalatin: Wittenberg, July 20, 1519

99   42. George Spalatin: Liebenswerda, October 9, or Wittenberg, October 10, 1519

99   43. Elector Frederick: Wittenberg, October 15, 1519

99   44. George Spalatin: Wittenberg, November 1, 1519

American Edition	St. Louis Edition	Weimar Edition	Erlangen Edition
48, 43-49	15, 390-393	Br 1, 108-112	
48, 49-52	21, 77-79	Br 1, 119-120	53, 1-2
48, 52-55	18, 1976-1979	Br 1, 132-134	
48, 56-59	15, 2399-2402	Br 1, 149-150	
48, 60-63	15, 2392-2394	Br 1, 172-174	
48, 64-70	15, 414-418	1, 525-527	
48, 70-73	15, 430-432	Br 1, 188	
48, 73-76	15, 432-434	Br 1, 189-191	
48, 76-80	21, 105-106	Br 1, 191-192	
48, 80-83	15, 2397-2399	Br 1, 195-196	
48, 83-87	15, 2416-2418	Br 1, 213-215	
48, 87-89	15, 592-594	Br 1, 222-223	
48, 90-93	15, 2408-2410	Br 1, 224-225	
48, 93-94	15, 2427	Br 1, 253	
48, 95-96	21, 120-121	Br 1, 262	
48, 96-100	15, 696-698	Br 1, 289-291	53, 5-7
48, 100-102	15, 705-708	Br 1, 291-293	
48, 103-106	15, 1726-1729	Br 1, 305-308	
48, 106-107	21, 144-145	Br 1, 325	
48, 108-111	15, 2442-2444	Br 1, 343-345	
48, 111-116	21, 155-157	Br 1, 358-360	
48, 116-119	18, 1582-1585	Br 1, 361-363	
48, 120-121	21, 165	Br 1, 386-387	53, 9-10
48, 122-124	21, 170-171	Br 1, 404	
48, 124-126	21, 174-175	Br 1, 408-409	
48, 126 31,318-325	15, 1162-1170	Br 1, 420-442	
48, 126-127	15, 752-753	Br 1, 524-525	
48, 127-129	15, 757-758	Br 1, 535-536	53, 28-29
48, 130-131	15, 2476-2477	Br 1, 548-549	

99 45. George Spalatin: Wittenberg, November 7, 1519

99 46. George Spalatin: Wittenberg, November 29, 1519

99 47. John Lang: Wittenberg, December 18, 1519

99 48. Thomas Fuchs: Wittenberg, December 23, 1519

99 49. George Spalatin: Wittenberg, December 31, 1519

99 50. George Spalatin: Wittenberg, January 14, 1520

99 51. John Lang: Wittenberg, January 26, 1520

99 52. George Spalatin: Wittenberg, about February 14, 1520

99 53. George Spalatin: Wittenberg, March 19, 1520

99 54. George Spalatin: Wittenberg, April 13, 1520

99 55. George Spalatin: Wittenberg, April 16, 1520

99 56. George Spalatin: Wittenberg, May 1, 1520

99 57. George Spalatin: Wittenberg, May 31, 1520

99 58. George Spalatin: Wittenberg, June 25, 1520

99 59. George Spalatin: Wittenberg, July 14, 1520

99 60. Wenceslaus Link: Wittenberg, August 19, 1520

99 61. George Spalatin: Wittenberg, August 23, 1520

99 62. George Spalatin: Wittenberg, August 24, 1520

99 63. Emperor Charles V: Wittenberg, August 30, 1520

99 64. George Spalatin: Lichtenberg, October 12, 1520

99 65. Duke John Frederick: Wittenberg, October 30, 1520

99 66. Lazarus Spengler: Wittenberg, November 17, 1520

99 67. George Spalatin: Wittenberg, December 10, 1520

99 68. George Spalatin: Wittenberg, December 29, 1520

99 69. John von Staupitz: Wittenberg, January 14, 1521

99 70. Elector Frederick: Wittenberg, January 25, 1521

99 71. George Spalatin: Frankfurt/Main, April 14, 1521

99 72. John Cuspinian: Worms, April 17, 1521

99 73. Lucas Cranach: Frankfurt/Main, April 28, 1521

99 74. Emperor Charles V: Friedberg, April 28, 1521

99 75. Philip Melanchthon: Wartburg, about May 8, 1521

99 76. Philip Melanchthon: Wartburg, about May 8, 1521

99 77. Philip Melanchthon: Wartburg, May 12, 1521

American Edition	St. Louis Edition	Weimar Edition	Erlangen Edition
48, 132-133	15, 2477-2478	Br 1, 551	
48, 133-134	21, 207-208	Br 1, 563-564	
48, 135-139	21, 214-216	Br 1, 596-597	
48, 139-141	21, 216-217	Br 1, 598-599	53, 29-30
48, 141-143	21, 219-220	Br 1, 604	
48, 143-148	19, 1774-1779	Br 1, 610-612	
48, 148-151	21, 224-225	Br 1, 619	
48, 151-153	21, 238-239	Br 2, 40-42	
48, 154-155	21, 246-247	Br 2, 72	
48, 156-159	21, 252-254	Br 2, 80-82	
48, 159-161	15, 2403-2405	Br 2, 82-83	
48, 161-162	21, 256-257	Br 2, 95-96	
48, 163-165	21, 262-263	Br 2, 111	
48, 165-167	21, 270-271	Br 2, 129-130	
48, 167-169	21, 278-279	Br 2, 142-143	
48, 169-171	21, 292-293	Br 2, 168	
48, 171-173	15, 2493-2494	Br 2, 169-170	
48, 173-174	21, 293-294	Br 2, 170-171	
48, 175-179	15, 1378-1382	Br 2, 172-178	
48, 179-181	15, 782-783	Br 2, 196-197	
48, 181-183	21, 303-304	Br 2, 204-206	53, 52-53
48, 184-185	21, 308-309	Br 2, 217-218	53, 53-54
48, 186-187	21, 324-325	Br 2, 2, 234	
48, 188-191	15, 1884-1887	Br 2, 242-243	
48, 191-194	15, 2422-2424	Br 2, 245-246	
48, 194-197	15, 1887-1890	Br 2, 253-255	53, 56-58
48, 197-198	15, 1827-1828	Br 2, 298	
48, 199-200	21, 348-349	Br 2, 299-300	
48, 200-203	15, 1935-1937	Br 2, 305	53, 64-65
48, 203-209	15, 1893-1899	Br 2, 307-310	53, 65-71
48, 210-213	21, 351-352	Br 2, 330-331	
48, 213-214	15, 1906-1907	Br 2, 331-332	
48, 215-217	15, 2513-2515	Br 2, 332-333	

99	78. Nicholas von Amsdorf: Wartburg, May 12, 1521
99	79. John Agricola: Wartburg, May 12, 1521
99	80. George Spalatin: Wartburg, May 14, 1521
99	81. Philip Melanchthon: Wartburg, May 26, 1521
99	82. Francis von Sickingen: Wartburg, June 1, 1521
99	83. The People of Wittenberg: Wartburg, June, 1521
99	84. George Spalatin: Wartburg, June 10, 1521
99	85. Philip Melanchthon: Wartburg, July 13, 1521
99	86. Nicholas von Amsdorf: Wartburg, July 15?, 1521
99	87. George Spalatin: Wartburg, July 15, 1521
99	88. George Spalatin: Wartburg, soon after July 15, 1521
99	89. George Spalatin: Wartburg, soon after July 15, 1521
99	90. George Spalatin: Wartburg, July 31, 1521
99	91. Philip Melanchthon: Wartburg, August 1, 1521
99	92. Philip Melanchthon: Wartburg, August 3, 1521
99	93. George Spalatin: Wartburg, August 6, 1521
99	94. George Spalatin: Wartburg, August 15, 1521
99	95. Philip Melanchthon: Wartburg, September 9, 1521
99	96. George Spalatin: Wartburg, September 9, 1521
99	97. Nicholas von Amsdorf: Wartburg, September 9, 1521
99	98. George Spalatin: Wartburg, September 17, 1521
99	99. George Spalatin: Wartburg, October 7, 1521
99	100. Nicholas Gerbel: Wartburg, November 1, 1521
99	101. George Spalatin: Wartburg, November 1, 1521
99	102. The Augustinians in Wittenberg: Wartburg, November, 1521
99	103. George Spalatin: Wartburg, November 11, 1521
99	104. Hans Luther: Wartburg, November 21, 1521
99	105. George Spalatin: Wartburg, November 22, 1521
99	106. Cardinal Albrecht, Archbishop of Mainz: Wartburg, December 1, 1521
99	107. George Spalatin: Wartburg, about December 5, 1521
99	108. George Spalatin: Wartburg, about December 12, 1521

American Edition	St. Louis Edition	Weimar Edition	Erlangen Edition
48, 218-220	15, 2516	Br 2, 334-335	
48, 220-222	15, 2520-2521	Br 2, 335-336	
48, 222-228	15, 2510-2513	Br 2, 336-338	
48, 228-244	15, 2542-2547	Br 2, 346-349	
48, 244-247	19, 814-817	8, 138-140	53, 74-77
48, 248-253	5, 306-311	8, 210-214	
48, 253-256	15, 2526-2528	Br 2, 354-355	
48, 256-263	15, 2528-2534	Br 2, 356-359	
48, 264-268	15, 2550-2554	Br 2, 361-363	
48, 268-270	15, 2538-2540	Br 2, 364-365	
48, 270-271	21, 356-357	Br 2, 366	
48, 272-273	21, 357-358	Br 2, 366-367	
48, 274-276	15, 2540-2542	Br 2, 368-369	
48, 277-282	15, 2585-2590	Br 2, 370-372	
48, 283-289	15, 2590-2596	Br 2, 373-376	
48 ,289-291	21, 358-360	Br 2, 377-378	
48, 291-296	15, 2521-2526	Br 2, 379-381	
48, 296-304	19, 1794-1801	Br 2, 382-386	
48, 305-310	15, 2535-2538	Br 2, 387-389	
48, 310-312	15, 2584-2585	Br 2, 390-391	
48, 312-315	21, 360-362	Br 2, 391-392	
48, 315-317	21, 363-364	Br 2, 394-395	
48, 317-322	15, 2517-2520	Br 2, 396-398	
48, 323-324	21, 364	Br 2, 399	
48, 324-325 36, 133-135	19, 1068-1071	8, 482-483	
48, 325-328	15, 2548-2550	Br 2, 402-403	
48, 329-336	19, 1500-1507	8, 573-576	53, 86-92
48, 337-338	19, 1800-1803	Br 2, 404-405	
48, 339-350	19, 548-553	Br 2, 405-408	53, 95-99
48, 350-352	19, 560-563	Br 2, 409-410	
48, 353-355	21, 367-369	Br 2, 411-412	

99   109. John Lang: Wartburg, December 18, 1521

99   110. Wenceslas Link: Wartburg, December 18, 1521

99   111. Nicholas von Amsdorf: Wartburg, January 13, 1522

99   112. Philip Melanchthon: Wartburg, January 13, 1522

99   113. Wolfgang Fabricius Capito: Wartburg, January 17, 1522

99   114. George Spalatin: Wartburg, January 17, 1522

99   115. George Spalatin: Wartburg, January 22?, 1522

99   116. Elector Frederick: Wartburg, about February 22, 1522

99   117. Elector Frederick: Borna, March 5, 1522

99   118. Elector Frederick: Wittenberg, March 7 or 8, 1522

99   119. Nicholas Hausmann: Wittenberg, March 17, 1522

99   120. George Spalatin: Wittenberg, March 30, 1522

99   121. George Spalatin: Wittenberg, May 20, 1522

99   122. An Anonymous Addressee: Wittenberg, May 28, 1522

99   123. George Spalatin: Wittenberg, June 7, 1522

99   124. John von Staupitz: Wittenberg, June 27, 1522

99   125. George Spalatin: Wittenberg, about September 20, 1522

99   126. Henning Teppen: Wittenberg, November 21, 1522

99   127. George Spalatin: Wittenberg, about December 12, 1522

99   128. Wenceslaus Link: Wittenberg, December 19, 1522

99   129. The Council of the City of Stettin:
       Wittenberg, January 11, 1523

99   130. The Council of the City of Leisnig:
       Wittenberg, January 29, 1523

99   131. Eobanus Hessus: Wittenberg, March 29, 1523

99   132. Elector Frederick: Wittenberg, May 29, 1523

99   133. John Oecolampadius: Wittenberg, June 20, 1523

99   134. Elector Frederick: Leisnig, August 11, 1523

99   135. John von Staupitz: Wittenberg, September 17, 1523

99   136. Gregory Brueck: Wittenberg, October 18, 1523

99   137. Nicholas Hausmann: Wittenberg, end of October, 1523

99   138. Elector Frederick: Wittenberg, mid-November, 1523

American Edition	St. Louis Edition	Weimar Edition	Erlangen Edition
48, 356-357	15, 2554-2555	Br 2, 413	
48, 357-359	21, 370-372	Br 2, 414-415	
48, 360-364	15, 2557-2560	Br 2, 422-423	
48, 364-372	15, 2599-2605	Br 2, 424-427	
48, 372-379	19, 554-561	Br 2, 428-434	
48, 380-381	15, 2606-2607	Br 2, 443-444	
48, 382-386	21, 378-382	Br 2, 445-447	
48, 386-388	15, 1984-1985	Br 2, 448-449	53, 103-104
48, 388-393	15, 1989-1993	Br 2, 453-457	53, 104-109
48, 393-399	15, 1998-2001	Br 2, 459-462	53, 109-112
48, 399-402	15, 2011-2013	Br 2, 474-475	
49, 3-4	15, 2555-2556	Br 2, 489-490	
49, 5	21, 412-413	Br 2, 537	
49, 6-8	18, 1978-1981	Br 2, 544-545	
49, 8-9	21, 421	Br 2, 556	53, 137
49, 10-13	15, 607-610	Br 2, 567-568	
49, 13-15	21, 446-447	Br 2, 598	
49, 16	21, 458-459	Br 2, 618	
49, 17-20	15, 2581-2583	Br 2, 630-631	
49, 20-25	15, 2578-2581	Br 2, 632-633	
49, 25-28	21, 471-472	Br 3, 13-14	53, 159-161
49, 28-32	21, 478	Br 3, 23	
49, 32-35	21, 491-493	Br 3, 49-50	
49, 35-42	15, 2187-2191	Br 3, 75-77	53, 163-167
49, 42-45	21, 517-519	Br 3, 96-97	
49, 45-47	21, 534-535	Br 3, 124-125	53, 194-195
49, 48-50	15, 610-612	Br 3, 155-156	
49, 50-55	10, 912-913	Br 3, 176-177	53, 219-220
49, 55-56	21, 571-572	Br 3, 183-184	
49, 57-59	21, 671-673	Br 3, 195-197	

99	139. Margrave Albrecht of Brandenburg: Wittenberg, December, 1523
99	140. George Spalatin: Wittenberg, end of 1523
99	141. George Spalatin: Wittenberg, January 14, 1524
99	142. George Spalatin: Wittenberg, March 14, 1524
99	143. Elector Frederick: Wittenberg, March 23, 1524
99	144. Erasmus of Rotterdam: Wittenberg, about April 18, 1524
99	145. Nicholas Gerbel: Wittenberg, May 6, 1524
99	146. Wolfgang Stein: Wittenberg, beginning of September, 1524
99	147. The Council of the City of Zerbst: Wittenberg, October 8, 1524
99	148. Nicholas Hausmann: Wittenberg, November 17, 1524
99	149. George Spalatin: Wittenberg, November 30, 1524
99	150. The Christians in Strassburg: Wittenberg, about December 15, 1524
99	151. Lazarus Spengler: Wittenberg, February 4, 1525
99	152. Theobald Billicanus: Wittenberg, March 5, 1525
99	153. George Spalatin: Wittenberg, April 16, 1525
99	154. John Ruehel: Seeburg, May 4, 1525
99	155. Nicholas von Amsdorf: Wittenberg, May 30, 1525
99	156. George Spalatin: Wittenberg, June 21, 1525
99	157. Nicholas von Amsdorf: Wittenberg, June 21, 1525
99	158. John Briessmann: Wittenberg, after August 15, 1525
99	159. Elector John: Wittenberg, September 6, 1525
99	160. Elector John: Wittenberg, October 31, 1525
99	161. Elector John: Wittenberg, November 30, 1525
99	162. Michael Stifel: Wittenberg, December 31, 1525
99	163. Gabriel Zwilling: Wittenberg, January 2, 1526
99	164. George Spalatin: Wittenberg, March 27, 1526
99	165. Caspar von Schwenkfeld: Wittenberg, April 14, 1526
99	166. John Agricola: Wittenberg, May 11, 1526
99	167. John Ruehel: Wittenberg, June 8, 1526
99	168. Michael Stifel: Wittenberg, August 11, 1526
99	169. Wenceslas Link: Wittenberg, January 1, 1527

American Edition	St. Louis Edition	Weimar Edition	Erlangen Edition
49, 59-68		Br 3, 214-219	
49, 68-70	21, 582-583	Br 3, 220	
49, 70-72	15, 2622-2623	Br 3, 234-235	
49, 72-74	15, 2623-2624	Br 3, 254	
49, 74-76	21, 601-602	Br 3, 258-259	53, 235-236
49, 76-81	18, 1596-1599	Br 3, 268-271	
49, 81-83	21, 619-620	Br 3, 284	
49, 83-85	21, 647-648	Br 3, 342-343	53, 268-269
49, 85-87	21, 650-651	Br 3, 355	
49, 87-91	18, 1984-1987	Br 3, 373-374	
49, 91-94	21, 665-667	Br 3, 393-394	
49, 94-96 40, 65-71	15, 2047-2053	15, 391-397	53, 270-277
49, 96-99	21, 715-716	Br 3, 432-433	53, 283-284
49, 99-102	21, 725-726	Br 3, 451-452	
49, 102-105	21, 736-738	Br 3, 474-475	
49, 106-112	16, 126-129	Br 3, 480-482	53, 291-294
49, 112-114	16, 133-135	Br 3, 517-518	
49, 115-116	21, 762-763	Br 3, 540	
49, 116-120	15, 2639-2640	Br 3, 541	
49, 120-125	21, 771-773	Br 3, 554-556	
49, 125-130	21, 775-776	Br 3, 569-570	56, viii-x
49, 130-137	21, 798-801	Br 3, 594-596	53, 329-332
49, 137-139	21, 812-813	Br 3, 628-629	53, 336-338
49, 139-141	21, 818-819	Br 3, 653	
49, 142		Br 4, 4	
49, 143-147	15, 2641-2644	Br 4, 41-42	
49, 148-150	20, 1660-1661	Br 4, 52-53	
49, 150-151	21, 863-864	Br 4, 73-74	
49, 151-153	21, 868-869	Br 4, 87	53, 380-381
49, 153-156	17, 1544	Br 4, 108-109	
49, 157-159	19, 1786-1787	Br 4, 147-148	

99 170. Nicholas Hausmann: Wittenberg, January 10, 1527

99 171. Nicholas Hausmann: Wittenberg, March 29, 1527

99 172. Wenceslas Link: Wittenberg, about May 4, 1527

99 173. Wenceslas Link: Wittenberg, July 5, 1527

99 174. Nicholas Hausmann: Wittenberg, July 13, 1527

99 175. Elector John: Wittenberg, September 16, 1527

99 176. Justus Jonas: Wittenberg, about November 10, 1527

99 177. John Brenz: Torgau, November 28, 1527

99 178. Justus Jonas: Wittenberg, December 10, 1527

99 179. Justus Jonas: Wittenberg, December 30, 1527

99 180. Nicholas von Amsdorf: Wittenberg, April 16, 1528

99 181. Elector John: Weimar, May 1 or 2, 1528

99 182. Duke John Frederick: Wittenberg, May 18, 1528

99 183. John Hess: Wittenberg, about June 13, 1528

99 184. Nicholas Gerbel: Wittenberg, July 28, 1528

99 185. Nicholas Hausmann: Wittenberg, August 5, 1528

99 186. Lazarus Spengler: Wittenberg, August 15, 1528

99 187. Elector John: Wittenberg, September 3, 1528

99 188. John Agricola: Wittenberg, September 11, 1528

99 189. Nicholas von Amsdorf: Wittenberg, November 1, 1528

99 190. Wenceslas Link: Wittenberg, March 7, 1529

99 191. Nicholas von Amsdorf: Wittenberg, May 5, 1529

99 192. Wenceslas Link: Wittenberg, May 6, 1529

99 193. Elector John: Wittenberg, May 22, 1529

99 194. Landgrave Philip of Hesse: Wittenberg, June 23, 1529

99 195. Thomas Loescher: Wittenberg, August 26, 1529

99 196. Mrs. Martin Luther: Marburg, October 4, 1529

99 197. Nicholas von Amsdorf: Wittenberg, October 27, 1529

99 198. Elector John: Wittenberg, November 18, 1529

99 199. Landgrave Philip of Hesse: Wittenberg, December 16, 1529

99 200. Elector John: Wittenberg, December 24, 1529

99 201. Some Pastors of the City of Luebeck: Wittenberg,
    January 12, 1530

American Edition	St. Louis Edition	Weimar Edition	Erlangen Edition
49, 159-161	21, 916-917	Br 4, 159	
49, 161-164	21, 929-930	Br 4, 180-181	53, 399-400
49, 164-165	21, 935-936	Br 4, 197-198	
49, 166-167	21, 984	Br 4, 220	
49, 167-169	21, 996-997	Br 4, 222	
49, 169-171	21, 1011-1012	Br 4, 248	
49, 171-177	15, 2645-2647	Br 4, 279-280	
49, 177-180	15, 2632-2633	Br 4, 285-286	
49, 180-185	17, 2228-2231	Br 4, 294-295	
49, 185-186	21, 1055-1056	Br 4, 311-312	
49, 187-188		Br 4, 443	
49, 189-195	21, 1147-1150	Br 4, 447-450	
49, 195-196	21, 1153	Br 4, 465	54, 5-6
49, 196-199	19, 1788-1789	Br 4, 480	
49, 199-202	21, 1180-1181	Br 4, 508	
49, 202-203	21, 1182	Br 4, 511	
49, 204-210	10, 2256-2261	Br 4, 533-536	54, 30-34
49, 210-211	21, 1197-1198	Br 4, 545-546	54, 34-35
49, 212-213	21, 1205-1206	Br 4, 557-558	
49, 213-214	21, 1231	Br 4, 597	
49, 214-217	21, 1269-1270	Br 5, 27-28	
49, 218-219	21, 1294-1295	Br 5, 61	54, 69
49, 219-221	21, 1297-1298	Br 5, 62-63	
49, 221-228	21, 1303-1306	Br 5, 75-77	54, 72-74
49, 228-231	17, 1935-1937	Br 5, 101-102	54, 83-85
49, 232-234	21, 1348-1349	Br 5, 137	
49, 234-239	21, 1366-1367	Br 5, 154	54, 107-108
49, 239-243	21, 1371-1372	Br 5, 167-168	
49, 244-250	10, 552-555	Br 5, 181-183	54, 110-112
49, 250-254	21, 1396-1397	Br 5, 203-204	
49, 254-260	21, 1384-1387	Br 5, 209-211	
49, 261-263	21, 1409-1411	Br 5, 220-221	

99	202. Nicholas Hausmann: Wittenberg, beginning of February, 1530
99	203. Hans Luther: Wittenberg, February 15, 1530
99	204. Elector John: Wittenberg, March 6, 1530
99	205. Nicholas Hausmann: Coburg, April 18, 1530
99	206. Philip Melanchthon: Coburg, April 24, 1530
99	207. George Spalatin: Coburg, April 24, 1530
99	208. Elector John: Coburg, May 15, 1530
99	209. Landgrave Philip of Hesse: Coburg, May 20, 1530
99	210. Elector John: Coburg, May 20, 1530
99	211. Mrs. Martin Luther: Coburg, June 5, 1530
99	212. Philip Melanchthon: Coburg, June 5, 1530
99	213. Philip Melanchthon: Coburg, June 7, 1530
99	214. John Luther: Coburg, about June 19, 1530
99	215. Philip Melanchthon: Coburg, June 29, 1530
99	216. George Spalatin: Coburg, June 30, 1530
99	217. John Agricola: Coburg, June 30, 1530
99	218. Philip Melanchthon: Coburg, July 3, 1530
99	219. Nicolas Hausmann: Coburg, July 6, 1530
99	220. Conrad Cordatus: Coburg, July 6, 1530
99	221. Lazarus Spengler: Coburg, July 8, 1530
99	222. Elector John: Coburg, July 9, 1530
99	223. Justus Jonas: Coburg, July 9, 1530
99	224. Justus Jonas, George Spalatin, Philip Melanchthon, John Agricola: Coburg, July 15, 1530
99	225. Philip Melanchthon: Coburg, July 21, 1530
99	226. Gregory Brueck: Coburg, August 5, 1530
99	227. Mrs. Martin Luther: Coburg, August 14, 1530
99	228. Mrs. Martin Luther: Coburg, August 15, 1530
99	229. Elector John: Coburg, August 26, 1530
99	230. George Spalatin: Coburg, August 26, 1530
99	231. Mrs. Martin Luther: Coburg, September 8, 1530

American Edition	St. Louis Edition	Weimar Edition	Erlangen Edition
49, 264-267	21, 1413-1414	Br 5, 236-237	
49, 267-271	10, 1794-1799	Br 5, 239-241	54, 130-133
49, 272-280	10, 544-549	Br 5, 258-261	54, 138-142
49, 280-287	16, 667-669	Br 5, 277-278	
49, 287-291	16, 2307-2309	Br 5, 285-286	
49, 292-295	16, 1754-1756	Br 5, 290-291	
49, 295-299	16, 657-658	Br 5, 319-320	54, 145-146
49, 299-304	17, 1960-1963	Br 5, 328-332	54, 151-154
49, 305-311	16, 690-694	Br 5, 324-327	54, 146-150
49, 311-316	21, 1464-1465	Br 5, 347-348	
49, 316-319	21, 1467-1469	Br 5, 350-351	
49, 320-321	21, 1470-1471	Br 5, 354	
49, 321-324	21, 1491-1492	Br 5, 377-378	54, 156-157
49, 324-333	16, 901-905	Br 5, 405-407	
49, 333-337	16, 908-910	Br 5, 414-415	
49, 338-342	16, 750-752	Br 5, 415-417	
49, 342-347	16, 913-914	Br 5, 435-436	
49, 348-352	16, 881-883	Br 5, 440	
49, 353-356	16, 914-916	Br 5, 441-442	
49, 356-359	21, 1513-1514	Br 5, 444-445	54, 168-169
49, 359-365	16, 814	Br 5, 453-455 Br 12, 117-119	54, 169-172
49, 366-372	16, 927	Br 5, 457-459	
49, 372-377	21, 1517-1519	Br 5, 479-480	
49, 378-393	16, 1013-1018	Br 5, 492-495	
49, 394-399	16, 1764-1767	Br 5, 530-532	54, 183-186
49, 399-400	16, 1084	Br 5, 544-545	54, 186
49, 400-403	21, 1541-1542	Br 5, 545-546	54, 187-188
49, 403-412	16, 1414-1417	Br 5, 572-574	54, 188-192
49, 412-414	16, 1406-1407	Br 5, 575-576	
49, 415-419	21. 1564-1565	Br 5, 608-609	56, 181-183

99	232. Nicholas Hausmann: Coburg, September 23, 1530
99	233. Mrs. Martin Luther: Coburg, September 24, 1530
99	234. Louis Senfl: Coburg, October 4, 1530
99	235. The Electoral Saxon Government: Torgau, about October 27, 1530
99	236. Landgrave Philip of Hesse: Torgau, October 28, 1530
99	237. Elector John: Wittenberg, about January 16, 1531
99	238. Martin Bucer: Wittenberg, January 22, 1531
99	239. Lazarus Spengler: Wittenberg, February 15, 1531
99	240. Wenceslas Link: Wittenberg, May 12, 1531
99	241. Mrs. Margaret Luther: Wittenberg, May 20, 1531
99	242. Gregory Brueck: Wittenberg, end of May, 1531
99	243. Elector John: Wittenberg, June 16, 1531
99	244. Michael Stifel: Wittenberg, June or July, 1531
99	245. Robert Barnes: Wittenberg, September 3, 1531
99	246. Elector John: Wittenberg, about February 12, 1532
99	247. Mrs. Martin Luther: Torgau, February 27, 1532
99	248. Thomas Zink: Wittenberg, April 22, 1532
99	249. Nicholas von Amsdorf: Wittenberg, June 13, 1532
99	250. Elector John: Wittenberg, June 29, 1532
99	251. The Regents and Councilors of the Margraviate of Brandenburg-Ansbach and to the Council of the City of Nuernberg: Wittenberg, August 1, 1532
99	252. Duke Joachim of Brandenburg: Wittenberg, August 3, 1532
99	253. Nicholas von Amsdorf: Wittenberg, November 2, 1532
99	254. John Loeser: Wittenberg, January 29, 1533
99	255. The Council of the City of Nuernberg: Wittenberg, April 18, 1533
99	256. John Schlaginhaufen: Wittenberg, March 10, 1534
99	257. Mrs. Martin Luther: Dessau, July 29, 1534
99	258. Elector John Frederick: Wittenberg, August 20, 1535
99	259. Philip Melanchthon: Wittenberg, August 29, 1535
99	260. Justus Jonas: Wittenberg, September 4, 1535

American Edition	St. Louis Edition	Weimar Edition	Erlangen Edition
49, 419-424	16, 1522-1523	Br 5, 631-632	
49, 424-425	21, 1571-1572	Br 5, 633-634	54, 194
49, 426-429	21, 1574-1576	Br 5, 639	
49, 429-433	10, 562-563	Br 5, 662	
49, 433-437	21, 1585-1586	Br 5, 660-661	
50, 3-6	17, 1975-1976	Br 6, 18-21	
50, 6-9	17, 1973-1975	Br 6, 24-26	
50, 9-12	10, 570-572	Br 6, 35-37	54, 213-214
50, 13-17	21, 1656-1658	Br 6, 95-97	
50, 17-21	10, 1798-1803	Br 6, 103-106	54, 232-236
50, 22-23	21, 1677	Br 6, 107-108	
50, 23-26	21, 1662-1664	Br 6, 122-124	
50, 26-27	21, 1672	Br 6, 143	
50, 27-40	21, 1688-1697	Br 6, 178-188	
50, 41-47	16, 1810-1812	Br 6, 259-261	54, 269-271
50, 47-50	21, 1731-1732	Br 6, 270-271	54, 275-276
50, 50-53	10, 2046-2047	Br 6, 300-302	54, 293-295
50, 53-56	21, 1751-1752	Br 6, 318-319	
50, 56-60	16, 1812-1814	Br 6, 324-327	54, 312-314
50, 61-67	21, 1761-1765	Br 6, 338-342	54, 316-320
50, 68-71	21, 1765-1767	Br 6, 343-345	54, 320-322
50, 72-73	21, 1782-1783	Br 6, 381-382	
50, 73-74	21, 1802-1803	Br 6, 425-426	55, 4-5
50, 75-78	21, 1811-1813	Br 6, 453-455	55, 8-10
50, 78-79	21, 3229	Br 7, 24	
50, 79-81	21, 1920	Br 7, 91	54, 61
50, 81-85	16, 1888-1889	Br 7, 237-238	54, 104
50, 85-92	21, 1995-1996	Br 7, 244-245	
50, 93-97	21, 1999-2000	Br 7, 249-250	

99   261. George Spalatin: Wittenberg, September 6, 1535

99   262. Elector John Frederick: Wittenberg, September 12, 1535

99   263. Gregory Brueck: Wittenberg, about September 15, 1535

99   264. Justus Jonas: Wittenberg, October 29, 1535

99   265. Justus Jonas: Wittenberg, November 10, 1535

99   266. Philip Melanchthon: Wittenberg, beginning
         of December, 1535

99   267. Elector John Frederick: Wittenberg, January 11, 1536

99   268. Nicholas Hausmann: Wittenberg, January 17, 1536

99   269. Caspar Mueller: Wittenberg, January 19, 1536

99   270. Francis Burchart: Wittenberg, January 25, 1536

99   271. Elector John Frederick: Wittenberg, March 28, 1536

99   272. Thomas Cromwell: Wittenberg, April 9, 1536

99   273. Francis Burchart: Wittenberg, April 20, 1536

99   274. George Spalatin: Wittenberg, June 10, 1536

99   275. Justus Jonas: Wittenberg, August 17, 1536

99   276. Nicholas Hausmann: Wittenberg, Torgau
         September 20, 1536

99   277. Hans Luther: Wittenberg, January 27, 1537

99   278. Justus Jonas: Altenburg, February 1, 1537

99   279. Elector John Frederick: Smalcald, about February 9, 1537

99   280. Mrs. Martin Luther: Tambach, February 27, 1537

99   281. George Spalatin: Wittenberg, March 21, 1537

99   282. Wolfgang Capito: Wittenberg, July 9, 1537

99   283. Nicholas Hausmann: Wittenberg, February 23, 1538

99   284. Edward Fox: Wittenberg, May 12, 1538

99   285. James Propst: Wittenberg, September 15, 1538

99   286. Elector John Frederick: Wittenberg, July 8, 1539

99   287. Martin Bucer: Wittenberg, October 14, 1539

99   288. Elector John Frederick: Wittenberg, October 23, 1539

99   289. Elector John Frederick: Wittenberg, October 23, 1539

99   290. Mrs. Martin Luther: Weimar, July 2, 1540

99   291. Mrs. Martin Luther: Eisenach, July 10, 1540

American Edition	St. Louis Edition	Weimar Edition	Erlangen Edition
50, 97-100	21, 2000-2001	Br 7, 251	
50, 100-102	17, 283-284	Br 7, 266-267	54, 105-107
50, 102-106	21, 3501-3502	Br 7, 267-268	
50, 107-109	21, 2016-2017	Br 7, 316-317	
50, 109-113	21, 2020-2021	Br 7, 321-322	
50, 113-117	21, 2024-2026	Br 7, 330-331	
50, 117-122	21, 2031-2033	Br 7, 341-343	55, 117-118
50, 122-124	21, 2036-2037	Br 7, 347	
50, 124-130	21, 2037-2039	Br 7, 348-350	55, 119-121
50, 130-131	21, 2040-2041	Br 7, 352	
50, 132-135	21, 2051-2052	Br 7, 381-384	55, 128-130
50, 136-138	21, 2057-2058	Br 7, 395-396	
50, 138-141	17, 282-283	Br 7, 400-404	55, 133-134
50, 141-143	21, 2069-2070	Br 7, 430	
50, 144-147	21, 2095-2096	Br 7, 503-504	
50, 148-151	21, 2105-2106	Br 7, 546-547	
50, 151-153	21, 2146-2147	Br 8, 18-20	
50, 153-157	21, 2147-2149	Br 8, 22-23	
50, 157-165	16, 1997-2000	Br 8, 35-38	
50, 165-169	21, 2156-2157	Br 8, 50-51	55, 174-175
50, 169-170	21, 2161-2162	Br 8, 59	
50, 171-174	21, 2175-2176	Br 8, 99-100	
50, 174-176	21, 2226-2227	Br 8, 199-200	
50, 177-180	21, 2238-2239	Br 8, 219-220	
50, 181-184	21, 2270-2271	Br 8, 291-292	
50, 185-187	21, 2352-2353	Br 8, 488-491	55, 234-235
50, 187-191	21, 2383-2385	Br 8, 568-569	
50, 192-194	17, 265-269	Br 8, 572-575	55, 243-247
50, 204-206	17, 269-270	Br 8, 577-578	55, 248-249
50, 207-212	21, 2485-2486	Br 9, 167-168	55, 225-227
50, 212-217	21, 2487-2489	Br 9, 171-173	

99	292. Mrs. Martin Luther: Eisenach, July 16, 1540
99	293. Mrs. Martin Luther: Eisenach, July 26, 1540
99	294. Mrs. Martin Luther: Wittenberg, September 18, 1541
99	295. Justus Jonas: Wittenberg, February 16, 1542
99	296. Marcus Crodel: Wittenberg, August 26, 1542
99	297. Marcus Crodel: Wittenberg, August 28, 1542
99	298. Marcus Crodel: Wittenberg, September 6, 1542
99	299. Justus Jonas: Wittenberg, September 23, 1542
99	300. Marcus Crodel: Wittenberg, December 26, 1542
99	301. John Luther: Wittenberg, December 27, 1542
99	302. Wenceslas Link: Wittenberg, June 20, 1543
99	303. James Propst: Wittenberg, December 5, 1544
99	304. Justus Jonas: Wittenberg, January 26, 1545
99	305. King Christian of Denmark: Wittenberg, April 14, 1545
99	306. Duke Albrecht of Prussia: Wittenberg, May 2, 1545
99	307. Elector John Frederick: Wittenberg, May 7, 1545
99	308. Nicholas von Amsdorf: Wittenberg, June 3, 1545
99	309. Nicholas von Amsdorf: Wittenberg, July 9, 1545
99	310. Justus Jonas: Wittenberg, July 16, 1545
99	311. Nicholas von Amsdorf: Wittenberg, July 17, 1545
99	312. Mrs. Martin Luther: Zeitz, July 28, 1545
99	313. Count Albrecht of Mansfeld: Wittenberg, December 6, 1545
99	314. Mrs. Martin Luther: Halle, January 25, 1546
99	315. George of Anhalt: Eisleben, January 29, 1546
99	316. Mrs. Martin Luther: Eisleben, February 1, 1546
99	317. Philip Melanchthon: Eisleben, February 1, 1546
99	318. Philip Melanchthon: Eisleben, February 3, 1546
99	319. Philip Melanchthon: Eisleben, February 6, 1546
99	320. Mrs. Martin Luther: Eisleben, February 6, 1546
99	321. Mrs. Martin Luther: Eisleben, February 7, 1546
99	322. Mrs. Martin Luther: Eisleben, February 10, 1546
99	323. George of Anhalt: Eisleben, February 10, 1546
99	324. Mrs. Martin Luther: Eisleben, February 14, 1546

American Edition	St. Louis Edition	Weimar Edition	Erlangen Edition
50, 218-220	21, 2490	Br 9, 174-175	55, 287-288
50, 221-223	21, 2501-2502	Br 9, 204-205	55, 288-289
50, 223-225	21, 2650	Br 9, 518-519	55, 332-333
50, 225-230	21, 2716-2718	Br 9, 620-622	
50, 230-233	21, 2782-2783	Br 10, 132-134	
50, 233-234	21, 2785	Br 10, 136-137	
50, 234-235	21, 2788-2789	Br 10, 147	
50, 236-238	21, 2790-2791	Br 10, 149-150	
50, 239-240	21, 2814	Br 10, 228-229	
50, 240-241	21, 2815	Br 10, 229	
50, 241-244	21, 2879-2880	Br 10, 334-335	
50, 244-246	21, 3043-3044	Br 10, 554	
50, 247-249	21, 3067-3068	Br 11, 29-30	
50, 250-252	21, 3077-3078	Br 11, 69-70	56, 130-131
50, 252-255	21, 3084-3085	Br 11, 83-86	56, 133-134
50, 255-261	21, 3088-3089	Br 11, 88	56, 134-135
50, 262-264	21, 3105-3106	Br 11, 115	
50, 264-267	21, 3113-3114	Br 11, 131-132	
50, 268-270	21, 3119-3120	Br 11, 141-143	
50, 270-272	21, 3122-3123	Br 11, 143-144	
50, 273-281	21, 3125-3126	Br 11, 148-150	56, 139-140
50, 281-284	21, 3161-3162	Br 11, 225-226	56, 146-147
50, 284-287	21, 3186	Br 11, 268-269	56 148-149
50, 288-289	21, 3188-3189	Br 11, 273	
50, 290-292	21, 3191-3192	Br 11, 275-276	56, 149-150
50, 292-295	21, 3190-3191	Br 11, 277-278	
50, 295-297		Br 11, 279-280	
50, 297-299	21, 3192-3194	Br 11, 285-286	
50, 299-300	21, 3194	Br 11, 283-284	56, 150-151
50, 301-304	21, 3194-3196	Br 11, 286-287	56, 151-153
50, 305-308	21, 3198-3199	Br 11, 290-291	56, 153-154
50, 309-310	21, 3197-3198	Br 11, 292	
50, 310-313	21, 3203-3204	Br 11, 299-300	56, 154-155

99   325. Philip Melanchthon: Eisleben, February 14, 1546

Early Sermons, 1510(?)-1517

Pr 1   Luther's First (?) Sermon, Matthew 7:12, 1510 (?) in Erfurt

Pr 20   Sermon on the Tenth Sunday after Trinity,
10 (?) Luke 18:9-14, July 27, 1516

Pr 29   Sermon on St. Thomas' Day, Psalm 19:1 December 21, 1516

Pr 47   Sermon on the Fourth Sunday after the Epiphany,
Matthew 8:23-27, February 1, 1517

Pr 52   Sermon on St. Matthew's Day, Matthew 11:25-30
February 24, 1517

Two Lenten Sermons, 1518

217   Sermon on the Man Born Blind, John 9:1-38, Preached
on the Wednesday after Laetare, March 17, 1518

217   Sermon on the Raising of Lazarus, John 11:1-45, Preached
on the Friday after Laetare, March 19, 1518

Sermons at Leipzig and Erfurt, 1519; 1521

476   Sermon Preached in the Castle at Leipzig on the
Day of St. Peter and St. Paul, Matthew 16:13-19,
June 29, 1519

203   Sermon Preached at Erfurt on the Journey to
Worms, John 20:19-20, April 7, 1521

Eight Sermons at Wittenberg, 1522

Pr 189   The First Sermon, March 9, 1522, Invocavit Sunday

Pr 190   The Second Sermon, March 10, 1522, Monday after Invocavit

Pr 191   The Third Sermon, March 11, 1522, Tuesday after Invocavit

Pr 192   The Fourth Sermon, March 12, 1522, Wednesday after Invocavit

Pr 193   The Fifth Sermon, March 13, 1522, Thursday after Invocavit

Pr 194   The Sixth Sermon, March 14, 1522, Friday after Invocavit

Pr 195   The Seventh Sermon, March 15, 1522, Saturday
before Reminiscere

Pr 196   The Eighth Sermon, March 16, 1522, Reminiscere
Sunday

Two Sermons Preached at Weimar, 1522

Pr 239   The First Sermon, Matthew 22:37-39, the Morning
of October 19, 1522

American Edition	St. Louis Edition	Weimar Edition	Erlangen Edition
50, 313-318	21, 3202-3203	Br 11, 301-302	
51, 5-13		4, 590-595	
51, 14-17	10, 1284-1289	1, 63-65	var 1, 101-104
51, 17-23	12, 1794-1801	1, 111-113	var 1, 156-161
51, 23-26	12, 1814-1817	1, 128-130	var 1, 200-202
51, 26-31	12, 1762-1769	1, 138-141	var 1, 171-176
51, 35-43	12, 1302-1313	1, 267-273	18, 196-205
51, 44-49	12, 1314-1321	1, 273-277	18, 205-211
51, 53-60	11, 2306-2313	2, 244-249	15, 396-403
			var 3, 217-224
51, 60-66	12, 1386-1393	7, 808-813	17, 98-104
51, 70-75	20, 8-17	10^{III}, 1-13	28, 205-215
51, 75-78	20, 17-22	10^{III}, 13-20	28, 216-221
51, 79-83	20, 22-28	10^{III}, 21-30	28, 221-228
51, 84-88	20, 28-34	10^{III}, 30-40	28, 228-235
51, 89-91	20, 34-38	10^{III}, 40-47	28, 235-239
51, 92-95	20, 39-43	10^{III}, 48-54	28, 239-244
51, 95-96	20, 43-45	10^{III}, 55-58	28, 244-247
51, 97-100	20, 46-51	10^{III}, 58-64	28, 247-251
51, 104-110		10^{III}, 341-346	E_2, 16, 420-429

American Edition	St. Louis Edition	Weimar Edition	Erlangen Edition
51, 111-117		10^{III}, 347-352	E_2, 16, 429-436
51, 119-132	11, 2174-2189	17, 38-45	15, 270-283
51, 137-141		30^{I}, 57-61	
51, 141-145		30^{I}, 61-66	
51, 145-150		30^{I}, 66-72	
51, 150-155		30^{I}, 72-77	
51, 155-161		30^{I}, 77-86	
51, 162-169		30^{I}, 86-94	
51, 169-176		30^{I}, 94-102	
51, 176-182		30^{I}, 103-109	
51, 182-188		30^{I}, 109-116	
51, 188-193		30^{I}, 116-122	
51, 193-208	12, 1328-1341	32, 28-39	17, 40-53
51, 209-218		32, 261-270	
51, 221-227		34, 156-165	
51, 231-243	12, 2072-2085	36, 237-254	18, 359-372
51, 243-255	12, 2086-2099	36, 255-270	18, 372-384
51, 257-287	9, 882-913	36, 352-375	19, 296-328

American Edition	St. Louis Edition	Weimar Edition	Erlangen Edition
51, 289-299		47, 757-771	8, 280-305
51, 301-312	12, 1408-1421	47, 772-779	17, 119-129
51, 313-329	7, 696-711	49, 124-135	19, 72-88
51, 331-354	12, 1962-1984	49, 588-615	17, 239-262
51, 355-367	10, 588-599	49, 797-805	20, 45-56
51, 369-380	12, 1168-1177	51, 123-134	16, 139-150
51, 381-392	12, 1254-1264	51, 187-194	16, 264-275
52, 3-6	11, xxxiv-xxxix	10^I, 1-8	7, 1-5
52, 7-31	11, 118-143	10^I, 58-95	10, 126-153
52, 32-40	11, 144-153	10^I, 128-141	10, 153-163
52, 41-88	11, 154-205	10^I, 180-247	10, 163-218
52, 89-101	11, 204-219	10^I, 270-289	10, 218-232
52, 102-148	11, 232-283	10^I, 379-448	10, 247-301
52, 149-158	11, 284-295	10^I, 504-519	10, 301-312
52, 159-286	11, 294-429	10^I, 555-728	10, 313-456
53, 7-14	10, 220-225	12, 35-37	22, 151-156
53, 15-40	10, 2232-2255	12, 205-220	var 7, 1-20
53, 41-50	10, 258-263	18, 417-421	53, 315-321
53, 51-90	10, 226-257	19, 72-113	22, 226-244
53, 95-103	10, 2136-2143	12, 42-48	22, 157-166
53, 104-105	10, 2256-2257	Br 3, 462-463	53, 285
53, 106-109	10, 2144-2147	19, 537-541	22, 290-294
53, 110-115	10, 720-725	30^{III}, 74-80	23, 207-213
53, 116-118		30^I, 343-345	

365	How One Should Teach Common Folk to Shrive Themselves, 1531
542	The Ordination of the Ministers of the Word, 1539
415, 232	Dear Lord God, Awaken Us
415, 232	Help, Dear Lord God, That We May Become and Remain Partakers
415, 232	Almighty Eternal God, We Heartily Pray Thee
415, 232	Merciful Everlasting God, Who Didst Not Spare Thine Own Son
415, 232	Almighty Father, Eternal God, Who Didst Allow
415, 232	Almighty God, Who by the Death of Thy Son
415, 232	Almighty Lord God, Grant to Us Who Believe
415, 232	Lord God, Dear Father Who Through Thy Holy Spirit
415, 232	Almighty Eternal God, Who Hast Taught Us
415, 232	Almighty God, Who Art the Protector
415, 232	O Thou Dear Lord God
415, 232	We Give Thanks to Thee, Almighty God
415, 232	Lord God, Heavenly Father, Who Createst Holy Desire
415, 232	Lord God, Heavenly Father, from Whom Without Ceasing We Receive
419	Lord God Almighty, Who Dost Not Disdain
419	Lord God, Heavenly Father, Who Hast No Pleasure
419	Lord God, Heavenly Father, Thou Knowest
419	Almighty Everlasting God, Who Through Thy Holy Spirit
712	O Almighty God, Father of Our Lord Jesus Christ, Look Upon This N.
712	O Almighty Eternal God, Father of Our Lord Jesus Christ, I Cry to Thee
712	Almighty Eternal God, Who According to Thy Righteous Judgment
712	Lord, Holy Father, Almighty Eternal God
728	O God, Who Hast Created Man and Woman
542	Merciful God, Heavenly Father, Thou Hast Said to Us

American Edition	St. Louis Edition	Weimar Edition	Erlangen Edition
53, 119-121	10, 14-17	30^{I}, 383-387	21, 17-19
53, 122-126	10, 1602-1605	38, 423-431	64, 290-293
53, 131	10, 1449	35, 552	56, 326
53, 131-132	10, 1470	35, 264	56, 357-358
53, 132	10, 1456	35, 533	56, 332
53, 132-133	10, 1456	35, 553	56, 332
53, 133	10, 1456	35, 553	56, 332
53, 134	10, 1447	35, 553-554	56, 320
53, 134-135	10, 1447	35, 554	56, 320
53, 135	10, 1459	35, 554	56, 320
53, 136	10, 1455	35, 554	56, 335
53, 136-137	10, 1461	19, 86	56, 347
53, 137	10, 1445	35, 556	56, 318
53, 137-138	10, 1445	19, 102	56, 31
53, 138	10, 1462	35, 233	56, 345
53, 138-139	10, 1460	35, 249	56, 347
53, 139-140	10, 1479	35, 555	56, 352-353
53, 140, 169	10, 1480-1481	30^{III}, 35	56, 362
53, 140, 169	10, 1480-1481	30^{III}, 36	56, 353
53, 141, 170	10, 1478-1479	30^{III}, 36	56, 362
53, 142	10, 2140	12, 43	22, 158-159
53, 142-143	10, 2144	12, 43-44	22, 291
53, 143-144	10, 2144-2145	12, 43-44	22, 291-292
53, 144	10, 2142	12, 44	22, 161
53, 144-145	10, 725	30^{III}, 80	23, 213
53, 145-146	10, 1604-1605	38, 429	64, 292

The Liturgical Chants

419   The Agnus Dei

419   The German Litany and the Latin Litany Corrected,
        1529

415, 232   The Te Deum, 1529?

444   The Magnificat, 1533

        The Communio, 1533

415   The Gloria in Excelsis, 1537

The Hymns

415, 232   A New Song Here Shall Be Begun, 1523

415, 232   Dear Christians, Let Us Now Rejoice, 1523

415, 232   From Trouble Deep I Cry to Thee, 1523

415, 232   Ah, God, from Heaven Look Down, 1523

415, 232   Although the Fools Say with Their Mouth, 1523

415, 232   Would That the Lord Would Grant Us Grace, 1523

415, 232   Come, the Heathen's Healing Light, 1523

415, 232   Jesus We Now Must Laud and Sing, 1523?

415, 232   All Praise to Thee, O Jesus Christ, 1523?

415, 232   Happy who in God's Fear Doth Stay, 1524

415, 232   Were God Not with Us at This Time, 1524

415, 232   In Peace and Joy I Now Depart, 1524

415, 232   Jesus Christ, Our God and Savior, 1524

American Edition	St. Louis Edition	Weimar Edition	Erlangen Edition
53, 151-152	10, 1478-1479	30^{III}, 33, 40	
53, 153-170	10, 1474-1481	30^{III}, 29-42	56, 360-366
53, 171-175	10, 1458-1461	35, 458-459 35, 521-524	56, 345-347
53, 176-179	7, 1376	7, 546	45, 215
53, 181-183			
53, 184-188 53, 292-294		35, 287-296	56, 368
53, 211-216	10, 1434-1436	35, 411-415 35, 487-488	56, 340-343
53, 217-220	10, 1436-1438	35, 422-423 35, 493-495	56, 309-310
53, 221-224	10, 1440-1441	35, 419-420 35, 492-493	56, 313-315
53, 225-228	10, 1438-1439	35, 415-417 35, 488-490	56, 311-312
53, 229-231	10, 1439-1440	35, 441-443 35, 505	56, 312-313
53, 232-234	10, 1441-1442	35, 418-419 35, 490-492	56, 318-319
53, 235-236	10, 1449	35, 430-431 35, 497-498	56, 325-326
53, 237-239	10, 1450-1451	35, 431-433 35, 498-499	56, 327-328
53, 240-241	10, 1442-1443	35, 434-435 35, 499	56, 328-329
53, 242-244	10, 1442	35, 437-438 35, 501-502	56, 335-336
53, 245-246	10, 1457-1458	35, 440-441 35, 504-505	56, 336-337
53, 247-248	10, 1455	35, 438-439 35, 503-504	56, 331-332
53, 249-251	10, 1443-1444	35, 435-437 35, 500-501	56, 315-317

415, 232	Let God Be Blest, 1524
415, 232	Death Held Our Lord in Prison, 1524
415, 232	Jesus Christ, Our Savior True, 1524
415, 232	Come, God Creator Holy Ghost, 1524
415, 232	Now Let Us Pray to the Holy Ghost, 1524
415, 232	Come, Holy Spirit Lord and God, 1524
415, 232	God the Father with Us Be, 1524
415, 232	In One True God We All Believe, 1524
415, 232	In the Midst of Life We Are, 1524
415, 232	These Are the Holy Ten Commands, 1524
415, 232	Man, Wouldst Thou Live All Blissfully, 1524
415, 232	Isaiah 'Twas the Prophet, 1526
415, 232	Our God He Is a Castle Strong, 1527/1528
415, 232	Grant Peace in Mercy, Lord, We Pray, 1528/1529
415, 232	Lord God, Thy Praise We Sing, 1531
415, 232	From Heaven on High I Come to You, 1534-1535
415, 232	To Me She's Dear, the Worthy Maid, 1535-1545
415, 232	All Glory, Laud, and Praise be Given, 1537
415, 232	Our Father in the Heaven Who Art, 1539

American Edition	St. Louis Edition	Weimar Edition	Erlangen Edition
53, 252-254	10, 1444-1445	35, 452-453 35, 514-515	56, 317-318
53, 255-257	10, 1447-1448	35, 443-445 35, 506-507	56, 321-322
53, 258-259	10, 1446-1447	35, 445 35, 507-508	56, 319-320
53, 260-262	10, 1452	35, 446-447 35, 508-509	56, 329-330
53, 263-264	10, 1458	35, 447-448 35, 510	56, 337-338
53, 265-267	10, 1451	35, 448-449 35, 510-512	56, 330-331
53, 268-270	10, 1454-1455	35, 450 35, 512-513	56, 334-335
53, 271-273	10, 1454	35, 451-452 35, 513-514	56, 333
53, 274-276	10, 1445-1446	35, 453-454 35, 515-516	56, 338-339
53, 277-279	10, 1452-1453	35, 426-428 35, 495-497	56, 322-324
53, 280-281	10, 1457	35, 428-429 35, 497	56, 324-325
53, 282, 82-83	10, 1459-1462	35, 455 35, 516-518	56, 343
53, 283-385	10, 1460-1462	35, 455-457 35, 518-520	56, 343-344
53, 286-287	10, 1462	35, 458 35, 521	56, 345
53, 288, 171-175	10, 1458-1461	35, 458 35, 521-524	56, 345-347
53, 289-291	10, 1462-1464	35, 459-461 35, 524-525	56, 348-349
53, 292-294	10, 1464	35, 462-463 35, 525-527	56, 350-351
53, 294, 184-188		35, 287-296	
53, 295-298	10, 1465-1466	35, 463-467 35, 527-528	56, 351-353

American Edition	St. Louis Edition	Weimar Edition	Erlangen Edition
53, 299-301	10, 1467-1468	35, 468-470 35, 490-491, 528	56, 355-356
53, 302-303	10, 1467	35, 470-471, 528	56, 353-354
53, 304-305	10, 1449	35, 467-468 35, 528	56, 354
53, 306-307	10, 1469	35, 471-473 35, 528	56, 357-358
53, 308-309	10, 1470	35, 473 35, 529	56, 358
53, 315-316	10, 1422-1425	35, 474-475	56, 296-297
53, 317-318	10, 1424-1425	35, 475-476	56, 298-299
53, 319-320	10, 1432-1434	35, 483-484	56, 295-296
53, 321-324		50, 368-374	
53, 325-331	10, 1424-1431	35, 478-483	56, 299-306
53, 332-334	10, 1430-1433	35, 476-477	56, 306-308
53, 335-341		35, 537	
54, 3-114		TR 1, 1-656	
54, 115-121		TR 1, 657-684	
54, 123-165		TR 2, 1232-1889	
54, 167-200		TR 2, 1950-3416	
54, 201-249		TR 3, 3465-3659	
54, 251-364		TR 3, 3683-4719	
54, 365-409		TR 4, 4858 to 5, 5341	
54, 411-464		TR 5, 5379-5603	
54, 465-476		TR 5, 5659-5675	
	22, 1-65		57, 1-107
	22, 64-137		57, 108-220
	22, 138-181		57, 220-280
	22, 182-239		57, 280-362
	22, 238-257		57, 362-385

American Edition	St. Louis Edition	Weimar Edition	Erlangen Edition
	22, 256-259		57, 385-391
	22, 260-353		58, 1-152
	22, 354-355		58, 153-162
	22, 356-383		58, 162-213
	22, 382-391		58, 214-239
	22, 392-415		58, 239-268
	22, 414-445		58, 269-338
	22, 416-489		58, 338-413
	22, 488-509		58, 413-445
	22, 510-535		59, 1-34
	22, 534-539		59, 34-44
	22, 540-555		59, 44-74
	22, 554-563		59, 74-87
	22, 562-595		59, 87-130
	22, 594-609		59, 131-155
	22, 610-627		59, 155-180
	22, 628-697		59, 181-285
	22, 696-701		59, 285-288
	22, 700-781		59, 289-348
			60, 1-75
	22, 780-785		60, 75-80
	22, 784-841		60, 80-176
	22, 840-935		60, 176-311
	22, 936-947		60, 312-327
	22, 946-949		60, 327-331
	22, 950-969		60, 331-356
	22, 970-983		60, 356-372
	22, 982-989		60, 372-382

American Edition	St. Louis Edition	Weimar Edition	Erlangen Edition
	22, 990-997		60, 382-390
	22, 996-999		60, 390-395
	22, 998-1007		60, 395-404
	22, 1006-1007		60, 404-405
	22, 1008-1095		61, 1-125
	22, 1094-1099		61, 125-132
	22, 1098-1113		61, 132-149
	22, 1112-1115		61, 150-152
	22, 1114-1119		61, 152-159
	22, 1118-1121		61, 159-164
	22, 1122-1215		61, 164-304
	22, 1214-1231		61, 305-327
	22, 1230-1283		61, 327-397
	22, 1284-1289		61, 397-403
	22, 1288-1299		61, 404-417
	22, 1298-1319		61, 417-447
	22, 1318-1327		62, 1-14
	22, 1328-1331		62, 15-18
	22, 1330-1339		62, 18-28
	22, 1338-1345		62, 28-35
	22, 1344-1349		62, 36-40
	22, 1348-1371		62, 41-71
	22, 1370-1381		62, 71-87
	22, 1382-1389		62, 88-97
	22, 1388-1401		62, 97-113
	22, 1400-1409		62, 113-124
	22, 1408-1417		62, 125-139
	22, 1418-1433		62, 139-159
	22, 1432-1437		62, 160-169
	22, 1438-1447		62, 169-180
	22, 1446-1453		62, 180-189

American Edition	St. Louis Edition	Weimar Edition	Erlangen Edition
	22, 1454-1467		62, 189-209
	22, 1468-1471		62, 209-214
	22, 1472-1521		62, 214-284
	22, 1522-1537		62, 285-307
	22, 1536-1541		62, 307-311
	22, 1540-1545		62, 311-317
	22, 1544-1553		62, 317-328
	22, 1554-1557		62, 329-334
	22, 1558-1561		62, 334-339
	22, 1560-1571		62, 339-352
	22, 1570-1591		62, 352-379
	22, 1590-1611		62, 379-405
	22, 1612-1633		62, 405-435
	22, 1634-1639		62, 435-443
	22, 1640-1647		62, 443-451
	22, 1646-1647		62, 451-452
	22, 1648-1653		62, 453-460
	22, 1654-1663		62, 461-474
	22, 1664-1667		
	22, 1668-1807		
	22, 1808-1993		

PART 2

Which works in the St. Louis edition are included in the American edition and where they may be found in the American, the Weimar, and the Erlangen editions.

St. Louis Edition	American Edition	Weimar Edition	Erlangen Edition
1, 1-437	1, 1-359	42, 1-263	ex 1, 1-2, 116
1, 436-921	2, 1-399	42, 264-549	ex 2, 116-3, 276
1, 920-1369	3, 1-365	42, 550-673 43, 1-137	ex 3, 277-5, 67
1, 1368-1765 2, 1-123	4, 1-409	43, 137-430	ex 5, 67-6, 243
2, 122-609	5, 1-386	43, 430-695	ex 6, 243-7, 354
2, 608-1159	6, 1-407	44, 1-304	ex 8, 1-9, 162
2, 1158-1655	7, 1-377	44, 304-581	ex 9, 162-10, 313
2, 1654-2091	8, 1-333	44, 581-825	ex 10, 313-11, 325
3, 2-17	35, 155-174	16, 363-393 "U"	33, 3-21
3, 1352-1361	43, 3-45	10^{II}, 375-428	22, 3-32 65, 266-268
3, 1370-1639	9, 1-311	14, 489-744	ex 13, 1-351
3, 1880-1973	15, 265-352	54, 28-100	37, 1-104
(4, 1-1913 — later works on the Psalms)	10, 1-464	3, 11-519	
	11, 1-553	3, 519-652 4, 1-414	
4, 124-137	35, 203-223	38, 9-17, 69	37, 250-266
4, 220-301	14, 279-349	5, 19-74	ex 14, 1-89
4, 1654-1743	14, 137-205	18, 479-530	37, 340-442
5, 1-75	14, 207-277	19, 552-615	38, 369-453
5, 74-237	12, 1-136	40^{II}, 193-212	ex 18, 8-127
5, 254-307	12, 145-194	45, 205-250 51, 267-295 17^{I}, 228-243	39, 4-61 39, 61-105 39, 106-122
5, 306-311	48, 248-253	8, 210-214	
5, 340-619	12, 197-410	40^{II}, 472-610 40^{II}, 315-470	ex 18, 130-260 ex 19, 10-154
5, 656-695	13, 1-37	8, 4-35	39, 178-220
5, 696-731	13, 39-72	31^{I}, 189-218	39, 224-265
5, 732-799	13, 73-141	40^{III}, 484-594	ex 18, 264-334

St. Louis Edition	American Edition	Weimar Edition	Erlangen Edition
5, 800-887	13, 143-224	51, 200-264	39, 265-364
5, 922-1055	13, 225-348	41, 79-239	40, 38-192
5, 1056-1097	13, 349-387	31^I, 393-426	40, 192-240
5, 1098-1131	13, 389-420	19, 297-336	40, 240-280
5, 1132-1173	14, 1-39	31^I, 223-257	40, 280-328
5, 1174-1251	14, 41-106	31^I, 65-182	41, 7-91
5, 1272-1283	43, 97-112	15, 69-78	41, 115-128 53, 233
5, 1284-1303	45, 311-337	15, 360-378	41, 128-150 53, 281
5, 1302-1333	14, 107-135	31^I, 430-456	41, 151-185
5, 1332-1339	12, 139-144	31^I, 580-586	
5, 1372-1579	15, 1-187	20, 7-203	ex 21, 1-248
5, 1580-1659	15, 189-264	31^{II}, 586-769	ex 21, 267-368
6, 4-9	35, 273-278	DB 11^I, 17-25	63, 52-59
6, 8-471	16, 1-349	31^{II}, 1-260	ex 22, 9-406
6, 470-851	17, 1-416	31^{II}, 261-585	ex 22,406-23,296
6, 896-917 6, 940-943	35, 294-316	DB 11^{II}, 3-49 DB 11^{II}, 125-131	41, 237-258 41, 294-324
6, 946-1029	18, 1-76	13, 1-66	ex 24, 1-88
6, 1414-1479	18, 77-123	13, 88-122	ex 25, 55-125
6, 1684-1773	18, 125-190	13, 158-206	ex 25, 377-481
7, 346-677	21, 1-294	32, 299-544	43, 1-368
7, 696-711	51, 313-329	49, 124-135	19, 72-88
7, 752-821	42, 15-81	2, 80-130	21, 156-227 45, 203-227
7, 1372-1445	21, 295-358	7, 544-604	45, 211-290
7, 1376	53, 176-179	7, 546	45, 215
7, 1538-2147	22, 1-530	46, 538-789 47, 1-231	45, 294-47, 226
7, 2192-2417	23, 1-197	33, 1-314	47, 226-394
8, 1-255	23, 198-422	33, 314-675	48, 1-409

St. Louis Edition	American Edition	Weimar Edition	Erlangen Edition
8, 264-745	24, 1-422	45, 465-733	49, 1-50, 154
		46, 1-111	
	25, 1-524	56, 1-528	
8, 1026-1085	28, 1-56	12, 92-142	51, 1-69
8, 1088-1273	28, 57-213	36, 481-696	51, 70-275
	28, 215-384	26, 4-120	
	29, 1-90	25, 6-69	
	29, 91-105	25, 69-78	
	29, 107-241	57^{III}, 97-238	
8, 1352-1661	27, 151-410	2, 445-618	gal 3, 126-483
9, 8-15	27, 145-149	40^{I}, 33-36	gal 1, 1-12
9, 16-601	26, 1-461	40^{I}, 40-688	gal 1, 12-2, 286
9, 600-771	27, 1-144	40^{II}, 1-184	gal 2, 286-3, 120
9, 882-913	51, 257-287	36, 352-375	19, 296-328
9, 958-1111	30, 1-145	12, 259-399	51, 324-494
9, 1342-1397	30, 147-199	14, 14-74	52, 212-272
9, 1398-1523	30, 217-327	20, 599-601	
9, 1742-1755	30, 201-215	14, 75-91	52, 272-287
	53, 116-118	30^{I}, 343-345	
10, 14-17	53, 119-121	30^{I}, 383-387	21, 17-19
10, 220-225	53, 7-14	12, 35-37	22, 151-156
10, 226-257	53, 51-90	19, 72-113	22, 226-249
10, 258-263	53, 41-50	18, 417-421	53, 315-321
10, 266-351	44, 115-217	6, 404-469	21, 274-360
10, 360-373	45, 51-74	8, 676-687	22, 43-59
10, 374-417	45, 75-129	11, 245-280	22, 59-105
10, 416-459	46, 207-258	30^{II}, 517-588	20, 1-45

St. Louis Edition	American Edition	Weimar Edition	Erlangen Edition
10, 458-485	45, 339-378	15, 27-53	22, 168-199
10, 488-531	46, 87-137	19^{II}, 623-662	22, 244-290
			53, 391-392
10, 544-549	49, 272-280	Br 5, 258-261	54, 138-142
10, 552-555	49, 244-250	Br 5, 181-183	54, 110-112
10, 562-563	49, 429-433	Br 5, 662	
10, 570-572	50, 9-12	Br 6, 35-37	54, 213-214
10, 588-599	51, 355-367	49, 797-805	20, 45-46
10, 598-628	45, 11-49	10^{II}, 275-304	20, 57-87
10, 628-629	45, 3-9	10^{II}, 265-266	20, 87-89
			53, 156-157
10, 630-637	44, 3-14	2, 166-171	16, 158-165
			var 3, 446-452
10, 712-721	45, 379-393	15, 163-169	53, 236-244
10, 720-725	53, 110-115	30^{III}, 74-80	23, 207-213
10, 725	53, 144-145	30^{III}, 80	23, 213
10, 730-735	43, 243-250	53, 205-208	23, 338-343
10, 754-809	46, 259-320	30^{III}, 205-248	23, 91-154
10, 824-855	45, 273-310	6, 36-60	20, 89-122
10, 912-913	49, 50-55	Br 3, 176-177	53, 219-220
10, 914-937	45, 231-273	15, 293-313	22, 199-226
		15, 321-322	
10, 954-961	45, 159-176	12, 11-15	22, 105-112
10, 960-977	45, 176-194	12, 18-30	22, 112-130
			53, 196-197
10, 992-1019	34, 197-229	50, 262-283	23, 251-281
10, 1168-1173	38, 235-277	39^{II}, 3-30	var 4, 458-461
10, 1232-1245	35, 3-22	2, 714-723	20, 179-193

St. Louis Edition	American Edition	Weimar Edition	Erlangen Edition
10, 1262-1277	31, 293-306	2, 145-152	var 2, 329-339
	51, 5-13	4, 590-595	
10, 1284-1289	51, 14-17	1, 63-65	var 1, 101-104
10, 1298-1389	44, 15-114	6, 202-276	20, 193-290
10, 1394-1415	43, 187-211	38, 358-375	23, 214-238
10, 1422-1425	53, 315-316	35, 474-475	56, 296-297
10, 1424-1425	53, 317-318	35, 475-476	56, 298-299
10, 1424-1431	53, 325-331	35, 478-483	56, 299-306
10, 1430-1433	53, 332-334	35, 476-477	56, 306-308
10, 1432-1434	53, 319-320	35, 483-484	56, 295-296
	53, 321-324	50, 368-374	
	53, 335-341	35, 537	
10, 1434-1436	53, 211-216	35, 411-415	56, 340-343
		35, 487-488	
10, 1436-1438	53, 217-220	35, 422-425	56, 309-310
		35, 493-495	
10, 1438-1439	53, 225-228	35, 415-417	56, 311-312
		35, 488-490	
10, 1439-1440	53, 229-231	35, 441-443	56, 312-313
		35, 505	
10, 1440-1441	53, 221-224	35, 419-420	56, 313-315
		35, 492-493	
10, 1441-1442	53, 232-234	35, 418-419	56, 318-319
		35, 490-492	
10, 1442	53, 242-244	35, 437-438	56, 335-336
		35, 501-502	
10, 1442-1443	53, 240-241	35, 434-435	56, 328-329
		35, 499	
10, 1443-1444	53, 249-251	35, 435-437	56, 315-317
		35, 500-501	
10, 1444-1445	53, 252-254	35, 452-453	56, 317-318
		35, 514-515	
10, 1445	53, 137	35, 556	56, 318
10, 1445	53, 137-138	19, 102	56, 318

415, 232	In the Midst of Life We Are, 1524
415, 232	Jesus Christ, Our Savior True, 1524
415, 232	Almighty God, Who by the Death of Thy Son
415, 232	Almighty Lord God, Grant to Us who Believe
415, 232	Death Held Our Lord in Prison, 1524
415, 232	Dear Lord God, Awake Us
415, 232	Come, the Heathen's Healing Light, 1523
415, 232	Jesus We Now Must Laud and Sing, 1523?
415, 232	Come, Holy Spirit Lord and God, 1524
415, 232	Come, God Creator Holy Ghost, 1524
415, 232	These Are the Holy Ten Commands, 1524
415, 232	In One True God We All Believe, 1524
415, 232	God the Father with Us Be, 1524
415, 232	Almighty Eternal God, Who Hast Taught Us
415, 232	In Peace and Joy I Now Depart, 1524
415, 232	Almighty Eternal God, We Heartily Pray Thee
415, 232	Merciful Everlasting God, Who Didst Not Spare Thine Own Son
415, 232	Almighty Father, Eternal God, Who Didst Allow
415, 232	Man, Wouldst Thou Live All Blissfully, 1524
415, 232	Were God Not with Us at This Time, 1524
415, 232	Now Let Us Pray to the Holy Ghost, 1524

FULLER
THEOLOGICAL SEMINARY
School of Theology

F.T.S. Box O
December 14, 1993

Professor Elsie Anne McKee
Princeton Theological Seminary
CN 821
Princeton, New Jersey 08542-0803

Dear Elsie:

I received copies of both of the letters you wrote for me, about one and two weeks ago, respectively. I thought your first letter was terrific, indeed, everything I'd hoped for; so when you forwarded the "new and improved" second epistle, I could only be overwhelmed. If I do not succeed in obtaining one of these grants, it will be no fault of yours, Elsie, and — regardless of outcome — the effort and polish you put into these letters will long cement my own loyalty and affection for you as friend and colleague. With all humility, I thank you.

I have just returned from the Sixteenth Century Studies Conference in St. Louis. There I had the pleasure of introducing my friend and recent Duke graduate, Craig Farmer, to everyone I knew. Craig

up on a couple of occasions, and both Muller and Wengert expressed admiration for your scholarship. And so I'm sorry you could not attend. One unexpected development was that I was asked by Merry Wiesner Hanks (whom I met only last year) to organize the theology papers for next year's conference in Toronto. This means, of course, I will be contacting everyone I know to serve as chair or commentator. So if you need an excuse to attend next year but don't wish to read a paper, I'll be happy to give you the pick of sessions to chair and/or papers to comment on!

About the enclosure: I can't imagine anything riskier than selecting a book for a fellow academic — you probably have a few already, I suppose — but I myself learned of this book's existence only recently, so I have some hope that it won't duplicate your holdings. It is also the sort of book I find handy to have around, as one might infer from my interest in "Calvin handbooks" and such. Anyway, perhaps it will one day save you a trip or two to the library to verify a reference and, if it does, I hope it will remind you of my appreciation.

In friendship,

John L. Thompson
Assistant Professor
of Historical Theology

135 North Oakland Avenue, Pasadena, California 91182 · Telephone: 818-584-5300   FAX: 818-584-5321

St. Louis Edition	American Edition	Weimar Edition	Erlangen Edition
10, 1445-1446	53, 274-276	35, 453-454 35, 515-516	56, 338-339
10, 1446-1447	53, 258-259	35, 445 35, 507-508	56, 319-320
10, 1447	53, 134	35, 553-554	56, 320
10, 1447	53, 134-135	35, 554	56, 320
10, 1447-1448	53, 255-257	35, 443-445 35, 506-507	56, 321-322
10, 1449	53, 131	35, 552	56, 326
10, 1449	53, 235-236	35, 430-431 35, 497-498	56, 325-326
10, 1450-1451	53, 237-239	35, 431-433 35, 498-499	56, 327-328
10, 1451	53, 265-267	35, 448-449 35, 510-512	56, 330-331
10, 1452	53, 260-262	35, 446-447 35, 508-509	56, 329-330
10, 1452-1453	53, 277-279	35, 426-428 35, 495-497	56, 322-324
10, 1454	53, 271-273	35, 451-452 35, 513-514	56, 333
10, 1454-1455	53, 268-270	35, 450 35, 512-513	56, 334-335
10, 1455	53, 136	35, 554	56, 335
10, 1455	53, 247-248	35, 438-439 35, 503-504	56, 331-332
10, 1456	53, 132	35, 533	56, 332
10, 1456	53, 132-133	35, 553	56, 332
10, 1456	53, 133	35, 553	56, 332
10, 1457	53, 280-281	35, 428-429 35, 497	56, 324-325
10, 1457-1458	53, 245-246	35, 440-441 35, 504-505	56, 336-337
10, 1458	53, 263-264	35, 447-448 35, 510	56, 337-338

415, 232 The Te Deum, 1529?

415, 232 Lord God, Thy Praise We Sing, 1531

415, 232 Lord God, Dear Father who Through Thy Holy Spirit

415, 232 Isaiah 'Twas the Prophet, 1526

415, 232 Communio, 1533

415, 232 The Gloria in Excelsis, 1537

415, 232 Lord God, Heavenly Father, from whom
     Without Ceasing We Receive

415, 232 Our God He Is a Castle Strong, 1527/1528

415, 232 Almighty God, Who Art the Protector

415, 232 Lord God, Heavenly Father, Who Createst Holy Desire

415, 232 Grant Peace in Mercy, Lord, We Pray, 1528/1529

415, 232 From Heaven on High I Come to You, 1534-1535

415, 232 To Me She's Dear, the Worthy Maid, 1535-1545

415, 232 All Glory, Laud, and Praise be Given, 1537

415, 232 Our Father in the Heaven Who Art, 1539

415, 232 Herod, Why Dreadest Thou a Foe, 1541

415, 232 To Jordan When Our Lord Had Come, 1541

415, 232 Lord, Keep Us Steadfast in Thy Word, 1541/1542

415, 232 From Heaven the Angel Troop Came Near, 1543

415, 232 Help, Dear Lord God, That We May Become and
     Remain Partakers

St. Louis Edition	American Edition	Weimar Edition	Erlangen Edition
10, 1458-1461	53, 171-175	35, 458-459 35, 521-524	56, 345-347
10, 1458-1461	53, 171-175 53, 288	35, 458 35, 521-524	56, 345-347
10, 1459	53, 135	35, 554	56, 320
10, 1459-1462	53, 82-83 53, 282 53, 182-183 53, 184-188 53, 294	35, 455 35, 516-518 35, 287-296	56, 343
10, 1460	53, 138-139	35, 249	56, 347
10, 1460-1462	53, 283-285	35, 455-457 35, 518-520	56, 343-344
10, 1461	53, 136-137	19, 86	56, 347
10, 1462	53, 138	35, 233	56, 345
10, 1462	53, 286-287	35, 458 35, 521	56, 345
10, 1462-1464	53, 289-291	35, 459-461 35, 524-525	56, 348-349
10, 1464	53, 292-294	35, 462-463 35, 525-527	56, 350-351
	53, 184-188 53, 294	35, 287-296	
10, 1465-1466	53, 295-298	35, 463-467 35, 527-528	56, 351-353
10, 1467	53, 302-303	35, 470-471 35, 528	56, 353-354
10, 1467-1468	53, 299-301	35, 468-470 35, 490-491 35, 528	56, 355-356
10, 1469	53, 304-305	35, 467-468 35, 528	56, 354
10, 1469	53, 306-307	35, 471-473 35, 528	56, 357-358
10, 1470	53, 131-132	35, 264	56, 357-358

St. Louis Edition	American Edition	Weimar Edition	Erlangen Edition
10, 1470	53, 308-309	35, 473 35, 529	56, 358
10, 1474-1481	53, 153-170	30^{III}, 29-42	56, 360-366
10, 1478-1479	53, 151-152	30^{III}, 33, 40	
10, 1478-1479	53, 141, 170	30^{III}, 36	56, 362
10, 1479	53, 139-140	35, 555	56, 353-353
10, 1480-1481	53, 140, 169	30^{III}, 35	56, 362
10, 1480-1481	53, 140, 169	30^{III}, 36	56, 353
10, 1538-1549	39, 301-314	11, 408-416	22, 140-151
10, 1554-1603	40, 3-44	12, 169-196	var 6, 492-535
10, 1602-1605	53, 122-126	38, 423-431	64, 290-293
10, 1604-1605	53, 145-146	38, 429	64, 292
10, 1628-1687	40, 263-320	26, 195-240	23, 1-70
10, 1692-1701	44, 231-242	7, 795-802	20, 301-308
10, 1712-1719	43, 167-177	30^{II}, 700-710	23, 154-162
10, 1732-1736	42, 179-186	7, 784-791	54, 116-117 64, 294-296
10, 1758-1761	43, 71-79	Br 3, 138-140	53, 197-201
10, 1776-1779	43, 179-186	32, 547-548	64, 298-300
10, 1794-1799	49, 267-271	Br 5, 239-241	54, 130-133
10, 1798-1803	50, 17-21	Br 6, 103-106	54, 232-236
10, 1820-1917	42, 117-166	6, 104-134	var 84-135 53, 31-34
10, 1960-1981	43, 139-165	23, 402-431	22, 294-316 53, 408
10, 1984-2001	42, 95-115	2, 685-697	21, 253-274 var 3, 453-473
10, 2002-2007	43, 47-55	10^{II}, 322-326	22, 32-38 53, 230
10, 2008-2029	43, 113-118	23, 339-379	22, 317-341 53, 408

St. Louis Edition	American Edition	Weimar Edition	Erlangen Edition
10, 2046-2047	50, 50-53	Br 6, 300-302	54, 293-295
10, 2112-2127	35, 23-43	2, 727-737	var 3, 394-410
10, 2136-2143	53, 95-103	12, 42-48	22, 157-166
10, 2140	53, 142	12, 43	22, 158-159
10, 2142	53, 144	12, 44	22, 161
10, 2144	53, 142-143	19, 539	22, 291
10, 2144-2145	53, 143-144	12, 43-44	22, 291-292
10, 2144-2147	53, 106-109	19, 537-541	22, 290-294
10, 2170-2209	38, 91-137	30^{II}, 595-626	23, 162-207
10, 2232-2255	53, 15-40	12, 205-220	var 7, 1-20
10, 2256-2257	53, 104-105	Br 3, 462-463	53, 285
10, 2256-2261	49, 204-210	Br 4, 533-536	54, 30-34
11, xxxiv-xxxix	52, 3-6	10^{I}, 1-8	7, 1-5
11, xxxviii-xlv	35, 113-124	10^{I}, 8-18	7, 5-12
11, 118-143	52, 7-31	10^{I}, 58-95	10, 126-153
11, 144-153	52, 32-40	10^{I}, 128-141	10, 153-163
11, 154-205	52, 41-88	10^{I}, 180-247	10, 163-218
11, 204-219	52, 89-101	10^{I}, 270-289	10, 218-232
11, 232-283	52, 102-148	10^{I}, 379-448	10, 247-301
11, 284-295	52, 149-158	10^{I}, 504-519	10, 301-312
11, 294-429	52, 159-286	10^{I}, 555-728	10, 313-456
11, 574-583	42, 3-14	2, 136-142	11, 144-152
			var 3, 410-419
	51, 104-110	10^{III}, 341-346	E_2 16, 420-429

St. Louis Edition	American Edition	Weimar Edition	Erlangen Edition
	51, 111-117	10^{III}, 347-352	E_2 16, 429-436
11, 2174-2189	51, 119-132	17, 38-45	15, 270-283
	51, 137-141	30^{I}, 57-61	
	51, 141-145	30^{I}, 61-66	
	51, 145-150	30^{I}, 66-72	
	51, 150-155	30^{I}, 72-77	
	51, 155-161	30^{I}, 77-86	
	51, 162-169	30^{I}, 86-94	
	51, 169-176	30^{I}, 94-102	
	51, 176-182	30^{I}, 103-109	
	51, 182-188	30^{I}, 109-116	
	51, 188-193	30^{I}, 116-122	
11, 2306-2313	51, 53-60	2, 244-249	15, 396-403 var 3, 217-224
12, 1168-1177	51, 369-380	51, 123-134	16, 139-150
12, 1254-1264	51, 381-392	51, 187-194	16, 264-275
12, 1302-1313	51, 35-43	1, 267-273	18, 196-205
12, 1314-1321	51, 44-49	1, 273-277	18, 205-211
12, 1328-1341	51, 193-208	32, 28-39	17, 40-53
	51, 209-218	32, 261-270	

St. Louis Edition	American Edition	Weimar Edition	Erlangen Edition
	51, 221-227	34^{II}, 156-165	
12, 1354-1361	42, 167-177	7, 692-697	17, 65-72
12, 1386-1393	51, 60-66	7, 808-813	17, 98-104
	51, 289-299	47, 757-771	8, 280-305
12, 1408-1421	51, 301-312	47, 772-779	17, 119-129
12, 1762-1769	51, 26-31	1, 138-141	var 1, 171-176
12, 1794-1801	51, 17-23	1, 111-115	var 1, 156-161
12, 1814-1817	51, 23-26	1, 128-130	var 1, 200-202
12, 1962-1984	51, 331-354	49, 588-615	17, 239-262
12, 2072-2085	51, 231-243	36, 237-254	18, 359-372
12, 2086-2099	51, 243-255	36, 255-270	18, 372-384
14, 2-17	35, 233-251	DB 8, 10-32	63, 7-25
14, 18-19	35, 251-253	DB 10^{I}, 5-6	63, 25-27
14, 20-25	35, 253-257	DB 10^{I}, 99-105	63, 27-32
14, 26-29	35, 258-261	DB 10^{I}, 7-10	63, 35-38
14, 28-31	35, 261-263	DB 10^{I}, 2-4	63, 38-40
14, 30-33	35, 263-264	DB 10^{II}, 104-106	63, 40-41
14, 32-41	35, 265-273	DB 11^{I}, 3-15	63, 42-52
14, 40-43	35, 279-282	DB 11^{I}, 191-195	63, 59-62
14, 44-45	35, 282-283	DB 11^{I}, 393	63, 62-64
14, 45-53	35, 284-293	DB 11^{I}, 395-409	63, 64-74
14, 54-55	35, 317-318	DB 11^{II}, 183	63, 74-75
14, 54-57	35, 318-319	DB 11^{II}, 213-215	63, 75-77

83	Preface to the Prophet Amos
83	Preface to the Prophet Obadiah
83	Preface to the Prophet Jonah
83	Preface to the Prophet Micah
83	Preface to the Prophet Nahum
83	Preface to the Prophet Zephaniah
83	Preface to the Prophet Haggai
83	Preface to the Prophet Zechariah
83	Preface to the Prophet Malachi
83	Preface to the Book of Judith
83	Preface to the Wisdom of Solomon
83	Preface to the Book of Tobit
83	Preface to the Book of Jesus Sirach
83	Preface to the Book of Baruch
83	Preface to the First Book of Maccabees
83	Preface to the Second Book of Maccabees
83	Preface to Parts of Esther and Daniel
83	Preface to the New Testament
83	Preface to the Acts of the Apostles
83	Preface to the Epistle of St. Paul to the Romans
83	Preface to the First Epistle of St. Paul to the Corinthians
83	Preface to the Second Epistle of St. Paul to the Corinthians
83	Preface to the Epistle of St. Paul to the Galatians
83	Preface to the Epistle of St. Paul to the Ephesians
83	Preface to the Epistle of St. Paul to the Philippians
83	Preface to the Epistle of St. Paul to the Colossians
83	Preface to the First Epistle of St. Paul to the Thessalonians
83	Preface to the Second Epistle of St. Paul to the Thessalonians
83	Preface to the First Epistle of St. Paul to Timothy
83	Preface to the Second Epistle of St. Paul to Timothy
83	Preface to the Epistle of St. Paul to Titus
83	Preface to the Epistle of.St. Paul to Philemon

St. Louis Edition	American Edition	Weimar Edition	Erlangen Edition
14, 56-59	35, 320-321	DB 11^{II}, 227-229	63, 77-78
14, 58-59	35, 321-322	DB 11^{II}, 251-253	63, 79-80
14, 60-61	35, 323-324	DB 11^{II}, 259-261	63, 80-81
14, 60-63	35, 324-325	DB 11^{II}, 271	63, 82
14, 62-63	35, 326	DB 11^{II}, 289	63, 83
14, 64-65	35, 328-329	DB 11^{II}, 311	63, 85-86
14, 64-67	35, 329-330	DB 11^{II}, 321	63, 86-87
14, 66-67	35, 330-331	DB 11^{II}, 329-331	63, 88-89
14, 68-69	35, 332-333	DB 11^{II}, 363-365	63, 89-90
14, 68-71	35, 337-339	DB 12, 5-7	63, 91-93
14, 72-77	35, 340-344	DB 12, 49-55	63, 93-98
14, 76-77	35, 345-347	DB 12, 109-111	63, 98-100
14, 78-81	35, 347-349	DB 12, 145-149	63, 100-102
14, 80-81	35, 349-350	DB 12, 291	63, 103-104
14, 80-83	35, 350-352	DB 12, 315-317	63, 104-106
14, 82-85	35, 352-353	DB 12, 417-419	63, 106-107
14, 84-85	35, 353-354	DB 12, 493	63, 107-108
14, 84-91	35, 357-362	DB 6, 2-10	63, 108-115
14, 92-95	35, 363-365	DB 6, 415-417	63, 116-119
14, 94-109	35, 365-380	DB 7, 2-27	63, 119-138
14, 110-113	35, 380-383	DB 7, 82-87	63, 138-141
14, 114-115	35, 383-384	DB 7, 138-139	63, 142-143
14, 114-115	35, 384	DB 7, 172-173	63, 143-144
14, 116-117	35, 385	DB 7, 190-191	63, 144
14, 116-117	35, 385	DB 7, 210-211	63, 145
14, 116-117	35, 386	DB 7, 224-225	63, 145-146
14, 118-119	35, 386-387	DB 7, 238-239	63, 146-147
14, 118-119	35, 387-388	DB 7, 250-251	63, 147-148
14, 120-121	35, 388	DB 7, 258-259	63, 148-149
14, 120-121	35, 389	DB 7, 272-273	63, 149
14, 122-123	35, 389-390	DB 7, 284-285	63, 150
14, 122-123	35, 390	DB 7, 292-293	63, 150-151

83	Preface to the First Epistle of St. Peter
83	Preface to the Second Epistle of St. Peter
83	Preface to the Three Epistles of St. John
83	Preface to the Epistle to the Hebrews
83	Preface to the Epistles of St. James and St. Jude
83	Preface to the Revelation of St. John
719	Preface to the Complete Edition of a German Theology, 1518
119	Preface to Galeatius Capella's History, 1538
35	Preface to the Wittenberg Edition of Luther's German Writings, 1539
753	Preface to the Complete Edition of Luther's Latin Writings, 1545
539	Obadiah (1)
348	Jonah (from the German text) (1) 1526
347	Jonah (from the Latin text) (2) 1525
505	Micah (2)
529	Nahum
392	On Rogationtide Prayer and Procession, 1519
266	Habakkuk (from the German Text) (1) 1526
83	Preface to the Prophet Habakkuk
265	Habakkuk (from the Latin Text) (2) 1525
783	Zephaniah (1)
269	Haggai
654	Zechariah (from the German text) 1527
653	Zechariah (from the Latin text) 1526
449	Malachi
99	Letter to Cardinal Albrecht, Archbishop of Mainz: Wittenberg, October 31, 1517
99	Letter to John von Staupitz: Wittenberg, May 30, 1518
99	Letter to George Spalatin: Wittenberg, August 8, 1518
99	Letter to George Spalatin: Wittenberg, August 28, 1518

St. Louis Edition	American Edition	Weimar Edition	Erlangen Edition
14, 122-125	35, 390-391	DB 7, 298-299	63, 151-152
14, 124-125	35, 391-392	DB 7, 314-315	63, 152-153
14, 126-127	35, 393	DB 7, 326-327	63, 153-154
14, 126-129	35, 394-395	DB 7, 344-345	63, 154-155
14, 128-131	35, 395-398	DB 7, 384-387	63, 156-158
14, 130-139	35, 399-411	DB 7, 406-421	63, 158-159
14, 182-185	31, 71-76	1, 378-389	63, 238-240
14, 376-381	34, 269-278	50, 383-385	63, 353-355
14, 432-437	34, 279-288	50, 657-661	1, 67-72
			63, 401-406
14, 438-449	34, 323-338	54, 179-187	var 1, 15-24
14, 808-823	18, 191-204	13, 215-223	25, 507-527
14, 836-911	19, 33-104	19, 185-251	41, 324-414
14, 912-943	19, 1-31	13, 241-258	27, 169-220
14, 978-983	18, 205-277	13, 299-343	26, 149-233
14, 1178-1257			
14, 1332-1373	18, 279-315	13, 371-394	27, 61-110
14, 1414-1421	42, 83-93	2, 175-179	20, 290-294
			var 3, 442-446
14, 1416-1507	19, 149-237	19, 349-435	42, 1-108
14, 1421-1423	35, 327-328	DB 11^{II}, 299-301	63, 84-85
14, 1506-1533	19, 105-148	12, 424-448	27, 169-220
14, 1604-1657	18, 317-364	13, 480-509	27, 283-350
14, 1708-1733	18, 365-387	13, 532-544	27, 391-416
14, 1768-1975	20, 153-347	23, 485-664	42, 108-362
14, 1976-2159	20, 1-152	13, 546-669	ex 28, 5-200
14, 2158-2195	18, 389-419	13, 675-703	ex 28, 287-323
15, 390-393	48, 43-49	Br 1, 108-112	
15, 414-418	48, 64-70	1, 525-527	
15, 430-432	48, 70-73	Br 1, 188	
15, 432-434	48, 73-76	Br 1, 189-191	

St. Louis Edition	American Edition	Weimar Edition	Erlangen Edition
15, 539-547	31, 253-292	2, 6-26	var 2, 367-392
15, 568-569			
15, 571-587			
15, 612-616			
15, 617-625			
15, 592-594	48, 87-89	Br 1, 222-223	
15, 607-610	49, 10-13	Br 2, 567-568	
15, 610-612	49, 48-50	Br 3, 155-156	
15, 696-698	48, 96-100	Br 1, 289-291	
15, 705-708q	48, 100-102	Br 1, 291-293	
15, 752-753	48, 126-127	Br 1, 524-525	
15, 757-758	48, 127-129	Br 1, 535-536	53, 28-29
15, 782-783	48, 179-181	Br 2, 196-197	
15, 1162-1170	48, 126	Br 1, 420-424	
	31, 318-325		
15, 1378-1382	48, 175-179	Br 2, 172-178	
15, 1476-1565	32, 3-99	7, 309-457	24, 52-150
15, 1619-1631	31, 379-395	7, 161-162	24, 150-164
15, 1662-1672	43, 57-70	10^{II}, 53-60	53, 119-129
15, 1726-1729	48, 103-106	Br 1, 305-308	
15, 1827-1828	48, 197-198	Br 2, 298	
15, 1884-1887	48, 188-191	Br 2, 242-243	
15, 1887-1890	48, 194-197	Br 2, 253-255	
15, 1893-1899	48, 203-209	Br 2, 307-310	
15, 1906-1907	48, 213-214	Br 2, 331-332	
15, 1916-1935	32, 101-131	7, 814-857	var 6, 5-23
15, 1935-1937	48, 200-203	Br 2, 305	
15, 1984-1985	48, 386-388	Br 2, 448-449	
15, 1989-1993	48, 388-393	Br 2, 453-457	53, 104-109
15, 1998-2001	48, 393-399	Br 2, 459-462	53, 109-112
15, 2011-2013	48, 399-402	Br 2, 474-475	

99 Letter to the Christians at Strassburg in
Opposition to the Fanatic Spirit, 1524

99 Letter to Elector Frederick: Wittenberg, May 29, 1523

99 Letter to George Spalatin: Wittenberg, May 18, 1518

99 Letter to George Spalatin: Wittenberg, September 2, 1518

99 Letter to George Spalatin: Wittenberg, February 22, 1518

99 Letter to George Spalatin: Wittenberg, April 16, 1520

99 Letter to George Spalatin: Wittenberg, October 31, 1518

99 Letter to George Spalatin: Augsburg, October 14, 1518

99 Letter to John von Staupitz: Wittenberg, January 14, 1521

99 Letter to George Spalatin: Wittenberg, November 25, 1518

99 Letter to John von Staupitz: Wittenberg, February 20, 1519

99 Letter to George Spalatin: Wittenberg, November 1, 1519

99 Letter to George Spalatin: Wittenberg, November 7, 1519

99 Letter to George Spalatin: Wittenberg, August 23, 1520

99 Letter to George Spalatin: Wartburg, May 14, 1521

99 Letter to Philip Melanchthon: Wartburg, May 12, 1521

99 Letter to Nicholas von Amsdorf: Wartburg, May 12, 1521

99 Letter to Nicholas Gerbel: Wartburg, November 1, 1521

99 Letter to John Agricola: Wartburg, May 12, 1521

99 Letter to George Spalatin: Wartburg, August 15, 1521

99 Letter to George Spalatin: Wartburg, June 10, 1521

99 Letter to Philip Melanchthon: Wartburg, July 13, 1521

99 Letter to George Spalatin: Wartburg, September 9, 1521

99 Letter to George Spalatin: Wartburg, July 15, 1521

99 Letter to George Spalatin: Wartburg, July 31, 1521

99 Letter to Philip Melanchthon: Wartburg, May 26, 1521

99 Letter to George Spalatin: Wartburg, November 11, 1521

99 Letter to Nicholas von Amsdorf: Wartburg, July 15?, 1521

99 Letter to John Lang: Wartburg, December 18, 1521

99 Letter to George Spalatin: Wittenberg, March 30, 1522

99 Letter to Nicholas von Amsdorf: Wartburg, January 13, 1522

99 Letter to Wenceslas Link: Wittenberg, December 19, 1522

St. Louis Edition	American Edition	Weimar Edition	Erlangen Edition
15, 2047-2053	40, 61-71 49, 94-96	15, 391-397	53, 270-277
15, 2187-2191	49, 35-42	Br 3, 75-77	53, 163-167
15, 2392-2394	48, 60-63	Br 1, 172-174	
15, 2397-2399	48, 80-83	Br 1, 195-196	
15, 2399-2402	48, 56-59	Br 1, 149-150	
15, 2403-2405	48, 159-161	Br 2, 82-83	
15, 2408-2410	48, 90-93	Br 1, 224-225	
15, 2416-2418	48, 83-87	Br 1, 213-215	
15, 2422-2424	48, 191-194	Br 2, 245-246	
15, 2427	48, 93-94	Br 1, 253	
15, 2442-2444	48, 108-111	Br 1, 343-345	
15, 2476-2477	48, 130-131	Br 1, 548-549	
15, 2477-2478	48, 132-133	Br 1, 551	
15, 2493-2494	48, 171-173	Br 2, 169-170	
15, 2510-2513	48, 222-228	Br 2, 336-338	
15, 2513-2515	48, 215-217	Br 2, 332-333	
15, 2516	48, 218-220	Br 2, 334-335	
15, 2517-2520	48, 317-322	Br 2, 396-398	
15, 2520-2521	48, 220-222	Br 2, 335-336	
15, 2521-2526	48, 291-296	Br 2, 379-381	
15, 2526-2528	48, 253-256	Br 2, 354-355	
15, 2528-2534	48, 256-263	Br 2, 356-359	
15, 2535-2538	48, 305-310	Br 2, 387-389	
15, 2538-2540	48, 268-270	Br 2, 364-365	
15, 2540-2542	48, 274-276	Br 2, 368-369	
15, 2542-2547	48, 228-244	Br 2, 346-349	
15, 2548-2550	48, 325-328	Br 2, 402-403	
15, 2550-2554	48, 264-268	Br 2, 361-363	
15, 2554-2555	48, 356-357	Br 2, 413	
15, 2555-2556	49, 3-4	Br 2, 489-490	
15, 2557-2560	48, 360-364	Br 2, 422-423	
15, 2578-2581	49, 20-25	Br 2, 632-633	

99 Letter to George Spalatin: Wittenberg, about December 12, 1522

99 Letter to Nicholas von Amsdorf: Wartburg, September 9, 1521

99 Letter to Philip Melanchthon: Wartburg, August 1, 1521

99 Letter to Philip Melanchthon: Wartburg, August 3, 1521

99 Letter to Philip Melanchthon: Wartburg, January 13, 1522

99 Letter to George Spalatin: Wartburg, January 17, 1522

99 Letter to George Spalatin: Wittenberg, January 14, 1524

99 Letter to George Spalatin: Wittenberg, March 14, 1524

99 Letter to John Brenz: Torgau, November 28, 1527

99 Letter to Nicholas von Amsdorf: Wittenberg, June 21, 1525

99 Letter to George Spalatin: Wittenberg, March 27, 1526

99 Letter to Justus Jonas: Wittenberg, about November 10, 1527

99 Letter to the Princes of Saxony Concerning
    the Rebellious Spirit, 1524

99 Admonition to Peace, A Reply to the Twelve
    Articles of the Peasants in Swabia, 1525

99 Against the Robbing and Murdering Hordes of Peasants, 1525

99 An Open Letter on the Harsh Book Against the Peasants, 1525

99 Letter to John Ruehel: Seeburg, May 4, 1525

99 Letter to Nicholas von Amsdorf: Wittenberg, May 30, 1525

99 Letter to Elector John: Coburg, May 15, 1530

99 Letter to Nicholas Hausmann: Coburg, April 18, 1530

99 Letter to Elector John: Coburg, May 20, 1530

99 Letter to John Agricola: Coburg, June 30, 1530

99 Letter to Elector John: Coburg, July 9, 1530

99 Letter to Nicolas Hausmann: Coburg, July 6, 1530

99 Letter to Philip Melanchthon: Coburg, June 29, 1530

99 Letter to George Spalatin: Coburg, June 30, 1530

99 Letter to Philip Melanchthon: Coburg,
    July 3, 1530

99 Letter to Conrad Cordatus: Coburg, July 6, 1530

99 Letter to Justus Jonas: Coburg, July 9, 1530

99 Exhortation to All Clergy Assembled at Augsburg, 1530

St. Louis Edition	American Edition	Weimar Edition	Erlangen Edition
15, 2581-2583	49, 17-20	Br 2, 630-631	
15, 2584-2585	48, 310-312	Br 2, 390-391	
15, 2585-2590	48, 277-282	Br 2, 370-372	
15, 2590-2596	48, 283-289	Br 2, 373-376	
15, 2599-2605	48, 364-372	Br 2, 424-427	
15, 2606-2607	48, 380-381	Br 2, 443-444	
15, 2622-2623	49, 70-72	Br 3, 234-235	
15, 2623-2624	49, 72-74	Br 3, 254	
15, 2632-2633	49, 177-180	Br 4, 285-286	
15, 2639-2640	49, 116-120	Br 3, 541	
15, 2641-2644	49, 143-147	Br 4, 41-42	
15, 2645-2647	49, 171-177	Br 4, 279-280	
16, 4-17	40, 45-59	15, 210-221	53, 255-268
16, 45-71	46, 3-43	18, 291-334	24, 257-286
16, 71-77	46, 45-55	18, 357-361	24, 287-294
16, 77-99	46, 57-85	18, 384-401	24, 294-319
16, 126-129	49, 106-112	Br 3, 480-482	53, 291-294
16, 133-135	49, 112-114	Br 3, 517-518	
16, 657-658	49, 295-299	Br 5, 319-320	54, 145-146
16, 667-669	49, 280-287	Br 5, 277-278	
16, 690-694	49, 305-311	Br 5, 324-327	54, 146-150
16, 750-752	49, 338-342	Br 5, 415-417	
16, 814	49, 359-365	Br 5, 453-455 Br 12, 117-119	54, 169-172
16, 881-883	49, 348-352	Br 5, 440	
16, 901-905	49, 324-333	Br 5, 405-407	
16, 908-910	49, 333-337	Br 5, 414-415	
16, 913-914	49, 342-347	Br 5, 435-436	
16, 914-916	49, 353-356	Br 5, 441-442	
16, 927	49, 366-372	Br 5, 457-459	
16, 946-992	34, 3-61	30^{II}, 268-356	24, 329-379

St. Louis Edition	American Edition	Weimar Edition	Erlangen Edition
16, 1013-1018	49, 378-393	Br 5, 492-495	
16, 1084	49, 399-400	Br 5, 544-545	54, 186
16, 1406-1407	49, 412-414	Br 5, 575-576	
16, 1414-1417	49, 403-412	Br 5, 572-574	54, 188-192
16, 1522-1523	49, 419-424	Br 5, 631-632	
16, 1624-1665	47, 3-55	30^{III}, 276-320	25, 1-50
16, 1666-1700	34, 63-104	30^{III}, 331-388	25, 51-88
16, 1754-1756	49, 292-295	Br 5, 290-291	
16, 1764-1767	49, 394-399	Br 5, 530-532	54, 183-186
16, 1810-1812	50, 41-47	Br 6, 259-261	54, 269-271
16, 1812-1814	50, 56-60	Br 6, 324-327	54, 312-314
16, 1888-1889	50, 81-85	Br 7, 237-238	54, 104
16, 1971-1994	34, 231-267	50, 288-308	25, 146-175
16, 1997-2000	50, 157-165	Br 8, 35-38	
16, 2144-2303	41, 3-178	50, 509-653	25, 219-388
16, 2307-2309	49, 287-291	Br 5, 285-286	
17, 265-269	50, 192-204	Br 8, 572-575	55, 243-247
17, 269-270	50, 204-206	Br 8, 577-578	55, 248-249
17, 282-283	50, 138-141	Br 7, 400-404	55, 133-134
17, 283-284	50, 100-102	Br 7, 266-267	55, 105-107
17, 1019-1132	41, 257-376	54, 206-299	26, 108-228
17, 1313-1381	41, 179-256	51, 469-572	26, 1-75
17, 1396-1419	43, 251-288	54, 389-411	26, 229-254 39, 221-223
17, 1544	49, 153-156	Br 4, 108-109	
17, 1935-1937	49, 228-231	Br 5, 101-102	54, 83-85
17, 1939-1943	38, 3-89	30^{III}, 110-171	65, 88-91
17, 1960-1963	49, 299-304	Br 5, 328-332	54, 151-154
17, 1973-1975	50, 6-9	Br 6, 24-26	
17, 1975-1976	50, 3-6	Br 6, 18-21	
17, 2187-2225	40, 225-262	26, 144-174	26, 254-294
17, 2228-2231	49, 180-185	Br 4, 294-295	

St. Louis Edition	American Edition	Weimar Edition	Erlangen Edition
18, 16-19	48, 36-38	Br 1, 88-89	
18, 18-27	31, 3-16	1, 224-228	var 1, 313-321
18, 36-71	31, 35-70	1, 353-374	var 1, 387-404
18, 70-81	31, 17-33	1, 233-238	var 1, 285-293
18, 100-269	31, 77-252	1, 529-628	var 2, 136-293
18, 718-721	31, 307-325	2, 158-161	var 3, 12-17
18, 1002-1053	39, 49-104	6, 285-324	27, 85-139
18, 1056-1201	32, 133-260	8, 43-128	var 5, 397-521
18, 1250-1255	39, 105-115	7, 262-265	27, 200-205
18, 1256-1271	39, 117-135	7, 271-283	27, 205-220
18, 1270-1353	39, 137-224	7, 621-688	27, 221-308
18, 1352-1363	39, 225-238	8, 247-254	27, 308-318
18, 1582-1585	48, 116-119	Br 1, 361-363	
18, 1596-1599	49, 76-81	Br 3, 268-271	
18, 1668-1969	33, 3-295	18, 600-787	var 7, 116-368
18, 1968-1971	48, 41-42	Br 1, 98-99	
18, 1972-1975	48, 23-26	Br 1, 69-71	
18, 1974-1975	48, 39-41	Br 1, 89-90	
18, 1976-1979	48, 52-55	Br 1, 132-134	
18, 1978-1981	49, 6-8	Br 2, 544-545	
18, 1984-1987	49, 87-91	Br 3, 373-374	
19, 4-129	36, 3-126	6, 497-573	var 5, 16-118
19, 426-449	35, 45-73	2, 742-758	27, 25-50
19, 548-553	48, 339-350	Br 2, 405-408	53, 95-99
19, 554-561	48, 372-379	Br 2, 428-434	

St. Louis Edition	American Edition	Weimar Edition	Erlangen Edition
19, 560-563	48, 350-352	Br 2, 409-410	
19, 598-621	35, 125-153	10^{II}, 72-92	28, 318-343
19, 668-727	39, 239-299	10^{II}, 105-158	28, 141-201
19, 786-807	39, 23-47	6, 157-169	var 4, 152-171
19, 808-815	44, 219-229	7, 290-298	24, 202-209
19, 814-817	48, 244-247	8, 138-140	53, 74-77
19, 884-901	39, 3-22	6, 63-75	27, 50-70
19, 902-957	40, 321-377	30^{II}, 465-507 30^{III}, 584-588	31, 126-184
19, 968-985	35, 175-202	30^{II}, 632-646	65, 102-123
19, 986-1011	31, 327-377	7, 1-38 7, 42-73	27, 173-199
19, 1036-1067	35, 75-111	6, 353-378	27, 139-173
19, 1068-1071	48, 324-325 36, 133-135	8, 482-483	
19, 1068-1177	36, 127-230	8, 482-563	28, 27-141
19, 1198-1215	36, 307-328	18, 22-36	29, 113-133
19, 1220-1285	38, 139-214	38, 195-256	31, 307-377
19, 1286-1299	38, 215-233	38, 262-272	31, 377-391
19, 1308-1337	36, 269-305	11, 431-456	28, 388-421
19, 1436-1450	34, 105-132	39^{I}, 44-62	var 4, 378-389
19, 1450-1455	34, 145-196	39^{I}, 82-126	var 4, 389-394
19, 1462-1467	34, 133-144	39^{I}, 175-180	var 4, 413-416
19, 1468-1473	34, 299-321	39^{II}, 187-203	var 4, 452-455
19, 1500-1507	48, 329-336	8, 573-576	53, 86-92
19, 1507-1665	44, 243-400	8, 577-669	var 6, 234-376 53, 86-92
19, 1674-1685	48, 81-96	15, 86-94	29, 102-113
19, 1689-1693	46, 139-154	19, 287-293	29, 318-327

St. Louis Edition	American Edition	Weimar Edition	Erlangen Edition
19, 1730-1745	45, 131-158	12, 232-244	29, 16-33
			53, 162
19, 1774-1779	48, 143-148	Br 1, 610-612	
19, 1786-1787	49, 157-159	Br 4, 147-148	
19, 1788-1789	49, 196-199	Br 4, 480	
19, 1794-1801	48, 296-304	Br 2, 382-386	
19, 1800-1803	48, 337-338	Br 2, 404-405	
19, 1808-1817	34, 339-360	54, 416-443	var 4, 480-492
20, 8-17	51, 70-75	10^{III}, 1-13	28, 205-215
20, 17-22	51, 75-78	10^{III}, 13-20	28, 216-221
20, 22-28	51, 79-83	10^{III}, 21-30	28, 221-228
20, 28-34	51, 84-88	10^{III}, 30-40	28, 228-235
20, 34-38	51, 89-91	10^{III}, 40-47	28, 235-239
20, 39-43	51, 92-95	10^{III}, 48-54	28, 239-244
20, 43-45	51, 95-96	10^{III}, 55-58	28, 244-247
20, 46-51	51, 97-100	10^{III}, 58-64	28, 247-251
20, 62-93	36, 231-267	10^{II}, 11-41	28, 285-318
20, 132-287	40, 73-223	18, 62-125	29, 134-297
		18, 134-214	
20, 734-763	36, 329-361	19, 482-523	29, 328-359
20, 762-893	37, 3-150	23, 64-283	30, 14-150
20, 894-1105	37, 151-372	26, 261-509	30, 151-373
20, 1610-1623	47, 99-119	50, 468-477	32, 1-14
20, 1660-1661	49, 148-150	Br 4, 52-53	
20, 1664-1677	40, 379-394	30^{III}, 518-527	31, 213-226
20, 1764-1791	38, 279-319	54, 141-167	32, 396-425
20, 1792-1821	45, 195-229	11, 314-336	29, 45-74
20, 1828-1861	47, 57-98	50, 312-337	31, 416-449

St. Louis Edition	American Edition	Weimar Edition	Erlangen Edition
20, 1860-2029	47, 121-306	53, 417-552	32, 99-274
20, 2108-2155	46, 155-205	30^{II}, 107-148	31, 31-80
20, 2194-2217	43, 213-241	51, 585-625	32, 74-99
21, 1-3	48, 3-5	Br 1, 10-11	
21, 5-7	48, 5-7	Br 1, 18	
21, 13-15	48, 8-11	Br 1, 27-29	
21, 18-19	48, 18-19	Br 1, 56	
21, 19-22	48, 11-14	Br 1, 33-36	
21, 26-29	48, 14-16	Br 1, 41-42	
21, 35-36	48, 17-18	Br 1, 50	
21, 38-41	48, 20-23	Br 1, 57-59	
21, 49-52	48, 27-32	Br 1, 72-73	
21, 53-57	48, 32-36	Br 1, 76-79	
21, 71-72	48, 42-43	Br 1, 102-103	
21, 77-79	48, 49-52	Br 1, 119-120	53, 1-2
21, 105-106	48, 76-80	Br 1, 191-192	
21, 120-121	48, 95-96	Br 1, 262	
21, 144-145	48, 106-107	Br 1, 325	
21, 155-157	48, 111-116	Br 1, 358-360	
21, 165	48, 120-121	Br 1, 386-387	53, 9-10
21, 170-171	48, 122-124	Br 1, 404	
21, 174-175	48, 124-126	Br 1, 408-409	
21, 207-208	48, 133-134	Br 1, 563-564	
21, 214-216	48, 135-139	Br 1, 596-597	
21, 216-217	48, 139-141	Br 1, 598-599	53, 29-30
21, 219-220	48, 141-143	Br 1, 604	
21, 224-225	48, 148-151	Br 1, 619	
21, 238-239	48, 151-153	Br 2, 40-42	
21, 246-247	48, 154-155	Br 2, 72	
21, 252-254	48, 156-159	Br 2, 80-82	
21, 256-257	48, 161-162	Br 2, 95-96	
21, 262-263	48, 163-165	Br 2, 111	

99 Letter to George Spalatin: Wittenberg, June 25, 1520

99 Letter to George Spalatin: Wittenberg, July 14, 1520

99 Letter to Wenceslas Link: Wittenberg, August 19, 1520

99 Letter to George Spalatin: Wittenberg, August 24, 1520

99 Letter to Duke John Frederick: Wittenberg, October 30, 1520

99 Letter to Lazarus Spengler: Wittenberg, November 17, 1520

99 Letter to George Spalatin: Wittenberg, December 10, 1520

99 Letter to John Cuspinian: Worms, April 17, 1521

99 Letter to Philip Melanchthon: Wartburg, about May 8, 1521

99 Letter to George Spalatin: Wartburg, soon after July 15, 1521

99 Letter to George Spalatin: Wartburg, soon after July 15, 1521

99 Letter to George Spalatin: Wartburg, August 6, 1521

99 Letter to George Spalatin: Wartburg, September 17, 1521

99 Letter to George Spalatin: Wartburg, October 7, 1521

99 Letter to George Spalatin: Wartburg, November 1, 1521

99 Letter to George Spalatin: Wartburg, about December 12, 1521

99 Letter to Wenceslas Link: Wartburg, December 18, 1521

99 Letter to George Spalatin: Wartburg, January 22?, 1522

99 Letter to George Spalatin: Wittenberg, May 20, 1522

99 Letter to George Spalatin: Wittenberg, June 7, 1522

99 Letter to George Spalatin: Wittenberg,
about September 20, 1522

99 Letter to Henning Teppen: Wittenberg, November 21, 1522

99 Letter to the Council of the City of Stettin:
Wittenberg, January 11, 1523

99 Letter to the Council of the City of Leisnig:
Wittenberg, January 29, 1523

99 Letter to Eobanus Hessus: Wittenberg, March 29, 1523

99 Letter to John Oecolampadius: Wittenberg, June 20, 1523

99 Letter to Elector Frederick: Leisnig, August 11, 1523

99 Letter to Nicholas Hausmann: Wittenberg, end of October, 1523

99 Letter to George Spalatin: Wittenberg, end of 1523

99 Letter to Elector Frederick: Wittenberg, March 14, 1524

St. Louis Edition	American Edition	Weimar Edition	Erlangen Edition
21, 270-271	48, 165-167	Br 2, 129-130	
21, 278-279	48, 167-169	Br 2, 142-143	
21, 292-293	48, 169-171	Br 2, 168	
21, 293-294	48, 173-174	Br 2, 170-171	
21, 303-304	48, 181-183	Br 2, 204-206	53, 52-53
21, 308-309	48, 184-185	Br 2, 217-218	53, 53-54
21, 324-325	48, 186-187	Br 2, 234	
21, 348-349	48, 199-200	Br 2, 299-300	
21, 351-352	48, 210-213	Br 2, 330-331	
21, 356-357	48, 270-271	Br 2, 366	
21, 357-358	48, 272-273	Br 2, 366-367	
21, 358-360	48, 289-291	Br 2, 377-378	
21, 360-362	48, 312-315	Br 2, 391-392	
21, 363-364	48, 315-317	Br 2, 394-395	
21, 364	48, 323-324	Br 2, 399	
21, 367-369	48, 353-355	Br 2, 411-412	
21, 370-372	48, 357-359	Br 2, 414-415	
21, 378-382	48, 382-386	Br 2, 445-447	
21, 412-413	49, 5	Br 2, 537	
21, 421	49, 8-9	Br 2, 556	53, 137
21, 446-447	49, 13-15	Br 2, 598	
21, 458-459	49, 16	Br 2, 618	
21, 471-472	49, 25-28	Br 3, 13-14	53, 159-161
21, 478	49, 28-32	Br 3, 23	
21, 491-493	49, 32-35	Br 3, 49-50	
21, 517-519	49, 42-45	Br 3, 96-97	
21, 534-535	49, 45-47	Br 3, 124-125	53, 194-195
21, 571-572	49, 55-56	Br 3, 183-184	
21, 582-583	49, 68-70	Br 3, 220	
21, 601-602	49, 74-76	Br 3, 258-259	53, 235-236

99   Letter to Nicholas Gerbel: Wittenberg, May 6, 1524

99   Letter to Wolfgang Stein: Wittenberg,
beginning of September, 1524

99   Letter to the Council of the City of Zerbst:
Wittenberg, October 8, 1524

99   Letter to George Spalatin: Wittenberg, November 30, 1524

99   Letter to Elector Frederick: Wittenberg, mid-November, 1523

99   Letter to Margrave Albrecht of Brandenburg:
Wittenberg, December, 1523

279   The Burning of Brother Henry, 1525

99   Letter to Lazarus Spengler: Wittenberg, February 4, 1525

99   Letter to Theobald Billicanus: Wittenberg, March 5, 1525

99   Letter to George Spalatin: Wittenberg, April 16, 1525

99   Letter to George Spalatin: Wittenberg, June 21, 1525

99   Letter to John Briesemann: Wittenberg, after August 15, 1525

99   Letter to Elector John: Wittenberg, September 6, 1525

99   Letter to Elector John: Wittenberg, October 31, 1525

99   Letter to Elector John: Wittenberg, November 30, 1525

99   Letter to Michael Stifel: Wittenberg, December 31, 1525

99   Letter to Gabriel Zwilling: Wittenberg, January 2, 1526

99   Letter to John Agricola: Wittenberg, May 11, 1526

99   Letter to John Ruehel: Wittenberg, June 8, 1526

99   Letter to Nicholas Hausmann: Wittenberg, January 10, 1527

99   Letter to Nicholas Hausmann: Wittenberg, March 29, 1527

99   Letter to Wenceslas Link: Wittenberg, about May 4, 1527

99   Letter to Wenceslas Link: Wittenberg, July 5, 1527

99   Letter to Nicholas Hausmann: Wittenberg, July 13, 1527

99   Letter to Elector John: Wittenberg, September 16, 1527

99   Letter to 179. Justus Jonas: Wittenberg, December 30, 1527

99   Letter to Nicholas von Amsdorf: Wittenberg, April 16, 1528

99   Letter to Elector John: Weimar, May 1 or 2, 1528

99   Letter to Duke John Frederick: Wittenberg, May 18, 1528

99   Letter to Nicholas Gerbel: Wittenberg, July 28, 1528

St. Louis Edition	American Edition	Weimar Edition	Erlangen Edition
21, 619-620	49, 81-83	Br 3, 284	
21, 647-648	49, 83-85	Br 3, 342-343	53, 268-269
21, 650-651	49, 85-87	Br 3, 355	
21, 665-667	49, 91-94	Br 3, 393-394	
21, 671-673	49, 57-59	Br 3, 195-197	
	49, 59-68	Br 3, 214-219	
21, 687-709	32, 261-286	18, 224-240	26, 313-337
21, 715-716	49, 96-99	Br 3, 432-433	53, 283-284
21, 725-726	49, 99-102	Br 3, 451-452	
21, 736-738	49, 102-105	Br 3, 474-475	
21, 762-763	49, 115-116	Br 3, 540	
21, 771-773	49, 120-125	Br 3, 554-556	
21, 775-776	49, 125-130	Br 3, 569-570	56, viii-x
21, 798-801	49, 130-137	Br 3, 594-596	53, 329-332
21, 812-813	49, 137-139	Br 3, 628-629	53, 336-338
21, 818-819	49, 139-141	Br 3, 653	
	49, 142	Br 4, 4	
21, 863-864	49, 150-151	Br 4, 73-74	
21, 868-869	49, 151-153	Br 4, 87	53, 380-381
21, 916-917	49, 159-161	Br 4, 159	
21, 929-930	49, 161-164	Br 4, 180-181	53, 399-400
21, 935-936	49, 164-165	Br 4, 197-198	
21, 984	49, 166-167	Br 4, 220	
21, 996-997	49, 167-169	Br 4, 222	
21, 1011-1012	49, 169-171	Br 4, 248	
21, 1055-1056	49, 185-186	Br 4, 311-312	
	49, 187-188	Br 4, 443	
21, 1147-1150	49, 189-195	Br 4, 447-450	
21, 1153	49, 195-196	Br 4, 465	54, 5-6
21, 1180-1181	49, 199-202	Br 4, 508	

99   Letter to Nicholas Hausmann: Wittenberg, August 5, 1528

99   Letter to Elector John: Wittenberg, September 3, 1528

99   Letter to John Agricola: Wittenberg, September 11, 1528

99   Letter to Nicholas von Amsdorf: Wittenberg, November 1, 1528

99   Letter to Wenceslas Link: Wittenberg, March 7, 1529

99   Letter to Nicholas von Amsdorf: Wittenberg, May 5, 1529

99   Letter to Wenceslas Link: Wittenberg, May 6, 1529

99   Letter to Elector John: Wittenberg, May 22, 1529

99   Letter to Thomas Loescher: Wittenberg, August 26, 1529

99   Letter to Mrs. Martin Luther: Marburg, October 4, 1529

99   Letter to Nicholas von Amsdorf: Wittenberg, October 27, 1529

99   Letter to Elector John: Wittenberg, December 24, 1529

99   Letter to Landgrave Philip von Hesse:
Wittenberg, December 16, 1529

99   Letter to some Pastors of the City of Luebeck:
Wittenberg, January 12, 1530

99   Letter to Nicholas Hausmann: Wittenberg,
beginning of February, 1530

99   Letter to Mrs. Martin Luther: Coburg, June 5, 1530

99   Letter to Philip Melanchthon: Coburg, June 5, 1530

99   Letter to Philip Melanchthon: Coburg, June 7, 1530

99   Letter to John Luther: Coburg, about June 19, 1530

99   Letter to Lazarus Spengler: Coburg, July 8, 1530

99   Letter to Justus Jonas, George Spalatin, Philip
Melanchthon, John Agricola: Coburg, July 15, 1530

99   Letter to Mrs. Martin Luther: Coburg, August 15, 1530

99   Letter to Mrs. Martin Luther: Coburg, September 8, 1530

99   Letter to Mrs. Martin Luther: Coburg, September 24, 1530

99   Letter to Louis Senfl: Coburg, October 4, 1530

99   Letter to Landgrave Philip of Hesse: Torgau, October 28, 1530

99   Letter to Wenceslas Link: Wittenberg, May 12, 1531

99   Letter to Elector John: Wittenberg, June 16, 1531

99   Letter to Michael Stifel: Wittenberg, June or July, 1531

St. Louis Edition	American Edition	Weimar Edition	Erlangen Edition
21, 1182	49, 202-203	Br 4, 511	
21, 1197-1198	49, 210-211	Br 4, 545-546	54, 34-35
21, 1205-1206	49, 212-213	Br 4, 557-558	
21, 1231	49, 213-214	Br 4, 597	
21, 1269-1270	49, 214-217	Br 5, 27-28	
21, 1294-1295	49, 218-219	Br 5, 61	54, 69
21, 1297-1298	49, 219-221	Br 5, 62-63	
21, 1303-1306	49, 221-228	Br 5, 75-77	54, 72-74
21, 1348-1349	49, 232-234	Br 5, 137	
21, 1366-1367	49, 234-239	Br 5, 154	54, 107-108
21, 1371-1372	49, 239-243	Br 5, 167-168	
21, 1384-1387	49, 254-260	Br 5, 209-211	
21, 1396-1397	49, 250-254	Br 5, 203-204	
21, 1409-1411	49, 261-263	Br 5, 220-221	
21, 1413-1414	49, 264-267	Br 5, 236-237	
21, 1464-1465	49, 311-316	Br 5, 347-348	
21, 1467-1469	49, 316-319	Br 5, 350-351	
21, 1470-1471	49, 320-321	Br 5, 354	
21, 1491-1492	49, 321-324	Br 5, 377-378	54, 156-157
21, 1513-1514	49, 356-359	Br 5, 444-445	54, 168-169
21, 1517-1519	49, 372-377	Br 5, 479-480	
21, 1541-1542	49, 400-403	Br 5, 545-546	54, 187-188
21, 1564-1565	49, 415-419	Br 5, 608-609	56, 181-183
21, 1571-1572	49, 424-425	Br 5, 633-634	54, 194
21, 1574-1576	49, 426-429	Br 5, 639	
21, 1585-1586	49, 433-437	Br 5, 660-661	
21, 1656-1658	50, 13-17	Br 6, 95-97	
21, 1662-1664	50, 23-26	Br 6, 122-124	
21, 1672	50, 26-27	Br 6, 143	

99 Letter to Gregory Brueck: Wittenberg, end of May, 1531

99 Letter to Robert Barnes: Wittenberg, September 3, 1531

99 Letter to Mrs. Martin Luther: Torgau, February 27, 1532

99 Letter to Nicholas von Amsdorf: Wittenberg, June 13, 1532

99 Letter to the Regents and Councilors, of the
Margraviate of Brandenburg-Ansbach and to the Council
of the City of Nuernberg: Wittenberg, August 1, 1532

99 Letter to Duke Joachim of Brandenburg:
Wittenberg, August 3, 1532

99 Letter to Nicholas von Amsdorf: Wittenberg, November 2, 1532

99 Letter to John Loeser: Wittenberg, January 29, 1533

99 Letter to the Council of the City of Nuernberg:
Wittenberg, April 18, 1533

99 Letter to Mrs. Martin Luther: Dessau, July 29, 1534

99 Letter to Philip Melanchthon: Wittenberg, August 29, 1535

99 Letter to Justus Jonas: Wittenberg, September 4, 1535

99 Letter to George Spalatin: Wittenberg, September 6, 1535

99 Letter to Justus Jonas: Wittenberg, October 29, 1535

99 Letter to Justus Jonas: Wittenberg, November 10, 1535

99 Letter to Philip Melanchthon: Wittenberg,
beginning of December, 1535

99 Letter to Elector John Frederick: Wittenberg, January 11, 1536

99 Letter to Nicholas Hausmann: Wittenberg, January 17, 1536

99 Letter to Caspar Mueller: Wittenberg, January 19, 1536

99 Letter to Francis Burchart: Wittenberg, January 25, 1536

99 Letter to Elector John Frederick: Wittenberg, March 28, 1536

99 Letter to Thomas Cromwell: Wittenberg, April 9, 1536

99 Letter to George Spalatin: Wittenberg, June 10, 1536

99 Letter to Justus Jonas: Wittenberg, August 17, 1536

99 Letter to Nicholas Hausmann: Wittenberg,
Torgau, September 20, 1536

99 Letter to Hans Luther: Wittenberg, January 27, 1537

99 Letter to Justus Jonas: Altenburg, February 1, 1537

99 Letter to Mrs. Martin Luther: Tambach, February 27, 1537

St. Louis Edition	American Edition	Weimar Edition	Erlangen Edition
21, 1677	50, 22-23	Br 6, 107-108	
21, 1688-1697	50, 27-40	Br 6, 178-188	
21, 1731-1732	50, 47-50	Br 6, 270-271	54, 275-276
21, 1751-1752	50, 53-56	Br 6, 318-319	
21, 1761-1765	50, 61-67	Br 6, 338-342	54, 316-320
21, 1765-1767	50, 68-71	Br 6, 343-345	54, 320-322
21, 1782-1783	50, 72-73	Br 6, 381-382	
21, 1802-1803	50, 73-74	Br 6, 425-426	55, 4-5
21, 1811-1813	50, 75-78	Br 6, 453-455	55, 8-10
21, 1920	50, 79-81	Br 7, 91	55, 61
21, 1995-1996	50, 85-92	Br 7, 244-245	
21, 1999-2000	50, 93-97	Br 7, 249-250	
21, 2000-2001	50, 97-100	Br 7, 251	
21, 2016-2017	50, 107-109	Br 7, 316-317	
21, 2020-2021	50, 109-113	Br 7, 321-322	
21, 2024-2026	50, 113-117	Br 7, 330-331	
21, 2031-2033	50, 117-122	Br 7, 341-343	55, 117-118
21, 2036-2037	50, 122-124	Br 7, 347	
21, 2037-2039	50, 124-130	Br 7, 348-350	55, 119-121
21, 2040-2041	50, 130-131	Br 7, 352	
21, 2051-2052	50, 132-135	Br 7, 381-384	55, 128-130
21, 2057-2058	50, 136-138	Br 7, 395-396	
21, 2069-2070	50, 141-143	Br 7, 430	
21, 2095-2096	50, 144-147	Br 7, 503-504	
21, 2105-2106	50, 148-151	Br 7, 546-547	
21, 2146-2147	50, 151-153	Br 8, 18-20	
21, 2147-2149	50, 153-157	Br 8, 22-23	
21, 2156-2157	50, 165-169	Br 8, 50-51	55, 174-175

99   Letter to George Spalatin: Wittenberg, March 21, 1537

99   Letter to Wolfgang Capito: Wittenberg, July 9, 1537

99   Letter to Nicholas Hausmann: Wittenberg, February 23, 1538

99   Letter to Edward Fox: Wittenberg, May 12, 1538

99   Letter to James Propst: Wittenberg, September 15, 1538

99   Letter to John Frederick: Wittenberg, July 8, 1539

99   Letter to Martin Bucer: Wittenberg, October 14, 1539

99   Letter to Mrs. Martin Luther: Weimar, July 2, 1540

99   Letter to Mrs. Martin Luther: Eisenach, July 10, 1540

99   Letter to Mrs. Martin Luther: Eisenach, July 16, 1540

99   Letter to Mrs. Martin Luther: Eisenach, July 26, 1540

99   Letter to Mrs. Martin Luther: Wittenberg, September 18, 1541

717   Luther's Will, 1542

99   Letter to Justus Jonas: Wittenberg, February 16, 1542

99   Letter to Marcus Crodel: Wittenberg, August 26, 1542

99   Letter to Marcus Crodel: Wittenberg, August 28, 1542

99   Letter to Marcus Crodel: Wittenberg, September 6, 1542

99   Letter to Justus Jonas: Wittenberg, September 23, 1542

99   Letter to Marcus Crodel: Wittenberg, December 26, 1542

99   Letter to John Luther: Wittenberg, December 27, 1542

99   Letter to Wenceslas Link: Wittenberg, June 20, 1543

99   Letter to James Propst: Wittenberg, December 5, 1544

99   Letter to Justus Jonas: Wittenberg, January 26, 1545

99   Letter to King Christian of Denmark: Wittenberg, April 14, 1545

99   Letter to Duke Albrecht of Prussia: Wittenberg, May 2, 1545

99   Letter to Elector John Frederick: Wittenberg, May 7, 1545

99   Letter to Nicholas von Amsdorf: Wittenberg, June 3, 1545

99   Letter to Nicholas von Amsdorf: Wittenberg, July 9, 1545

99   Letter to Justus Jonas: Wittenberg, July 16, 1545

99   Letter to Nicholas von Amsdorf: Wittenberg, July 17, 1545

99   Letter to Mrs. Martin Luther: Zeitz, July 28, 1545

99   Letter to Count Albrecht of Mansfeld:
    Wittenberg, December 6, 1545

St. Louis Edition	American Edition	Weimar Edition	Erlangen Edition
21, 2161-2162	50, 169-170	Br 8, 59	
21, 2175-2176	50, 171-174	Br 8, 99-100	
21, 2226-2227	50, 174-176	Br 8, 199-200	
21, 2238-2239	50, 177-180	Br 8, 219-220	
21, 2270-2271	50, 181-184	Br 8, 291-292	
21, 2352-2353	50, 185-187	Br 8, 488-491	55, 234-235
21, 2383-2385	50, 187-191	Br 8, 568-569	
21, 2485-2486	50, 207-212	Br 9, 167-168	55, 225-227
21, 2487-2489	50, 212-217	Br 9, 171-173	
21, 2490	50, 218-220	Br 9, 174-175	55, 287-288
21, 2501-2502	50, 221-223	Br 9, 204-205	55, 288-289
21, 2650	50, 223-225	Br 9, 518-519	55, 332-333
21, 2695-2698	50, 289-297	9, 572-574	56, 2-5
21, 2716-2718	50, 225-230	Br 9, 620-622	
21, 2782-2783	50, 230-233	Br 10, 132-134	
21, 2785	50, 233-234	Br 10, 136-137	
21, 2788-2789	50, 234-235	Br 10, 147	
21, 2790-2791	50, 236-238	Br 10, 149-150	
21, 2814	50, 239-240	Br 10, 228-229	
21, 2815	50, 240-241	Br 10, 229	
21, 2879-2880	50, 241-244	Br 10, 334-335	
21, 3043-3044	50, 244-246	Br 10, 554	
21, 3067-3068	50, 247-249	Br 11, 29-30	
21, 3077-3078	50, 250-252	Br 11, 69-70	56, 130-131
21, 3084-3085	50, 252-255	Br 11, 83-84	56, 133-134
21, 3088-3089	50, 255-261	Br 11, 88	56, 134-135
21, 3105-3106	50, 262-264	Br 11, 115	
21, 3113-3114	50, 264-267	Br 11, 131-132	
21, 3119-3120	50, 268-270	Br 11, 141-143	
21, 3122-3123	50, 270-272	Br 11, 143-144	
21, 3125-3126	50, 273-281	Br 11, 148-150	56, 139-140
21, 3161-3162	50, 281-284	Br 11, 225-226	56, 146-147

99	Letter to Mrs. Martin Luther: Halle, January 25, 1546
99	Letter to George of Anhalt: Eisleben, January 29, 1546
99	Letter to Philip Melanchthon: Eisleben, February 1, 1546
99	Letter to Mrs. Martin Luther: Eisleben, February 1, 1546
99	Letter to Philip Melanchthon: Eisleben, February 3, 1546
99	Letter to Philip Melanchthon: Eisleben, February 6, 1546
99	Letter to Mrs. Martin Luther: Eisleben, February 6, 1546
99	Letter to Mrs. Martin Luther: Eisleben, February 7, 1546
99	Letter to George of Anhalt: Eisleben, February 10, 1546
99	Letter to Mrs. Martin Luther: Eisleben, February 10, 1546
99	Letter to Philip Melanchthon: Eisleben, February 14, 1546
99	Letter to Mrs. Martin Luther: Eisleben, February 14, 1546
99	Letter to John Schlaginhaufen: Wittenberg, March 10, 1534
423	An Italian Lie Concerning Dr. Martin Luther's Death, 1545
99	Letter to Gregory Brueck: Wittenberg, about September 15, 1535
725	Table Talk Recorded by Veit Dietrich, 1531-1533
725	Table Talk Recorded by George Roerer, 1531-1535
725	Table Talk Recorded by John Schlaginhaufen, 1531-1532
725	Table Talk Collected by Conrad Cordatus, 1532-1533
725	Table Talk Recorded by Anthony Lauterbach and Jerome Weller, 1536-1537
725	Table Talk Recorded by Anthony Lauterbach, 1538-1539
725	Table Talk Recorded by John Mathesius, 1540
725	Table Talk Recorded by Caspar Heydenreich, 1542-1543
725	Table Talk Recorded by Jerome Resold, 1544

Tischreden

725	Cap. 1. Von Gottes Wort oder der heiligen Schrift
725	Cap. 2. Von Gottes Werken
725	Cap. 3. Von der Schoepfung
725	Cap. 4. Von der Welt und ihrer Art
725	Cap. 5. Von der Abgoetterei

St. Louis Edition	American Edition	Weimar Edition	Erlangen Edition
21, 3186	50, 284-287	Br 11, 268-269	56, 148-149
21, 3188-3189	50, 288-289	Br 11, 273	
21, 3190-3191	50, 292-295	Br 11, 277-278	
21, 3191-3192	50, 290-292	Br 11, 275-276	56, 149-150
	50, 295-297	Br 11, 279-280	
21, 3192-3194	50, 297-299	Br 11, 285-286	
21, 3194	50, 299-300	Br 11, 283-284	56, 150-151
21, 3194-3196	50, 301-304	Br 11, 286-287	56, 151-153
21, 3197-3198	50, 309-310	Br 11, 292	
21, 3198-3199	50, 305-308	Br 11, 290-291	
21, 3202-3203	50, 313-318	Br 11, 301-302	
21, 3203-3204	50, 310-313	Br 11, 299-300	56, 154-155
21, 3229	50, 78-79	Br 7, 24	
21, 3374-3377	34, 361-366	54, 192-194	32, 425-430
21, 3501-3502	50, 102-106	Br 7, 267-268	
	54, 3-114	TR 1, 656	
	54, 115-121	TR 1, 657-684	
	54, 123-165	TR 2, 1232-1889	
	54, 167-200	TR 2, 1950-3416	
	54, 201-249	TR 3, 3465-3659	
	54, 251-364	TR 3, 3683-4719	
	54, 365-409	TR 4, 4848 to 5, 5341	
	54, 411-464	TR 5, 5379-5603	
	54, 465-476	TR 5, 5659-5675	
22, 1-65			57, 1-107
22, 64-137			57, 108-220
22, 138-181			57, 220-280
22, 182-239			57, 280-362
22, 238-257			57, 362-385

St. Louis Edition	American Edition	Weimar Edition	Erlangen Edition
22, 256-259			57, 385-391
22, 260-353			58, 1-152
22, 354-355			58, 153-162
22, 356-383			58, 162-213
22, 382-391			58, 214-239
22, 392-415			58, 239-268
22, 414-445			58, 269-338
22, 416-489			58, 338-413
22, 488-509			58, 413-445
22, 510-535			59, 1-34
22, 534-539			59, 34-44
22, 540-555			59, 44-74
22, 554-563			59, 74-87
22, 562-595			59, 87-130
22, 594-609			59, 131-155
22, 610-627			59, 155-180
22, 628-697			59, 181-285
22, 696-701			58, 285-288
22, 700-781			59, 289-348
			60, 1-75
22, 780-785			60, 75-80
22, 784-841			60, 80-176
22, 840-935			60, 176-311
22, 936-947			60, 312-327
22, 946-949			60, 327-331
22, 950-969			60, 331-356
22, 970-983			60, 356-372
22, 982-989			60, 372-382
22, 990-997			60, 382-390
22, 996-999			60, 390-395

St. Louis Edition	American Edition	Weimar Edition	Erlangen Edition
22, 998-1007			60, 395-404
22, 1006-1007			60, 404-405
22, 1008-1095			61, 1-125
22, 1094-1099			61, 125-132
22, 1098-1113			61, 132-149
22, 1112-1115			61, 150-152
22, 1114-1119			61, 152-159
22, 1118-1121			61, 159-164
22, 1122-1215			61, 164-304
22, 1214-1231			61, 305-327
22, 1230-1283			61, 327-397
22, 1284-1289			61, 397-403
22, 1288-1299			61, 404-417
22, 1298-1319			61, 417-447
22, 1318-1327			62, 1-14
22, 1328-1331			62, 15-18
22, 1330-1339			62, 18-28
22, 1338-1345			62, 28-35
22, 1344-1349			62, 36-40
22, 1348-1371			62, 41-71
22, 1370-1381			62, 71-87
22, 1382-1389			62, 88-97
22, 1388-1401			62, 97-113
22, 1400-1409			62, 113-124
22, 1408-1417			62, 125-139
22, 1418-1433			62, 139-159
22, 1432-1437			62, 160-169
22, 1438-1447			62, 169-180
22, 1446-1453			62, 180-189
22, 1454-1467			62, 189-209

St. Louis Edition	American Edition	Weimar Edition	Erlangen Edition
22, 1468-1471			62, 209-214
22, 1472-1521			62, 214-284
22, 1522-1537			62, 285-307
22, 1536-1541			62, 307-311
22, 1540-1545			62, 311-317
22, 1544-1553			62, 317-328
22, 1554-1557			62, 329-334
22, 1558-1561			62, 334-339
22, 1560-1571			62, 339-352
22, 1570-1591			62, 352-379
22, 1590-1611			62, 379-405
22, 1612-1633			62, 405-435
22, 1634-1639			62, 435-443
22, 1640-1647			62, 443-451
22, 1646-1647			62, 451-452
22, 1648-1653			62, 453-460
22, 1654-1663			62, 461-474
22, 1664-1667			
22, 1668-1807			
22, 1808-1993			

PART 3

Which works in the Weimar edition are included in the American edition and where they may be found in the American, the St. Louis, and the Erlangen editions.

Weimar Edition	American Edition	St. Louis Edition	Erlangen Edition
1, 63-65	51, 14-17	10, 1284-1289	var 1, 101-104
1, 111-115	51, 17-23	12, 1794-1801	var 1, 156-161
1, 128-130	51, 23-26	12, 1814-1817	var 1, 200-202
1, 138-141	51, 26-31	12, 1762-1769	var 1, 171-176
1, 224-228	31, 3-16	18, 18-27	var 1, 313-321
1, 233-238	31, 17-33	18, 70-81	var 1, 285-293
1, 267-273	51, 35-43	12, 1302-1313	18, 196-205
1, 273-277	51, 44-49	12, 1314-1321	18, 205-211
1, 353-374	31, 35-70	18, 36-71	var 1, 387-404
1, 378-379	31, 71-76	14, 182-185	63, 238-240
1, 525-527	48, 64-70	15, 414-418	
1, 529-628	31, 77-252	18, 100-269	var 2, 136-293
2, 6-26	31, 253-292	15, 612-616	var 2, 367-392
		15, 568-569	
		15, 571-587	
		15, 617-625	
		15, 539-547	
2, 80-130	42, 15-81	7, 752-821	21, 156-227
			45, 203-207
2, 136-142	42, 3-14	11, 574-583	11, 144-152
			var 3, 410-419
2, 145-152	31, 293-306	10, 1262-1277	var 2, 329-339
2, 158-161	31, 307-325	18, 718-721	var 3, 12-17
Br 1, 420-424		15, 1162-1170	
2, 166-171	44, 3-14	10, 630-637	16, 158-165
			var 3, 446-452
2, 175-179	42, 83-93	14, 1414-1421	20, 290-294
			var 3, 442-446

132

Weimar Edition	American Edition	St. Louis Edition	Erlangen Edition
2, 244-249	51, 53-60	11, 2306-2313	15, 396-403
			var 3, 217-224
2, 445-618	27, 151-410	8, 1352-1661	gal 3, 126-483
2, 685-697	42, 95-115	10, 1984-2001	21, 253-274
			var 3, 453-473
2, 714-723	35, 3-22	10, 1232-1245	20, 179-193
2, 727-737	35, 23-43	10, 2112-2127	var 3, 394-410
2, 742-758	35, 45-73	19, 426-449	27, 25-50
3, 11-519	10, 1-464	(4, 1-1913 —	
3, 519-652	11, 1-553	later works	
4, 1-414		on the Psalms)	
4, 590-595	51, 5-13		
5, 19-74	14, 279-349	4, 220-301	14, 1-89
6, 36-60	45, 231-310	10, 914-937	22, 199-226
15, 293-313		10, 824-855	20, 89-122
15, 321-322			
6, 63-75	39, 3-22	19, 894-901	27, 50-70
6, 104-134	42, 117-166	10, 1820-1917	var 4, 84-135
			53, 31-34
6, 157-169	39, 23-47	19, 786-807	var 4, 152-171
6, 202-276	44, 15-114	10, 1298-1389	20, 193-290
6, 285-324	39, 49-104	18, 1002-1053	27, 85-139
6, 353-378	35, 75-111	19, 1036-1067	27, 139-173
6, 404-469	44, 115-217	10, 266-351	21, 274-360
6, 497-573	36, 3-126	19, 4-129	var 5, 16-118
7, 1-38	31, 327-377	19, 986-1011	27, 173-199
7, 42-73			
7, 161-182	31, 379-395	15, 1619-1631	24, 150-164
7, 262-265	39, 105-115	18, 1250-1255	27, 200-205

Weimar Edition	American Edition	St. Louis Edition	Erlangen Edition
7, 271-283	39, 117-135	18, 1256-1271	27, 205-220
7, 290-298	44, 219-229	19, 808-815	24, 202-209
7, 309-457	32, 3-99	15, 1476-1565	24, 52-150
7, 538-604	21, 295-355	7, 1372-1445	45, 211-290
7, 621-688	39, 137-224	18, 1270-1353	27, 221-308
7, 692-697	42, 167-177	12, 1354-1361	17, 65-72
7, 784-791	42, 179-186	10, 1732-1736	54, 116-117
			64, 294-296
7, 795-802	44, 231-242	10, 1692-1701	20, 301-308
7, 808-813	51, 60-66	12, 1386-1393	17, 98-104
7, 814-857	32, 101-131	15, 1916-1935	var 6, 5-23
8, 4-35	13, 1-37	5, 656-695	39, 178-220
8, 43-128	32, 133-260	18, 1056-1201	var 5, 397-521
8, 138-140	48, 244-247	19, 814-817	53, 74-77
8, 210-214	48, 248-253	5, 306-311	
8, 247-254	39, 225-238	18, 1352-1363	27, 308-318
8, 482-483	48, 324-325	19, 1068-1071	
	36, 133-135		
8, 482-563	36, 127-230	19, 1068-1177	28, 27-141
8, 573-576	48, 329-336	19, 1500-1507	53, 86-92
8, 577-669	44, 243-400	19, 1507-1665	var 6, 234-376
			53, 86-92
8, 676-687	45, 51-74	10, 360-373	22, 43-59
9, 572-574	34, 289-297	21, 2695-2698	56, 2-5
10^{I}, 1-8	52, 3-6	11, xxxiv-xxxix	7, 1-5

Weimar Edition	American Edition	St. Louis Edition	Erlangen Edition
10ᴵ, 8-18	35, 113-124	11, xxxviii-xlv	7, 5-12
10ᴵ, 58-95	52, 7-31	11, 118-143	10, 126-153
10ᴵ, 128-141	52, 32-40	11, 144-153	10, 153-163
10ᴵ, 180-247	52, 41-88	11, 154-205	10, 163-218
10ᴵ, 270-289	52, 89-101	11, 204-219	10, 218-232
10ᴵ, 379-448	52, 102-148	11, 232-283	10, 247-301
10ᴵ, 504-519	52, 149-158	11, 284-295	10, 301-312
10ᴵ, 555-728	52, 159-286	11, 294-429	10, 313-456
10ᴵᴵ, 11-41	36, 231-267	20, 62-93	28, 285-318
10ᴵᴵ, 53-60	43, 57-70	15, 1662-1672	53, 119-129
10ᴵᴵ, 72-92	35, 125-153	19, 598-621	28, 318-343
10ᴵᴵ, 105-158	39, 239-299	19, 668-727	28, 141-201
10ᴵᴵ, 265-266	45, 3-9	10, 628-629	20, 87-89 53, 156-157
10ᴵᴵ, 275-304	45, 11-49	10, 598-628	20, 57-87
10ᴵᴵ, 322-326	43, 47-55	10, 2002-2007	22, 32-38 53, 230
10ᴵᴵ, 375-428	43, 3-45	3, 1352-1361	22, 3-32 65, 266-268
10ᴵᴵᴵ, 1-13	51, 70-75	20, 8-17	28, 205-215
10ᴵᴵᴵ, 13-20	51, 75-78	20, 17-22	28, 216-221
10ᴵᴵᴵ, 21-30	51, 79-83	20, 22-28	28, 221-228
10ᴵᴵᴵ, 30-40	51, 84-88	20, 28-34	28, 228-235
10ᴵᴵᴵ, 40-47	51, 89-91	20, 34-38	28, 235-239
10ᴵᴵᴵ, 48-54	51, 92-95	20, 39-43	28, 239-244
10ᴵᴵᴵ, 55-58	51, 95-96	20, 43-45	28, 244-247
10ᴵᴵᴵ, 58-64	51, 97-100	20, 46-51	28, 247-251

Weimar Edition	American Edition	St. Louis Edition	Erlangen Edition
10^{III}, 341-346	51, 104-110		E$_2$ 16, 420-429
10^{III}, 347-352	51, 111-117		E$_2$ 16, 429-436
11, 245-280	45, 75-129	10, 374-417	22, 59-105
11, 314-336	45, 195-229	20, 1792-1821	29, 45-74
11, 408-416	39, 301-314	10, 1538-1549	22, 140-151
11, 431-456	36, 269-305	19, 1304-1337	28, 388-421
12, 11-15	45, 159-176	10, 954-961	22, 105-122
12, 16-30	45, 176-194	10, 960-977	22, 112-130 53, 196-197
12, 35-37	53, 7-14	10, 220-225	22, 151-156
12, 42-48	53, 95-103	10, 2136-2143	22, 157-166
12, 43	53, 142	10, 2140	22, 158-159
12, 43-44	53, 143-144	10, 2144-2145	22, 291-292
12, 44	53, 144	10, 2142	22, 161
12, 92-142	28, 1-56	8, 1026-1085	51, 1-69
12, 169-196	40, 3-44	10, 1554-1603	var 6, 492-535
12, 205-220	53, 15-40	10, 2232-2255	var 7, 1-20
12, 232-244	45, 131-158	19, 1730-1745	29, 16-33 53, 162
12, 259-399	30, 1-145	9, 958-1111	51, 324-494
13, 1-66	18, 1-76	6, 946-1029	ex 24, 1-88
13, 88-122	18, 77-123	6, 1414-1479	ex 25, 55-125
13, 158-206	18, 125-190	6, 1684-1773	ex 25, 377-481
13, 215-223	18, 191-204	14, 808-823	ex 25, 507-527

Weimar Edition	American Edition	St. Louis Edition	Erlangen Edition
13, 241-258	19, 1-31	14, 912-943	ex 26, 43-76
13, 299-343	18, 205-277	14, 973-983 14, 1178-1257	ex 26, 149-233
13, 371-394	18, 279-315	14, 1332-1373	ex 27, 61-110
13, 424-448	19, 105-148	14, 1506-1533	ex 27, 169-220
13, 480-509	18, 317-364	14, 1604-1657	ex 27, 283-350
13, 532-544	18, 365-387	14, 1708-1733	ex 27, 391-416
13, 546-669	20, 1-152	14, 1976-2159	ex 28, 5-200
13, 675-703	18, 389-419	14, 2158-2195	ex 28, 287-323
14, 14-74	30, 147-199	9, 1342-1397	52, 212-272
14, 75-91	30, 201-215	9, 1742-1755	52, 272-287
14, 489-744	9, 1-311	3, 1370-1639	ex 13, 1-351
15, 27-53	45, 339-378	10, 458-485	22, 168-199
15, 69-78	43, 97-112	5, 1272-1283	41, 115-128 53, 233
15, 86-94	43, 81-96	19, 1674-1685	29, 102-113
15, 163-169	45, 379-393	10, 712-721	53, 236-244
15, 210-221	40, 45-49	16, 4-17	53, 255-268
15, 293-313 15, 321-322 6, 36-60	45, 231-310	10, 914-937 10, 824-855	22, 199-226 20, 89-122
15, 360-378	45, 311-337	5, 1284-1303	41, 128-150 53, 281
15, 391-397	40, 61-71 49, 94-96	15, 2047-2053	53, 270-277
16, 363-393"U"	35, 155-174	3, 2-17	33, 3-21
17^{I}, 38-45	51, 119-132	11, 2174-2189	15, 270-283

Weimar Edition	American Edition	St. Louis Edition	Erlangen Edition
51, 267-295	12, 145-194	5, 254-307	39, 61-105
17^I, 228-243	12, 145-		39, 106-122
18, 22-36	36, 307-328	19, 1198-1215	29, 113-133
18, 62-125	40, 73-223	20, 132-287	29, 134-297
18, 134-214			
18, 224-240	32, 261-286	21, 687-709	26, 313-337
18, 291-334	46, 3-43	16, 45-71	24, 257-286
18, 357-361	46, 45-55	16, 71-77	24, 287-294
18, 384-401	46, 57-85	16, 77-99	24, 294-319
18, 417-421	53, 41-50	10, 258-263	53, 315-321
18, 479-530	14, 137-205	4, 1654-1743	37, 340-442
18, 600-787	33, 3-295	18, 1668-1969	var 7, 116-368
19, 72-113	53, 51-90	10, 226-257	22, 226-244
19, 86	53, 136-137	10, 1461	56, 347
19, 102	53, 137-138	10, 1445	56, 318
19, 185-251	19, 33-104	14, 836-911	41, 324-414
19, 287-293	46, 139-154	19, 1689-1693	29, 318-327
19, 297-336	13, 389-420	5, 1098-1131	40, 240-280
19, 349-435	19, 149-237	14, 1416-1507	42, 1-108
19, 482-523	36, 329-361	20, 734-763	29, 328-359
19, 537-541	53, 106-109	10, 2144-2147	22, 290-294
19, 539	53, 142-143	10, 2144	22, 158-159
19, 552-615	14, 207-277	5, 1-75	38, 369-453
19, 623-662	46, 87-137	10, 488-531	22, 244-290
			53, 391-392
20, 7-203	15, 1-187	5, 1372-1579	ex 21, 1-248
20, 599-801	30, 217-327	9, 1398-1523	
23, 64-283	37, 3-150	20, 762-893	30, 14-150
23, 339-379	43, 113-138	10, 2008-2029	22, 317-341
			53, 408

144

Weimar Edition	American Edition	St. Louis Edition	Erlangen Edition
30^{II}, 595-626	38, 91-137	10, 2170-2209	23, 162-207
30^{II}, 632-646	35, 175-202	19, 968-985	65, 102-123
30^{II}, 700-710	43, 167-177	10, 1712-1719	23, 154-162
30^{III}, 29-42	53, 153-170	10, 1474-1481	56, 360-366
30^{III}, 35	53, 140, 169	10, 1480-1481	56, 362
30^{III}, 36	53, 140, 169	10, 1480-1481	56, 353
30^{III}, 36	53, 141, 170	10, 1478-1479	56, 362
30^{III}, 74-80	53, 110-115	10, 720-725	23, 207-213
30^{III}, 80	53, 144-145	10, 725	23, 213
30^{III}, 110-171	38, 3-89	17, 1939-1943	65, 88-91
30^{III}, 205-248	46, 259-320	10, 754-809	23, 91-154
30^{III}, 276-320	47, 3-55	16, 1624-1665	25, 1-50
30^{III}, 331-388	34, 63-104	16, 1666-1700	25, 51-88
30^{III}, 518-527	40, 379-394	20, 1664-1677	31, 213-226
30^{III}, 584-588 30^{II}, 465-507	40, 321-377	19, 902-957	31, 126-184
31^{I}, 65-182	14, 41-106	5, 1174-1251	41, 7-91
31^{I}, 189-218	13, 39-72	5, 696-731	39, 224-265
31^{I}, 223-257	14, 1-39	5, 1132-1173	40, 290-328
31^{I}, 393-426	13, 349-387	5, 1056-1097	40, 192-240
31^{I}, 430-456	14, 107-135	5, 1302-1333	41, 151-185
31^{I}, 580-586	12, 139-144	5, 1332-1339	
31^{II}, 586-769	15, 189-264	15, 1580-1659	ex 21, 267-368
32, 28-39	51, 193-208	12, 1328-1341	17, 40-53
32, 261-270	51, 209-218		
32, 299-544	21, 1-294	7, 346-677	43, 1-368
32, 547-548	43, 179-186	10, 1776-1779	64, 298-300
33, 1-314	23, 1-197	7, 2192-2417	47, 226-394
33, 314-675	23, 198-422	8, 1-255	48, 1-409

Pr 1270　Sermon on the Epistle for the Twelfth Sunday after Trinity
2 Corinthians 3:4-6, Preached on the Afternoon of
August 17, 1531

415, 232　Lord God, Heavenly Father, Who Createst Holy Desire

415, 232　Lord God, Heavenly Father, from Whom
Without Ceasing We Receive

415, 232　Help, Dear Lord God, That We May Become and
Remain Partakers

415　The Gloria in Excelsis, 1537

415　All Glory, Laud, and Praise be Given, 1537

415, 232　A New Song Here Shall Be Begun, 1523

415, 232　Ah, God, from Heaven Look Down, 1523

415, 232　Would That the Lord Would Grant Us Grace, 1523

415, 232　From Trouble Deep I Cry to Thee, 1523

415, 232　Dear Christians, Let Us Now Rejoice, 1523

415, 232　These Are the Holy Ten Commands, 1524

415, 232　Man, Wouldst Thou Live All Blissfully, 1524

415, 232　Come, the Heathen's Healing Light, 1523

415, 232　Jesus We Now Must Laud and Sing, 1523?

415, 232　All Praise to Thee, O Jesus Christ, 1523?

415, 232　Jesus Christ, Our God and Savior, 1524

415, 232　Happy Who in God's Fear Doth Stay, 1524

415, 232　In Peace and Joy I Now Depart, 1524

Weimar Edition	American Edition	St. Louis Edition	Erlangen Edition
34^{II}, 156-165	51, 221-227		
35, 233	53, 138	10, 1462	56, 345
35, 249	53, 138-139	10, 1460	56, 347
35, 264	53, 131-132	10, 1470	56, 357-358
35, 287-296	53, 184-188		56, 368
35, 287-296	53, 184-188, 294		56, 368
35, 411-415 35, 487-488	53, 211-216	10, 1434-1436	56, 340-343
35, 415-417 35, 488-490	53, 225-228	10, 1438-1439	56, 311-312
35, 418-419 35, 490-492	53, 232-234	10, 1441-1442	56, 318-319
35, 419-420 35, 492-493	53, 221-224	10, 1440-1441	56, 313-315
35, 422-423 35, 493-495	53, 217-220	10, 1436-1438	56, 309-310
35, 426-428 35, 495-497	53, 277-279	10, 1452-1453	56, 322-324
35, 428-429 35, 497	53, 280-281	10, 1457	56, 324-325
35, 430-431 35, 497-498	53, 235-236	10, 1449	56, 325-326
35, 431-433 35, 498-499	53, 237-239	10, 1450-1451	56, 327-328
35, 434-435 35, 499	53, 240-241	10, 1442-1443	56, 328-329
35, 435-437 35, 500-501	53, 249-251	10, 1443-1444	56, 315-317
35, 437-438 35, 501-502	53, 242-244	10, 1442	56, 335-336
35, 438-439 35, 503-504	53, 247-248	10, 1455	56, 331-332

Weimar Edition	American Edition	St. Louis Edition	Erlangen Edition
35, 440-441 35, 504-505	53, 245-246	10, 1457-1458	56, 336-337
35, 441-443 35, 505	53, 229-231	10, 1439-1440	56, 312-313
35, 443-445 35, 506-507	53, 255-257	10, 1447-1448	56, 321-322
35, 445 35, 507-508	53, 258-259	10, 1446-1447	56, 319-320
35, 446-447 35, 508-509	53, 260-262	10, 1452	56, 329-330
35, 447-448 35, 510	53, 263-264	10, 1458	56, 337-338
35, 448-449 35, 510-512	53, 265-267	10, 1451	56, 330-331
35, 450 35, 512-513	53, 268-270	10, 1454-1455	56, 334-335
35, 451-452 35, 513-514	53, 271-273	10, 1454	56, 333
35, 452-453 35, 514-515	53, 252-254	10, 1444-1445	56, 317-318
35, 453-454 35, 515-516	53, 274-276	10, 1445-1446	56, 338-339
35, 455 35, 516-518	53, 282, 82-83	10, 1459-1462	56, 343
35, 455-457 35, 518-520	53, 283-385	10, 1460-1462	56, 343-345
35, 458 35, 521	53, 286-287	10, 1462	56, 345
35, 458 35, 521-524	53, 288, 171-175	10, 1458-1461	56, 345-347
35, 458-459 35, 521-524	53, 171-175	10, 1458-1461	56, 345-347
45, 215	53, 176-179 53, 181-183	7, 1376	45, 215
35, 459-461 35, 524-525	53, 289-291	10, 1462-1464	56, 348-349

Weimar Edition	American Edition	St. Louis Edition	Erlangen Edition
35, 462-463 35, 525-527	53, 292-294	10, 1464	56, 350-351
35, 463-467 35, 527-528	53, 295-298	10, 1465-1466	56, 351-353
35, 467-468 35, 528	53, 304-305	10, 1469	56, 354
35, 468-470 35, 490-491, 528	53, 299-301	10, 1467-1468	56, 355-356
35, 470-471, 528	53, 302-303	10, 1467	56, 353-354
35, 471-473, 528	53, 306-307	10, 1469	56, 357-358
35, 473, 529	53, 308-309	10, 1470	56, 358
35, 474-475	53, 315-316	10, 1422-1425	56, 296-297
35, 475-476	53, 317-318	10, 1424-1425	56, 298-299
35, 476-477	53, 332-334	10, 1430-1433	56, 306-308
35, 478-483	53, 325-331	10, 1424-1431	56, 299-306
35, 483-484	53, 319-320	10, 1432-1434	56, 295-296
35, 537	53, 335-341		
35, 552	53, 131	10, 1449	56, 326
35, 553	53, 132	10, 1456	56, 332
35, 553	53, 132-133	10, 1456	56, 332
35, 553	53, 133	10, 1456	56, 332
35, 553-554	53, 134	10, 1447	56, 320
35, 554	53, 134-135	10, 1447	56, 320
35, 554	53, 135	10, 1459	56, 338
35, 554	53, 136	10, 1455	56, 335
35, 555	53, 139-140	10, 1479	56, 352-353
35, 556	53, 137	10, 1445	56, 318
36, 237-254	51, 231-243	12, 2072-2085	18, 359-372
36, 255-270	51, 243-255	12, 2086-2099	18, 372-384

Weimar Edition	American Edition	St. Louis Edition	Erlangen Edition
36, 352-375	51, 257-287	9, 882-913	19, 296-328
36, 481-696	28, 57-213	8, 1088-1273	51, 70-275
38, 9-17, 69	35, 203-223	4, 134-137 4, 198-199	37, 250-266
38, 195-256	38, 139-214	19, 1220-1285	31, 307-377
38, 262-272	38, 215-233	19, 1286-1299	31, 377-391
38, 358-375	43, 187-211	10, 1394-1415	23, 214-238
38, 423-431	53, 122-126	10, 1602-1605	64, 290-293
38, 429	53, 145-146	10, 1604-1605	64, 292
39^{I}, 44-62	34, 105-132	19, 1436-1450	var 4, 378-389
39^{I}, 82-126	34, 145-196	19, 1450-1455	var 4, 389-394
39^{I}, 175-180	34, 133-144	19, 1462-1467	var 4, 413-416
39^{II}, 3-30	38, 235-277	10, 1168-1173	var 4, 458-461
39-^{II}, 187-203	34, 299-321	19, 1468-1473	var 4, 452-455
40^{I}, 33-36	27, 145-149	9, 8-15	gal 1, 1-12
40^{I}, 40-688	26, 1-461	9, 16-601	gal 1, 12-2, 286
40^{II}, 1-184	27, 1-144	9, 600-771	gal 2, 286-3, 120
40^{II}, 193-212 45, 205-250	12, 1-136	5, 74-237	ex 18, 8-127 39, 4-61
40^{II}, 315-470 472-610	12, 197-410	5, 340-619	ex 18, 130-260 ex 19, 10-154
40^{III}, 484-594	13, 73-141	5, 732-799	ex 18, 264-334
41, 79-239	13, 225-348	5, 922-1055	40, 38-192
42, 1-263	1, 1-359	1, 1-437	ex 1, 1-2, 116
42, 264-549	2, 1-399	1, 436-921	ex 2, 116-3, 276
42, 550-673 43, 1-137	3, 1-365	1, 920-1369	ex 3, 277-5, 67
43, 137-430	4, 1-409	1, 1368-1765 2, 1-123	ex 5, 67-6, 243
43, 430-695	5, 1-386	2, 122-609	ex 6, 243-7, 354
44, 1-304	6, 1-607	2, 608-1159	ex 8, 1-9, 162

Weimar Edition	American Edition	St. Louis Edition	Erlangen Edition
44, 304-581	7, 1-377	2, 1158-1655	ex 9, 162-10, 313
44, 581-825	8, 1-333	2, 1654-2091	ex 10, 313-11, 325
45, 205-250	12, 1-136	5, 74-237	ex 18, 8-127
40^{II}, 193-212			39, 4-61
45, 465-733 46, 1-111	24, 1-422	8, 264-745	49, 1-50, 154
46, 538-789 47, 1-231	22, 1-530	7, 1538-2147	45, 294-422 46, 1-47, 226
47, 757-771	51, 289-299		8, 280-305
47, 772-779	51, 301-312	12, 1408-1421	17, 119-129
49, 124-135	51, 313-329	7, 696-711	19, 72-88
49, 588-615	51, 331-354	12, 1962-1984	17, 239-262
49, 797-805	51, 355-367	10, 588-599	20, 45-46
50, 262-283	34, 197-229	10, 992-1019	23, 251-201
50, 288-308	34, 231-267	16, 1971-1994	25, 146-175
50, 312-337	47, 57-98	20, 1828-1861	31, 416-449
50, 368-374	53, 321-324		
50, 383-385	34, 269-278	14, 376-381	63, 353-355
50, 468-477	47, 99-119	20, 1610-1623	32, 1-14
50, 509-653	41, 3-178	16, 2144-2303	25, 219-388
50, 657-661	34, 279-288	14, 432-437	1, 67-72 63, 401-406
51, 123-134	51, 369-380	12, 1168-1177	16, 139-150
51, 187-194	51, 381-392	12, 1254-1264	16, 264-275
51, 200-264	13, 143-224	5, 800-887	39, 265-364
51, 267-295	12, 145-194	5, 254-307	39, 61-105

Weimar Edition	American Edition	St. Louis Edition	Erlangen Edition
17^I, 228-243			39, 106-122
51, 469-572	41, 179-256	17, 1313-1381	26, 1-75
51, 585-625	43, 213-241	20, 2194-2217	32, 74-99
53, 205-208	43, 243-250	10, 730-735	23, 338-343
53, 417-552	47, 121-306	20, 1860-2029	32, 99-274
54, 28-100	15, 265-352	3, 1880-1973	37, 1-104
54, 141-167	38, 279-319	20, 1764-1791	32, 396-425
54, 179-187	34, 323-338	14, 438-449	var 1, 15-24
54, 192-194	34, 361-366	21, 3374-3377	32, 425-430
54, 206-299	41, 257-376	17, 1019-1132	26, 108-228
54, 389-411	43, 251-288	17, 1396-1419	26, 229-254 39, 221-223
54, 415-443	34, 339-360	19, 1808-1817	var 4, 480-492
56, 1-528	25, 1-524		
57^{III}, 97-238	29, 107-241		
Br 1, 10-11	48, 3-5	21, 1-3	
Br 1, 18	48, 5-7	21, 5-7	
Br 1, 27-29	48, 8-11	21, 13-15	
Br 1, 33-36	48, 11-14	21, 19-22	
Br 1, 41-42	48, 14-16	21, 26-29	
Br 1, 50	48, 17-18	21, 35-36	
Br 1, 56	48, 18-19	21, 18-19	
Br 1, 57-59	48, 20-23	21, 38-41	
Br 1, 69-71	48, 23-26	18, 1972-1975	
Br 1, 72-73	48, 27-32	21, 49-52	
Br 1, 76-79	48, 32-36	21, 53-57	
Br 1, 88-89	48, 36-38	18, 16-19	
Br 1, 89-90	48, 39-41	18, 1974-1975	
Br 1, 98-99	48, 41-42	18, 1968-1971	
Br 1, 102-103	48, 42-43	21, 71-72	

99   16. Cardinal Albrecht, Archbishop of Mainz:
      Wittenberg, October 31, 1517

99   17. Elector Frederick: Wittenberg, about November 6, 1517

99   18. George Spalatin: Wittenberg, January 18, 1518

99   19. George Spalatin: Wittenberg, February 22, 1518

99   20. George Spalatin: Wittenberg, May 18, 1518

99   21. John von Staupitz: Wittenberg, May 30, 1518

99   22. George Spalatin: Wittenberg, August 8, 1518

99   23. George Spalatin: Wittenberg, August 28, 1518

99   24. George Spalatin: Wittenberg, August 31, 1518

99   25. George Spalatin: Wittenberg, September 2, 1518

99   26. George Spalatin: Augsburg, October 14, 1518

99   27. The Papal Legate, Cardinal Cajetan:
      Augsburg, October 18, 1518

99   28. George Spalatin: Wittenberg, October 31, 1518

99   29. George Spalatin: Wittenberg, November 25, 1518

99   30. George Spalatin: Wittenberg, December 9, 1518

99   31. Elector Frederick: Altenburg, January 5 or 6, 1519

99   32. Pope Leo X: Altenburg, January 5 or 6, 1519

99   33. Elector Frederick: Wittenberg,
      between January 13 and 19, 1519

99   34. George Spalatin: Wittenberg, February 7, 1519

99   35. John von Staupitz: Wittenberg, February 20, 1519

99   36. George Spalatin: Wittenberg, March 13, 1519

99   37. Erasmus of Rotterdam: Wittenberg, March 27, 1519

99   38. Elector Frederick: Wittenberg, about May 15, 1519

99   39. George Spalatin: Wittenberg, May 22, 1519

99   40. Martin Glaser: Wittenberg, May 30, 1519

99   41. George Spalatin: Wittenberg, July 20, 1519

99   42. George Spalatin: Liebenswerda, October 9,
      or Wittenberg, October 10, 1519

99   43. Elector Frederick: Wittenberg, October 15, 1519

Weimar Edition	American Edition	St. Louis Edition	Erlangen Edition
Br 1, 108-112	48, 43-49	15, 390-393	
Br 1, 119-120	48, 49-52	21, 77-79	53, 1-2
Br 1, 132-134	48, 52-55	18, 1976-1979	
Br 1, 149-150	48, 56-59	15, 2399-2402	
Br 1, 172-174	48, 60-63	15, 2392-2394	
1, 525-527	48, 64-70	15, 414-418	
Br 1, 188	48, 70-73	15, 430-432	
Br 1, 189-191	48, 73-76	15, 432-434	
Br 1, 191-192	48, 76-80	21, 105-106	
Br 1, 195-196	48, 80-83	15, 2397-2399	
Br 1, 213-215	48, 83-87	15, 2416-2418	
Br 1, 222-223	48, 87-89	15, 592-594	
Br 1, 224-225	48, 90-93	15, 2408-2410	
Br 1, 253	48, 93-94	15, 2427	
Br 1, 262	48, 95-96	21, 120-121	
Br 1, 289-291	48, 96-100	15, 696-698	53, 5-7
Br 1, 291-293	48, 100-102	15, 705-708	
Br 1, 305-308	48, 103-106	15, 1726-1729	
Br 1, 325	48, 106-107	21, 144-145	
Br 1, 343-345	48, 108-111	15, 2442-2444	
Br 1, 358-360	48, 111-116	21, 155-157	
Br 1, 361-363	48, 116-119	18, 1582-1585	
Br 1, 386-387	48, 120-121	21, 165	53, 9-10
Br 1, 404	48, 122-124	21, 170-171	
Br 1, 408-409	48, 124-126	21, 174-175	
Br 1, 420-442	48, 126 31, 318-325	15, 1162-1170	
Br 1, 524-525	48, 126-127	15, 752-753	
Br 1, 535-536	48, 127-129	15, 757-758	53, 28-29

99	44. George Spalatin: Wittenberg, November 1, 1519
99	45. George Spalatin: Wittenberg, November 7, 1519
99	46. George Spalatin: Wittenberg, November 29, 1519
99	47. John Lang: Wittenberg, December 18, 1519
99	48. Thomas Fuchs: Wittenberg, December 23, 1519
99	49. George Spalatin: Wittenberg, December 31, 1519
99	50. George Spalatin: Wittenberg, January 14, 1520
99	51. John Lang: Wittenberg, January 26, 1520
99	52. George Spalatin: Wittenberg, about February 14, 1520
99	53. George Spalatin: Wittenberg, March 19, 1520
99	54. George Spalatin: Wittenberg, April 13, 1520
99	55. George Spalatin: Wittenberg, April 16, 1520
99	56. George Spalatin: Wittenberg, May 1, 1520
99	57. George Spalatin: Wittenberg, May 31, 1520
99	58. George Spalatin: Wittenberg, June 25, 1520
99	59. George Spalatin: Wittenberg, July 14, 1520
99	60. Wenceslas Link: Wittenberg, August 19, 1520
99	61. George Spalatin: Wittenberg, August 23, 1520
99	62. George Spalatin: Wittenberg, August 24, 1520
99	63. Emperor Charles V: Wittenberg, August 30, 1520
99	64. George Spalatin: Lichtenberg, October 12, 1520
99	65. Duke John Frederick: Wittenberg, October 30, 1520
99	66. Lazarus Spengler: Wittenberg, November 17, 1520
99	67. George Spalatin: Wittenberg, December 10, 1520
99	68. George Spalatin: Wittenberg, December 29, 1520
99	69. John von Staupitz: Wittenberg, January 14, 1521
99	70. Elector Frederick: Wittenberg, January 25, 1521
99	71. George Spalatin: Frankfurt/Main, April 14, 1521
99	72. John Cuspinian: Worms, April 17, 1521
99	73. Lucas Cranach: Frankfurt/Main, April 28, 1521
99	74. Emperor Charles V: Friedberg, April 28, 1521
99	75. Philip Melanchthon: Wartburg, about May 8, 1521

Weimar Edition	American Edition	St. Louis Edition	Erlangen Edition
Br 1, 548-549	48, 130-131	15, 2476-2477	
Br 1, 551	48, 132-133	15, 2477-2478	
Br 1, 563-564	48, 133-134	21, 207-208	
Br 1, 596-597	48, 135-139	21, 214-216	
Br 1, 598-599	48, 139-141	21, 216-217	53, 29-30
Br 1, 604	48, 141-143	21, 219-220	
Br 1, 610-612	48, 143-148	19, 1774-1779	
Br 1, 619	48, 148-151	21, 224-225	
Br 2, 40-42	48, 151-153	21, 238-239	
Br 2, 72	48, 154-155	21, 246-247	
Br 2, 80-82	48, 156-159	21, 252-254	
Br 2, 82-83	48, 159-161	15, 2403-2405	
Br 2, 95-96	48, 161-162	21, 256-257	
Br 2, 111	48, 163-165	21, 262-263	
Br 2, 129-130	48, 165-167	21, 270-271	
Br 2, 142-143	48, 167-169	21, 278-279	
Br 2, 168	48, 169-171	21, 292-293	
Br 2, 169-170	48, 171-173	15, 2493-2494	
Br 2, 170-171	48, 173-174	21, 293-294	
Br 2, 172-178	48, 175-179	15, 1378-1382	
Br 2, 196-197	48, 179-181	15, 782-783	
Br 2, 204-206	48, 181-183	21, 303-304	53, 52-53
Br 2, 217-218	48, 184-185	21, 308-309	53, 53-54
Br 2, 234	48, 186-187	21, 324-325	
Br 2, 242-243	48, 188-191	15, 1884-1887	
Br 2, 245-246	48, 191-194	15, 2422-2424	
Br 2, 253-255	48, 194-197	15, 1887-1890	53, 56-58
Br 2, 298	48, 197-198	15, 1827-1828	
Br 2, 299-300	48, 199-200	21, 348-349	
Br 2, 305	48, 200-203	15, 1935-1937	53, 64-65
Br 2, 307-310	48, 203-209	15, 1893-1899	53, 65-71
Br 2, 330-331	48, 210-213	21, 351-352	

99	76. Philip Melanchthon: Wartburg, about May 8, 1521
99	77. Philip Melanchthon: Wartburg, May 12, 1521
99	78. Nicholas von Amsdorf: Wartburg, May 12, 1521
99	79. John Agricola: Wartburg, May 12, 1521
99	80. George Spalatin: Wartburg, May 14, 1521
99	81. Philip Melanchthon: Wartburg, May 26, 1521
99	82. Francis von Sickingen: Wartburg, June 1, 1521
99	83. The People of Wittenberg: Wartburg, June, 1521
99	84. George Spalatin: Wartburg, June 10, 1521
99	85. Philip Melanchthon: Wartburg, July 13, 1521
99	86. Nicholas von Amsdorf: Wartburg, July 15?, 1521
99	87. George Spalatin: Wartburg, July 15, 1521
99	88. George Spalatin: Wartburg, soon after July 15, 1521
99	89. George Spalatin: Wartburg, soon after July 15, 1521
99	90. George Spalatin: Wartburg, July 31, 1521
99	91. Philip Melanchthon: Wartburg, August 1, 1521
99	92. Philip Melanchthon: Wartburg, August 3, 1521
99	93. George Spalatin: Wartburg, August 6, 1521
99	94. George Spalatin: Wartburg, August 15, 1521
99	95. Philip Melanchthon: Wartburg, September 9, 1521
99	96. George Spalatin: Wartburg, September 9, 1521
99	97. Nicholas von Amsdorf: Wartburg, September 9, 1521
99	98. George Spalatin: Wartburg, September 17, 1521
99	99. George Spalatin: Wartburg, October 7, 1521
99	100. Nicholas Gerbel: Wartburg, November 1, 1521
99	101. George Spalatin: Wartburg, November 1, 1521
99	102. The Augustinians in Wittenberg: Wartburg, November, 1521
99	103. George Spalatin: Wartburg, November 11, 1521
99	104. Hans Luther: Wartburg, November 21, 1521
99	105. George Spalatin: Wartburg, November 22, 1521
99	106. Cardinal Albrecht, Archbishop of Mainz: Wartburg, December 1, 1521

Weimar Edition	American Edition	St. Louis Edition	Erlangen Edition
Br 2, 331-332	48, 213-214	15, 1906-1907	
Br 2, 332-333	48, 215-217	15, 2513-2515	
Br 2, 334-335	48, 218-220	15, 2516	
Br 2, 335-336	48, 220-222	15, 2520-2521	
Br 2, 336-338	48, 222-228	15, 2510-2513	
Br 2, 346-349	48, 228-244	15, 2542-2547	
8, 136-140	48, 244-247	19, 814-817	53, 74-77
8, 210-214	48, 248-253	5, 306-311	
Br 2, 354-355	48, 253-256	15, 2526-2528	
Br 2, 356-359	48, 256-263	15, 2528-2534	
Br 2, 361-363	48, 264-268	15, 2550-2554	
Br 2, 364-365	48, 268-270	15, 2538-2540	
Br 2, 366	48, 270-271	21, 356-357	
Br 2, 366-367	48, 272-273	21, 357-358	
Br 2, 368-369	48, 274-276	15, 2540-2542	
Br 2, 370-372	48, 277-282	15, 2585-2590	
Br 2, 373-376	48, 283-289	15, 2590-2596	
Br 2, 377-378	48, 289-291	21, 358-360	
Br 2, 379-381	48, 291-296	15, 2521-2526	
Br 2, 382-386	48, 296-304	19, 1794-1801	
Br 2, 387-389	48, 305-310	15, 2535-2538	
Br 2, 390-391	48, 310-312	15, 2584-2585	
Br 2, 391-392	48, 312-315	21, 360-362	
Br 2, 394-395	48, 315-317	21, 363-364	
Br 2, 396-398	48, 317-322	15, 2517-2520	
Br 2, 399	48, 323-324	21, 364	
8, 482-483	48, 324-325 36, 133-135	19, 1068-1071	
Br 2, 402-403	48, 325-328	15, 2548-2550	
8, 573-576	48, 329-336	19, 1500-1507	53, 86-92
Br 2, 404-405	48, 337-338	19, 1800-1803	
Br 2, 405-408	48, 339-350	19, 548-553	53, 95-99

99   107. George Spalatin: Wartburg, about December 5, 1521

99   108. George Spalatin: Wartburg, about December 12, 1521

99   109. John Lang: Wartburg, December 18, 1521

99   110. Wenceslas Link: Wartburg, December 18, 1521

99   111. Nicholas von Amsdorf: Wartburg, January 13, 1522

99   112. Philip Melanchthon: Wartburg, January 13, 1522

99   113. Wolfgang Fabricius Capito: Wartburg, January 17, 1522

99   114. George Spalatin: Wartburg, January 17, 1522

99   115. George Spalatin: Wartburg, January 22?, 1522

99   116. Elector Frederick: Wartburg, about February 22, 1522

99   117. Elector Frederick: Borna, March 5, 1522

99   118. Elector Frederick: Wittenberg, March 7 or 8, 1522

99   119. Nicholas Hausmann: Wittenberg, March 17, 1522

99   120. George Spalatin: Wittenberg, March 30, 1522

99   121. George Spalatin: Wittenberg, May 20, 1522

99   122. An Anonymous Addressee: Wittenberg, May 28, 1522

99   123. George Spalatin: Wittenberg, June 7, 1522

99   124. John von Staupitz: Wittenberg, June 27, 1522

99   125. George Spalatin: Wittenberg, about September 20, 1522

99   126. Henning Teppen: Wittenberg, November 21, 1522

99   127. George Spalatin: Wittenberg, about December 12, 1522

99   128. Wenceslas Link: Wittenberg, December 19, 1522

99   129. The Council of the City of Stettin:
      Wittenberg, January 11, 1523

99   130. The Council of the City of Leisnig:
      Wittenberg, January 29, 1523

99   131. Eobanus Hessus: Wittenberg, March 29, 1523

99   132. Elector Frederick: Wittenberg, May 29, 1523

99   133. John Oecolampadius: Wittenberg, June 20, 1523

99   134. Elector Frederick: Leisnig, August 11, 1523

99   To All Christians in Worms, 1523

99   135. John von Staupitz: Wittenberg, September 17, 1523

99   136. Gregory Brueck: Wittenberg, October 18, 1523

Weimar Edition	American Edition	St. Louis Edition	Erlangen Edition
Br 2, 409-410	48, 350-352	19, 560-563	
Br 2, 411-412	48, 353-355	21, 367-369	
Br 2, 413	48, 356-357	15, 2554-2555	
Br 2, 414-415	48, 357-359	21, 370-372	
Br 2, 422-423	48, 360-364	15, 2557-2560	
Br 2, 424-427	48, 364-372	15, 2599-2605	
Br 2, 428-434	48, 372-379	19, 554-561	
Br 2, 443-444	48, 380-381	15, 2606-2607	
Br 2, 445-447	48, 382-386	21, 378-382	
Br 2, 448-449	48, 386-388	15, 1984-1985	53, 103-104
Br 2, 453-457	48, 388-393	15, 1989-1993	53, 104-109
Br 2, 459-462	48, 393-399	15, 1998-2001	53, 109-112
Br 2, 474-475	48, 399-402	15, 2011-2013	
Br 2, 489-490	49, 3-4	15, 2555-2556	
Br 2, 537	49, 5	21, 412-413	
Br 2, 544-545	49, 6-8	18, 1978-1981	
Br 2, 556	49, 8-9	21, 421	53, 137
Br 2, 567-568	49, 10-13	15, 607-610	
Br 2, 598	49, 13-15	21, 446-447	
Br 2, 618	49, 16	21, 458-459	
Br 2, 630-631	49, 17-20	15, 2581-2583	
Br 2, 632-633	49, 20-25	15, 2578-2581	
Br 3, 13-14	49, 25-28	21, 471-472	53, 159-161
Br 3, 23	49, 28-32	21, 478	
Br 3, 49-50	49, 32-35	21, 491-493	
Br 3, 75-77	49, 35-42	15, 2187-2191	53, 163-167
Br 3, 96-97	49, 42-45	21, 517-519	
Br 3, 124-125	49, 45-47	21, 534-535	53, 194-195
Br 3, 138-140	43, 71-79	10, 1758-1761	
Br 3, 155-156	49, 48-50	15, 610-612	
Br 3, 176-177	49, 50-55	10, 912-913	53, 219-220

99   137. Nicholas Hausmann: Wittenberg, end of October, 1523

99   138. Elector Frederick: Wittenberg, mid-November, 1523

99   139. Margrave Albrecht of Brandenburg,
      Wittenberg, December, 1523

99   140. George Spalatin: Wittenberg, end of 1523

99   141. George Spalatin: Wittenberg, January 14, 1524

99   142. George Spalatin: Wittenberg, March 14, 1524

99   143. Elector Frederick: Wittenberg, March 23, 1524

99   144. Erasmus of Rotterdam: Wittenberg, about April 18, 1524

99   145. Nicholas Gerbel: Wittenberg, May 6, 1524

99   146. Wolfgang Stein: Wittenberg, beginning of September, 1524

99   147. The Council of the City of Zerbst:
      Wittenberg, October 8, 1524

99   148. Nicholas Hausmann: Wittenberg, November 17, 1524

99   149. George Spalatin: Wittenberg, November 30, 1524

99   150. The Christians in Strassburg: Wittenberg,
      about December 15, 1524

99   151. Lazarus Spengler: Wittenberg, February 4, 1525

99   152. Theobald Billicanus: Wittenberg, March 5, 1525

      An Exhortation to the Communicants, 1525

99   153. George Spalatin: Wittenberg, April 16, 1525

99   154. John Ruehel: Seeburg, May 4, 1525

99   155. Nicholas von Amsdorf: Wittenberg, May 30, 1525

99   156. George Spalatin: Wittenberg, June 21, 1525

99   157. Nicholas von Amsdorf: Wittenberg, June 21, 1525

99   158. John Briessmann: Wittenberg, after August 15, 1525

99   159. Elector John: Wittenberg, September 6, 1525

99   160. Elector John: Wittenberg, October 31, 1525

99   161. Elector John: Wittenberg, November 30, 1525

99   162. Michael Stifel: Wittenberg, December 31, 1525

99   163. Gabriel Zwilling: Wittenberg, January 2, 1526

99   164. George Spalatin: Wittenberg, March 27, 1526

99   165. Caspar von Schwenkfeld: Wittenberg, April 14, 1526

Weimar Edition	American Edition	St. Louis Edition	Erlangen Edition
Br 3, 183-184	49, 55-56	21, 571-572	
Br 3, 195-197	49, 57-59	21, 671-673	
Br 3, 214-219	49, 59-68		
Br 3, 220	49, 68-70	21, 582-583	
Br 3, 234-235	49, 70-72	15, 2622-2623	
Br 3, 254	49, 72-74	15, 2623-2624	
Br 3, 258-259	49, 74-76	21, 601-602	53, 235-236
Br 3, 268-271	49, 76-81	18, 1596-1599	
Br 3, 284	49, 81-83	21, 619-620	
Br 3, 342-343	49, 83-85	21, 647-648	53, 268-269
Br 3, 355	49, 85-87	21, 650-651	
Br 3, 373-374	49, 87-91	18, 1984-1987	
Br 3, 393-394	49, 91-94	21, 665-667	
15, 391-397	49, 94-96 40, 65-71	15, 2047-2053	53, 270-277
Br 3, 432-433	49, 96-99	21, 715-716	53, 283-284
Br 3, 451-452	49, 99-102	21, 725-726	
Br 3, 462-463	53, 104-105	10, 2256-2257	53, 285
Br 3, 474-475	49, 102-105	21, 736-738	
Br 3, 480-482	49, 106-112	16, 126-129	53, 291-294
Br 3, 517-518	49, 112-114	16, 133-135	
Br 3, 540	49, 115-116	21, 762-763	
Br 3, 541	49, 116-120	15, 2639-2640	
Br 3, 554-556	49, 120-125	21, 771-773	
Br 3, 569-570	49, 125-130	21, 775-776	56, viii-x
Br 3, 594-596	49, 130-137	21, 798-801	53, 329-332
Br 3, 628-629	49, 137-139	21, 812-813	53, 336-338
Br 3, 653	49, 139-141	21, 818-819	
Br 4, 4	49, 142		
Br 4, 41-42	49, 143-147	15, 2641-2644	
Br 4, 52-53	49, 148-150	20, 1660-1661	

99 166. John Agricola: Wittenberg, May 11, 1526

99 167. John Ruehel: Wittenberg, June 8, 1526

99 168. Michael Stifel: Wittenberg, August 11, 1526

99 169. Wenceslas Link: Wittenberg, January 1, 1527

99 170. Nicholas Hausmann: Wittenberg, January 10, 1527

99 171. Nicholas Hausmann: Wittenberg, March 29, 1527

99 172. Wenceslas Link: Wittenberg, about May 4, 1527

99 173. Wenceslas Link: Wittenberg, July 5, 1527

99 174. Nicholas Hausmann: Wittenberg, July 13, 1527

99 175. Elector John: Wittenberg, September 16, 1527

99 176. Justus Jonas: Wittenberg, about November 10, 1527

99 177. John Brenz: Torgau, November 28, 1527

99 178. Justus Jonas: Wittenberg, December 10, 1527

99 179. Justus Jonas: Wittenberg, December 30, 1527

99 180. Nicholas von Amsdorf: Wittenberg, April 16, 1528

99 181. Elector John: Weimar, May 1 or 2, 1528

99 182. Duke John Frederick: Wittenberg, May 18, 1528

99 183. John Hess: Wittenberg, about June 13, 1528

99 184. Nicholas Gerbel: Wittenberg, July 28, 1528

99 185. Nicholas Hausmann: Wittenberg, August 5, 1528

99 186. Lazarus Spengler: Wittenberg, August 15, 1528

99 187. Elector John: Wittenberg, September 3, 1528

99 188. John Agricola: Wittenberg, September 11, 1528

99 189. Nicholas von Amsdorf: Wittenberg, November 1, 1528

99 190. Wenceslas Link: Wittenberg, March 7, 1529

99 191. Nicholas von Amsdorf: Wittenberg, May 5, 1529

99 192. Wenceslas Link: Wittenberg, May 6, 1529

99 193. Elector John: Wittenberg, May 22, 1529

99 194. Landgrave Philip of Hesse: Wittenberg, June 23, 1529

99 195. Thomas Loescher: Wittenberg, August 26, 1529

99 196. Mrs. Martin Luther: Marburg, October 4, 1529

99 197. Nicholas von Amsdorf: Wittenberg, October 27, 1529

99 198. Elector John: Wittenberg, November 18, 1529

Weimar Edition	American Edition	St. Louis Edition	Erlangen Edition
Br 4, 73-74	49, 150-151	21, 863-864	
Br 4, 87	49, 151-153	21, 868-869	53, 380-381
Br 4, 108-109	49, 153-156	17, 1544	
Br 4, 147-148	49, 157-159	19, 1786-1787	
Br 4, 159	49, 159-161	21, 916-917	
Br 4, 180-181	49, 161-164	21, 929-930	53, 399-400
Br 4, 197-198	49, 164-165	21, 935-936	
Br 4, 220	49, 166-167	21, 984	
Br 4, 222	49, 167-169	21, 996-997	
Br 4, 248	49, 169-171	21, 1011-1012	
Br 4, 279-280	49, 171-177	15, 2645-2647	
Br 4, 285-286	49, 177-180	15, 2632-2633	
Br 4, 294-295	49, 180-185	17, 2228-2231	
Br 4, 311-312	49, 185-186	21, 1055-1056	
Br 4, 443	49, 187-188		
Br 4, 447-450	49, 189-195	21, 1147-1150	
Br 4, 465	49, 195-196	21, 1153	54, 5-6
Br 4, 480	49, 196-199	19, 1788-1789	
Br 4, 508	49, 199-202	21, 1180-1181	
Br 4, 511	49, 202-203	21, 1182	
Br 4, 533-536	49, 204-210	10, 2256-2261	54, 30-34
Br 4, 545-546	49, 210-211	21, 1197-1198	54, 34-35
Br 4, 557-558	49, 212-213	21, 1205-1206	
Br 4, 597	49, 213-214	21, 1231	
Br 5, 27-28	49, 214-217	21, 1269-1270	
Br 5, 61	49, 218-219	21, 1294-1295	54, 69
Br 5, 62-63	49, 219-221	21, 1297-1298	
Br 5, 75-77	49, 221-228	21, 1303-1306	54, 72-74
Br 5, 101-102	49, 228-231	17, 1935-1937	54, 83-85
Br 5, 137	49, 232-234	21, 1348-1349	
Br 5, 154	49, 234-239	21, 1366-1367	54, 107-108
Br 5, 167-168	49, 239-243	21, 1371-1372	
Br 5, 181-183	49, 244-250	10, 552-555	54, 110-112

99 199. Landgrave Philip of Hesse: Wittenberg, December 16, 1529

99 200. Elector John: Wittenberg, December 24, 1529

99 201. Some Pastors of the City of Luebeck:
Wittenberg, January 12, 1530

99 202. Nicholas Hausmann: Wittenberg,
beginning of February, 1530

99 203. Hans Luther: Wittenberg, February 15, 1530

99 204. Elector John: Wittenberg, March 6, 1530

99 205. Nicholas Hausmann: Coburg, April 18, 1530

99 206. Philip Melanchthon: Coburg, April 24, 1530

99 207. George Spalatin: Coburg, April 24, 1530

99 208. Elector John: Coburg, May 15, 1530

99 209. Landgrave Philip of Hesse: Coburg, May 20, 1530

99 210. Elector John: Coburg, May 20, 1530

99 211. Mrs. Martin Luther: Coburg, June 5, 1530

99 212. Philip Melanchthon: Coburg, June 5, 1530

99 213. Philip Melanchthon: Coburg, June 7, 1530

99 214. John Luther: Coburg, about June 19, 1530

99 215. Philip Melanchthon: Coburg, June 29, 1530

99 216. George Spalatin: Coburg, June 30, 1530

99 217. John Agricola: Coburg, June 30, 1530

99 218. Philip Melanchthon: Coburg, July 3, 1530

99 219. Nicolas Hausmann: Coburg, July 6, 1530

99 220. Conrad Cordatus: Coburg, July 6, 1530

99 221. Lazarus Spengler: Coburg, July 8, 1530

99 222. Elector John: Coburg, July 9, 1530

99 223. Justus Jonas: Coburg, July 9, 1530

99 224. Justus Jonas, George Spalatin, Philip
Melanchthon, John Agricola: Coburg, July 15, 1530

99 225. Philip Melanchthon: Coburg, July 21, 1530

99 226. Gregory Brueck: Coburg, August 5, 1530

99 227. Mrs. Martin Luther: Coburg, August 14, 1530

99 228. Mrs. Martin Luther: Coburg, August 15, 1530

Weimar Edition	American Edition	St. Louis Edition	Erlangen Edition
Br 5, 203-204	49, 250-254	21, 1396-1397	
Br 5, 209-211	49, 254-260	21, 1384-1387	
Br 5, 220-221	49, 261-263	21, 1409-1411	
Br 5, 236-237	49, 264-267	21, 1413-1414	
Br 5, 239-241	49, 267-271	10, 1794-1799	54, 130-133
Br 5, 258-261	49, 272-280	10, 544-549	54, 138-142
Br 5, 277-278	49, 280-287	16, 667-669	
Br 5, 285-286	49, 287-291	16, 2307-2309	
Br 5, 290-291	49, 292-293	16, 1754-1756	
Br 5, 319-320	49, 295-299	16, 657-658	54, 145-146
Br 5, 328-332	49, 299-304	17, 1960-1963	54, 151-154
Br 5, 324-327	49, 305-311	16, 690-694	54, 146-150
Br 5, 347-348	49, 311-316	21, 1464-1465	
Br 5, 350-351	49, 316-319	21, 1467-1469	
Br 5, 354	49, 320-321	21, 1470-1471	
Br 5, 377-378	49, 321-324	21, 1491-1492	54, 156-157
Br 5, 405-407	49, 324-333	16, 901-905	
Br 5, 414-415	49, 333-337	16, 908-910	
Br 5, 415-417	49, 338-342	16, 750-752	
Br 5, 435-436	49, 342-347	16, 913-914	
Br 5, 440	49, 348-352	16, 881-883	
Br 5, 441-442	49, 353-356	16, 914-916	
Br 5, 444-445	49, 356-359	21, 1513-1514	54, 168-169
Br 5, 453-455 Br 12, 117-119	49, 359-365	16, 814	54, 169-172
Br 5, 457-459	49, 366-372	16, 927	
Br 5, 479-480	49, 372-377	21, 1517-1519	
Br 5, 492-495	49, 378-393	16, 1013-1018	
Br 5, 530-532	49, 394-399	16, 1764-1767	54, 183-186
Br 5, 544-545	49, 399-400	16, 1084	54, 186
Br 5, 545-546	49, 400-403	21, 1541-1542	54, 187-188

99   229. Elector John: Coburg, August 26, 1530

99   230. George Spalatin: Coburg, August 26, 1530

99   231. Mrs. Martin Luther: Coburg, September 8, 1530

99   232. Nicholas Hausmann: Coburg, September 23, 1530

99   233. Mrs. Martin Luther: Coburg, September 24, 1530

99   234. Louis Senfl: Coburg, October 4, 1530

99   235. The Electoral Saxon Government: Torgau,
about October 27, 1530

99   236. Landgrave Philip of Hesse: Torgau, October 28, 1530

99   237. Elector John: Wittenberg, about January 16, 1531

99   238. Martin Bucer: Wittenberg, January 22, 1531

99   239. Lazarus Spengler: Wittenberg, February 15, 1531

99   240. Wenceslas Link: Wittenberg, May 12, 1531

99   241. Mrs. Margaret Luther: Wittenberg, May 20, 1531

99   242. Gregory Brueck: Wittenberg, end of May, 1531

99   243. Elector John: Wittenberg, June 16, 1531

99   244. Michael Stifel: Wittenberg, June or July, 1531

99   245. Robert Barnes: Wittenberg, September 3, 1531

99   246. Elector John: Wittenberg, about February 12, 1532

99   247. Mrs. Martin Luther: Torgau, February 27, 1532

99   248. Thomas Zink: Wittenberg, April 22, 1532

99   249. Nicholas von Amsdorf: Wittenberg, June 13, 1532

99   250. Elector John: Wittenberg, June 29, 1532

99   251. The Regents and Councilors, of the Margraviate
of Brandenburg-Ansbach and to the Council of the
City of Nuernberg: Wittenberg, August 1, 1532

99   252. Duke Joachim of Brandenburg: Wittenberg, August 3, 1532

99   253. Nicholas von Amsdorf: Wittenberg, November 2, 1532

99   254. John Loeser: Wittenberg, January 29, 1533

99   255. The Council of the City of Nuernberg:
Wittenberg, April 18, 1533

99   256. John Schlaginhaufen: Wittenberg, March 10, 1534

99   257. Mrs. Martin Luther: Dessau, July 29, 1534

Weimar Edition	American Edition	St. Louis Edition	Erlangen Edition
Br 5, 572-574	49, 403-412	16, 1414-1417	54, 188-192
Br 5, 575-576	49, 412-414	16, 1406-1407	
Br 5, 608-609	49, 415-419	21, 1564-1565	56, 181-183
Br 5, 631-632	49, 419-424	16, 1522-1523	
Br 5, 633-634	49, 424-425	21, 1571-1572	54, 194
Br 5, 639	49, 426-429	21, 1574-1576	
Br 5, 662	49, 429-433	10, 562-563	
Br 5, 660-661	49, 433-437	21, 1585-1586	
Br 6, 18-21	50, 3-6	17, 1975-1976	
Br 6, 24-26	50, 6-9	17, 1973-1975	
Br 6, 35-37	50, 9-12	10, 570-572	54, 213-214
Br 6, 95-97	50, 13-17	21, 1656-1658	
Br 6, 103-106	50, 17-21	10, 1798-1803	54, 232-236
Br 6, 107-108	50, 22-23	21, 1677	
Br 6, 122-124	50, 23-26	21, 1662-1664	
Br 6, 143	50, 26-27	21, 1672	
Br 6, 178-188	50, 27-40	21, 1688-1697	
Br 6, 259-261	50, 41-47	16, 1810-1812	54, 269-271
Br 6, 270-271	50, 47-50	21, 1731-1732	54, 275-276
Br 6, 300-302	50, 50-53	10, 2046-2047	54, 293-295
Br 6, 318-319	50, 53-56	21, 1751-1752	
Br 6, 324-327	50, 56-60	16, 1812-1814	54, 312-314
Br 6, 338-342	50, 61-67	21, 1761-1765	54, 316-320
Br 6, 343-345	50, 68-71	21, 1765-1767	54, 320-322
Br 6, 381-382	50, 72-73	21, 1782-1783	
Br 6, 425-426	50, 73-74	21, 1802-1803	55, 4-5
Br 6, 453-455	50, 75-78	21, 1811-1813	55, 8-10
Br 7, 24	50, 78-79	21, 3229	
Br 7, 91	50, 79-81	21, 1920	55, 61

99	258. Elector John Frederick: Wittenberg, August 20, 1535
99	259. Philip Melanchthon: Wittenberg, August 29, 1535
99	260. Justus Jonas: Wittenberg, September 4, 1535
99	261. George Spalatin: Wittenberg, September 6, 1535
99	262. Elector John Frederick: Wittenberg, September 12, 1535
99	263. Gregory Brueck: Wittenberg, about September 15, 1535
99	264. Justus Jonas: Wittenberg, October 28, 1535
99	265. Justus Jonas: Wittenberg, November 10, 1535
99	266. Philip Melanchthon: Wittenberg, beginning of December, 1535
99	267. Elector John Frederick: Wittenberg, January 11, 1536
99	268. Nicholas Hausmann: Wittenberg, January 17, 1536
99	269. Caspar Mueller: Wittenberg, January 19, 1536
99	270. Francis Burchart: Wittenberg, January 25, 1536
99	271. Elector John Frederick: Wittenberg, March 28, 1536
99	272. Thomas Cromwell: Wittenberg, April 9, 1536
99	273. Francis Burchart: Wittenberg, April 20, 1536
99	274. George Spalatin: Wittenberg, June 10, 1536
99	275. Justus Jonas: Wittenberg, August 17, 1536
99	276. Nicholas Hausmann: Wittenberg, Torgau September 20, 1536
99	277. John Luther: Wittenberg, January 27, 1537
99	278. Justus Jonas: Altenburg, February 1, 1537
99	279. Elector John Frederick: Smalcald, about February 9, 1537
99	280. Mrs. Martin Luther: Tambach, February 27, 1537
99	281. George Spalatin: Wittenberg, March 21, 1537
99	282. Wolfgang Capito: Wittenberg, July 9, 1537
99	283. Nicholas Hausmann: Wittenberg, February 23, 1538
99	284. Edward Fox: Wittenberg, May 12, 1538
99	285. James Propst: Wittenberg, September 15, 1538
99	286. Elector John Frederick: Wittenberg, July 8, 1539
99	287. Martin Bucer: Wittenberg, October 14, 1539
99	288. Elector John Frederick: Wittenberg, October 23, 1539

Weimar Edition	American Edition	St. Louis Edition	Erlangen Edition
Br 7, 237-238	50, 81-85	16, 1888-1889	55, 104
Br 7, 244-245	50, 85-92	21, 1995-1996	
Br 7, 249-250	50, 93-97	21, 1999-2000	
Br 7, 251	50, 97-100	21, 2000-2001	
Br 7, 266-267	50, 100-102	17, 283-284	54, 105-107
Br 7, 267-268	50, 102-106	21, 3501-3502	
Br 7, 316-317	50, 107-109	21, 2016-2017	
Br 7, 321-322	50, 109-113	21, 2020-2021	
Br 7, 330-331	50, 113-117	21, 2024-2026	
Br 7, 341-343	50, 117-122	21, 2031-2033	55, 117-118
Br 7, 347	50, 122-124	21, 2036-2037	
Br 7, 348-350	50, 124-130	21, 2037-2039	55, 119-121
Br 7, 352	50, 130-131	21, 2040-2041	
Br 7, 381-384	50, 132-135	21, 2051-2052	55, 128-130
Br 7, 395-396	50, 136-138	21, 2057-2058	
Br 7, 400-404	50, 138-141	17, 282-283	55, 133-134
Br 7, 430	50, 141-143	21, 2069-2070	
Br 7, 503-504	50, 144-147	21, 2095-2096	
Br 7, 546-547	50, 148-151	21, 2105-2106	
Br 8, 18-20	50, 151-153	21, 2146-2147	
Br 8, 22-23	50, 153-157	21, 2147-2149	
Br 8, 35-38	50, 157-165	16, 1997-2000	
Br 8, 50-51	50, 165-169	21, 2156-2157	55, 174-175
Br 8, 59	50, 169-170	21, 2161-2162	
Br 8, 99-100	50, 171-174	21, 2175-2176	
Br 8, 199-200	50, 174-176	21, 2226-2227	
Br 8, 219-220	50, 177-180	21, 2238-2239	
Br 8, 291-292	50, 181-184	21, 2270-2271	
Br 8, 488-491	50, 185-187	21, 2352-2353	55, 234-235
Br 8, 568-569	50, 187-191	21, 2383-2385	
Br 8, 572-575	50, 192-194	17, 265-269	55, 243-247

99	289. John Frederick: Wittenberg, October 23, 1539
99	290. Mrs. Martin Luther: Weimar, July 2, 1540
99	291. Mrs. Martin Luther: Eisenach, July 10, 1540
99	292. Mrs. Martin Luther: Eisenach, July 16, 1540
99	293. Mrs. Martin Luther: Eisenach, July 26, 1540
99	294. Mrs. Martin Luther: Wittenberg, September 18, 1541
99	295. Justus Jonas: Wittenberg, February 16, 1542
99	296. Marcus Crodel: Wittenberg, August 26, 1542
99	297. Marcus Crodel: Wittenberg, August 28, 1542
99	298. Marcus Crodel: Wittenberg, September 6, 1542
99	299. Justus Jonas: Wittenberg, September 23, 1542
99	300. Marcus Crodel: Wittenberg, December 26, 1542
99	301. John Luther: Wittenberg, December 27, 1542
99	302. Wenceslas Link: Wittenberg, June 20, 1543
99	303. James Propst: Wittenberg, December 5, 1544
99	304. Justus Jonas: Wittenberg, January 26, 1545
99	305. King Christian of Denmark: Wittenberg, April 14, 1545
99	306. Duke Albrecht of Prussia: Wittenberg, May 2, 1545
99	307. Elector John Frederick: Wittenberg, May 7, 1545
99	308. Nicholas von Amsdorf: Wittenberg, June 3, 1545
99	309. Nicholas von Amsdorf: Wittenberg, July 9, 1545
99	310. Justus Jonas: Wittenberg, July 16, 1545
99	311. Nicholas von Amsdorf: Wittenberg, July 17, 1545
99	312. Mrs. Martin Luther: Zeitz, July 28, 1545
99	313. Count Albrecht of Mansfeld: Wittenberg, December 6, 1545
99	314. Mrs. Martin Luther: Halle, January 25, 1546
99	315. George of Anhalt: Eisleben, January 29, 1546
99	316. Mrs. Martin Luther: Eisleben, February 1, 1546
99	317. Philip Melanchthon: Eisleben, February 1, 1546
99	318. Philip Melanchthon: Eisleben, February 3, 1546
99	319. Philip Melanchthon: Eisleben, February 6, 1546
99	320. Mrs. Martin Luther: Eisleben, February 6, 1546

Weimar Edition	American Edition	St. Louis Edition	Erlangen Edition
Br 8, 577-578	50, 204-206	17, 269-270	55, 248-249
Br 9, 167-168	50, 207-212	21, 2485-2486	55, 225-227
Br 9, 171-173	50, 212-217	21, 2487-2489	
Br 9, 174-175	50, 218-220	21, 2490	55, 287-288
Br 9, 204-205	50, 221-223	21, 2501-2502	55, 288-289
Br 9, 518-519	50, 223-225	21, 2650	55, 332-333
Br 9, 620-622	50, 225-230	21, 2716-2718	
Br 10, 132-134	50, 230-233	21, 2782-2783	
Br 10, 136-137	50, 233-234	21, 2785	
Br 10, 147	50, 234-235	21, 2788-2789	
Br 10, 149-150	50, 236-238	21, 2790-2791	
Br 10, 228-229	50, 239-240	21, 2814	
Br 10, 229	50, 240-241	21, 2815	
Br 10, 334-335	50, 241-244	21, 2879-2880	
Br 10, 554	50, 244-246	21, 3043-3044	
Br 11, 29-30	50, 247-249	21, 3067-3068	
Br 11, 69-70	50, 250-252	21, 3077-3078	56, 130-131
Br 11, 83-84	50, 252-255	21, 3084-3085	56, 133-134
Br 11, 88	50, 255-261	21, 3088-3089	56, 134-135
Br 11, 115	50, 262-264	21, 3105-3106	
Br 11, 131-132	50, 264-267	21, 3113-3114	
Br 11, 141-142	50, 268-270	21, 3119-3120	
Br 11, 143-144	50, 270-272	21, 3122-3123	
Br 11, 148-150	50, 273-281	21, 3125-3126	56, 139-140
Br 11, 225-226	50, 281-284	21, 3161-3162	56, 146-147
Br 11, 268-269	50, 284-287	21, 3186	56, 148-149
Br 11, 273	50, 288-289	21, 3188-3189	
Br 11, 275-276	50, 290-292	21, 3191-3192	56, 149-150
Br 11, 277-278	50, 292-295	21, 3190-3191	
Br 11, 279-280	50, 295-297		
Br 11, 285-286	50, 297-299	21, 3192-3194	
Br 11, 283-284	50, 299-300	21, 3194	56, 150-151

99   321. Mrs. Martin Luther: Eisleben, February 7, 1546

99   322. Mrs. Martin Luther: Eisleben, February 10, 1546

99   323. George of Anhalt: Eisleben, February 10, 1546

99   324. Mrs. Martin Luther: Eisleben, February 14, 1546

99   325. Philip Melanchthon: Eisleben, February 14, 1546

The German Bible

83   Preface to the New Testament

83   Preface to the Acts of the Apostles

83   Preface to the Epistle of St. Paul to the Romans

83   Preface to the First Epistle of St. Paul to the Corinthians

83   Preface to the Second Epistle to the Corinthians

83   Preface to the Epistle of St. Paul to the Galatians

83   Preface to the Epistle of St. Paul to the Ephesians

83   Preface to the Epistle of St. Paul to the Philippians

83   Preface to the Epistle of St. Paul to the Colossians

83   Preface to the First Epistle of St. Paul to the Thessalonians

83   Preface to the Second Epistle of St. Paul to the Thessalonians

83   Preface to the First Epistle of St. Paul to Timothy

83   Preface to the Second Epistle of St. Paul to Timothy

83   Preface to the Epistle of St. Paul to Titus

83   Preface to the Epistle of St. Paul to Philemon

83   Preface to the First Epistle of St. Peter

83   Preface to the Second Epistle of St. Peter

83   Preface to the Three Epistles of St. John

83   Preface to the Epistle to the Hebrews

83   Preface to the Epistles of St. James and St. Jude

83   Preface to the Revelation of St. John I

83   Preface to the Revelation of St. John II

83   Prefaces to the Old Testament

83   Preface to the Book of Job

83   Preface to the Psalter

83   Preface to the Books of Solomon

Weimar Edition	American Edition	St. Louis Edition	Erlangen Edition
Br 11, 286-287	50, 301-304	21, 3194-3196	56, 151-153
Br 11, 290-291	50, 305-308	21, 3198-3199	56, 153-154
Br 11, 292	50, 309-310	21, 3197-3198	
Br 11, 299-300	50, 310-313	21, 3203-3204	56, 154-155
Br 11, 301-302	50, 313-318	21, 3202-3203	
DB 6, 2-10	35, 357-362	14, 84-91	63, 108-115
DB 6, 415-417	35, 363-365	14, 92-95	63, 116-119
DB 7, 2-27	35, 365-380	14, 94-109	63, 119-138
DB 7, 82-87	35, 380-383	14, 110-113	63, 138-141
DB 7, 138-139	35, 383-384	14, 114-115	63, 142-143
DB 7, 172-173	35, 384	14, 114-115	63, 143-144
DB 7, 190-191	35, 385	14, 116-117	63, 144
DB 7, 210-211	35, 385	14, 116-117	63, 145
DB 7, 224-225	35, 386	14, 116-117	63, 145-146
DB 7, 238-239	35, 386-387	14, 118-119	63, 146-147
DB 7, 250-251	35, 387-388	14, 118-119	63, 147-148
DB 7, 258-259	35, 388	14, 120-121	63, 149
DB 7, 272-273	35, 389	14, 120-121	63, 150
DB 7, 284-285	35, 389-390	14, 122-123	63, 150
DB 7, 292-293	35, 390	14, 122-123	63, 150-151
DB 7, 298-299	35, 390-391	14, 122-125	63, 151-152
DB 7, 314-315	35, 391-392	14, 124-125	63, 152-153
DB 7, 326-327	35, 393	14, 126-127	63, 153-154
DB 7, 344-345	35, 394-395	14, 126-129	63, 154-155
DB 7, 384-387	35, 395-398	14, 128-131	63, 156-158
DB 7, 404	35, 398-399	14, 140-141	63, 169-170
DB 7, 406-421	35, 399-411	14, 130-139	63, 158-169
DB 8, 10-32	35, 233-251	14, 2-17	63, 7-25
DB 10^{I}, 5-6	35, 251-253	14, 18-19	63, 25-27
DB 10^{I}, 99-105	35, 253-257	14, 20-25	63, 27-32
DB 10^{II}, 7-10	35, 258-261	14, 26-29	63, 35-38

Weimar Edition	American Edition	St. Louis Edition	Erlangen Edition
DB 10^{II}, 2-4	35, 261-263	14, 28-31	63, 38-40
DB 10^{II}, 104-106	35, 263-264	14, 30-33	63, 40-41
DB 11^{I}, 3-15	35, 265-273	14, 32-41	63, 42-52
DB 11^{I}, 17-25	35, 273-278	6, 4-9	63, 52-59
DB 11^{I}, 191-195	35, 279-282	14, 40-43	63, 59-62
DB 11^{I}, 393	35, 282-283	14, 44-45	63, 62-64
DB 11^{I}, 395-409	35, 284-293	14, 45-53	63, 64-74
DB 11^{II}, 3-49	35, 294-313	6, 896-917	41, 237-258
DB 11^{II}, 125-131	35, 313-316	6, 940-943	41, 294-324
DB 11^{II}, 183	35, 317-318	14, 54-55	63, 74-75
DB 11^{II}, 213-215	35, 318-319	14, 54-57	63, 75-77
DB 11^{II}, 227-229	35, 320-321	14, 56-59	63, 77-78
DB 11^{II}, 251-253	35, 321-322	14, 58-59	63, 79-80
DB 11^{II}, 259-261	35, 323-324	14, 60-61	63, 80-81
DB 11^{II}, 271	35, 324-325	14, 60-63	63, 82
DB 11^{II}, 289	35, 326	14, 62-63	63, 83
DB 11^{II}, 299-301	35, 327-328	14, 1421-1423	63, 84-85
DB 11^{II}, 311	35, 328-329	14, 64-65	63, 85-86
DB 11^{II}, 321	35, 329-330	14, 64-67	63, 86-87
DB 11^{II}, 329-331	35, 330-331	14, 66-67	63, 88-89
DB 11^{II}, 363-365	35, 332-333	14, 68-69	63, 89-90
DB 12, 5-7	35, 337-339	14, 68-71	63, 91-93
DB 12, 49-55	35, 340-344	14, 72-77	63, 93-98
DB 12, 109-111	35, 345-347	14, 76-77	63, 98-100
DB 12, 145-149	35, 347-349	14, 78-81	63, 100-102
DB 12, 291	35, 349-350	14, 80-81	63, 103-104
DB 12, 315-317	35, 350-352	14, 80-83	63, 104-106
DB 12, 417-419	35, 352-353	14, 82-85	63, 106-107
DB 12, 493	35, 353-354	14, 84-85	63, 107-108
TR 1, 1-656	54, 3-114		
TR 1, 657-684	54, 115-121		

725   Table Talk Recorded by John Schlaginhaufen, 1531-1532

725   Table Talk Collected by Conrad Cordatus, 1532-1533

725   Table Talk Recorded by Anthony Lauterbach and
       Jerome Weller, 1536-1537

725   Table Talk Recorded by Anthony Lauterbach, 1538-1539

725   Table Talk Recorded by John Mathesius, 1540

725   Table Talk Recorded by Caspar Heydenreich, 1542-1543

725   Table Talk Recorded by Jerome Resold, 1544

Tischreden

725   Cap. 1. Von Gottes Wort oder der heiligen Schrift

725   Cap. 2. Von Gottes Werken

725   Cap. 3. Von der Schoepfung

725   Cap. 4. Von der Welt und ihrer Art

725   Cap. 5. Von der Abgoetterei

725   Cap. 6. Von der heiligen Dreifaltigkeit

725   Cap. 7. Von dem Herrn Christo

725   Cap. 8. Von dem Heiligen Geist

725   Cap. 9. Von der Suende, und deren Unterschied, Art und Strafe

725   Cap. 10. Von dem freien Willen

725   Cap. 11. Von dem Heiligen Catechismo

725   Cap. 12. Von dem Gesetz und Evangelio

725   Cap. 13. Dasz der Glaube an Christum allein
       vor Gott gerecht mache

725   Cap. 14. Von guten Werken

725   Cap. 15. Von dem Gebet

725   Cap. 16. Vom Bekenntnis der Lehre, und Bestaendigkeit

725   Cap. 17. Von der heiligen Taufe

725   Cap. 18. Von der Ohrenbeichte

725   Cap. 19. Von dem Sacrament des Altars, des wahren
       Leibs und Bluts Jesu Christi

725   Cap. 20. Von der christlichen Kirche

725   Cap. 21. Von der Excommunication und Bann, oder
       der Kirchen Jurisdiction

Weimar Edition	American Edition	St. Louis Edition	Erlangen Edition
TR 2, 1232-1889	54, 123-165		
TR 2, 1950-3416	54, 167-200		
TR 3, 3465-3659	54, 201-249		
TR 3, 3683-4719	54, 251-364		
TR 4, 4848 to 5, 5341	54, 365-409		
TR 5, 5379-5603	54, 411-464		
TR 5, 5659-5675	54, 465-476		
		22, 1-65	57, 1-107
		22, 64-137	57, 108-220
		22, 138-181	57, 220-280
		22, 182-239	57, 280-362
		22, 238-257	57, 362-385
		22, 256-259	57, 385-391
		22, 260-353	58, 1-152
		22, 354-355	58, 153-162
		22, 356-383	58, 162-213
		22, 382-391	58, 214-239
		22, 392-415	58, 239-268
		22, 414-445	58, 269-338
		22, 416-489	58, 338-413
		22, 488-509	58, 413-445
		22, 510-535	59, 1-34
		22, 534-539	59, 34-44
		22, 540-555	59, 44-74
		22, 554-563	59, 74-87
		22, 562-595	59, 87-130
		22, 594-609	59, 131-155
		22, 610-627	59, 155-180

Weimar Edition	American Edition	St. Louis Edition	Erlangen Edition
		22, 628-697	59, 181-285
		22, 696-701	58, 285-288
		22, 700-781	59, 289-348
			60, 1-75
		22, 780-785	60, 75-80
		22, 784-841	60, 80-176
		22, 840-935	60, 176-311
		22, 936-947	60, 312-327
		22, 946-949	60, 327-331
		22, 950-969	60, 331-356
		22, 970-983	60, 356-372
		22, 982-989	60, 372-382
		22, 990-997	60, 382-390
		22, 996-999	60, 390-395
		22, 998-1007	60, 395-404
		22, 1006-1007	60, 404-405
		22, 1008-1095	61, 1-125
		22, 1094-1099	61, 125-132
		22, 1098-1113	61, 132-149
		22, 1112-1115	61, 150-152
		22, 1114-1119	61, 152-159
		22, 1118-1121	61, 159-164
		22, 1122-1215	61, 164-304
		22, 1214-1231	61, 305-327
		22, 1230-1283	61, 327-397
		22, 1284-1289	61, 397-403
		22, 1288-1299	61, 404-417
		22, 1298-1319	61, 417-447
		22, 1318-1327	62, 1-14
		22, 1328-1331	62, 15-18

Weimar Edition	American Edition	St. Louis Edition	Erlangen Edition
		22, 1330-1339	62, 18-28
		22, 1338-1345	62, 28-35
		22, 1344-1349	62, 36-40
		22, 1348-1371	62, 41-71
		22, 1370-1381	62, 71-87
		22, 1382-1389	62, 88-97
		22, 1388-1401	62, 97-113
		22, 1400-1409	62, 113-124
		22, 1408-1417	62, 125-139
		22, 1418-1433	62, 139-159
		22, 1432-1437	62, 160-169
		22, 1438-1447	62, 169-180
		22, 1446-1453	62, 180-189
		22, 1454-1467	62, 189-209
		22, 1468-1471	62, 209-214
		22, 1472-1521	62, 214-284
		22, 1522-1537	62, 285-307
		22, 1536-1541	62, 307-311
		22, 1540-1545	62, 311-317
		22, 1544-1553	62, 317-328
		22, 1554-1557	62, 329-334
		22, 1558-1561	62, 334-339
		22, 1560-1571	62, 339-352
		22, 1570-1591	62, 352-379
		22, 1590-1611	62, 379-405
		22, 1612-1633	62, 405-435
		22, 1634-1639	62, 435-443
		22, 1640-1667	62, 443-451
		22, 1646-1647	62, 451-452
		22, 1648-1653	62, 453-460
		22, 1654-1663	62, 461-474

189

Sprueche der heiligen Schrift so in den Tischreden
nuetzlich erklaeret und ausgelegt sind

Appendix No. I Uebersetzung der Stuecke aus M. Anton
Lauterbachs Tagebuche auf das Jahr 1538, welche in
den Tischreden nicht befindlich sind

Appendix No. II. Uebersetzung der Stuecke aus den
Tagebuche ueber D. Martin Luther, gefuehrt von D. Conrad
Cordatus 1537, welche in den Tischreden sich nicht finden.

Weimar Edition	American Edition	St. Louis Edition	Erlangen Edition
		22, 1664-1667	
		22, 1668-1807	
		22, 1808-1993	

PART 4

Which works in the Erlangen edition are included in the American edition and where they may be found in the American, the St. Louis and the Weimar editions.

Erlangen Edition	American Edition	St. Louis Edition	Weimar Edition
1, 67-72 63, 401-406	34, 279-288	14, 432-437	50, 657-661
7, 1-5	52, 3-6	11, xxxiv-xxxix	10^I, 1-8
7, 5-12	35, 113-124	11, xxxviii-xlv	10^I, 8-18
8, 280-305	51, 289-299		47, 757-771
10, 126-153	52, 7-31	11, 118-143	10^I, 58-95
10, 153-163	52, 32-40	11, 144-153	10^I, 128-141
10, 163-218	52, 41-88	11, 154-205	10^I, 180-247
10, 218-232	52, 89-101	11, 204-219	10^I, 270-289
10, 247-301	52, 102-148	11, 232-283	10^I, 379-448
10, 301-312	52, 149-158	11, 284-295	10^I, 504-519
10, 313-456	52, 159-286	11, 294-429	10^I, 555-728
11, 144-152 var 3, 410-419	42, 3-14	11, 574-583	2, 136-142
15, 270-283	51, 119-132	11, 2174-2189	17^I, 38-45
15, 396-403 var 3, 217-224	51, 53-60	11, 2306-2313	2, 244-249
16, 139-150	51, 369-380	12, 1168-1177	51, 123-134
16, 158-165 var 3, 446-452	44, 3-14	10, 630-637	2, 166-171
16, 264-275	51, 381-392	12, 1254-1264	51, 187-194
17, 40-53	51, 193-208	12, 1328-1341	32, 28-39
17, 65-72	42, 167-177	12, 1354-1361	7, 692-697
17, 98-104	51, 60-66	12, 1386-1393	7, 808-813
17, 119-129	51, 301-312	12, 1408-1421	47, 772-779

Erlangen Edition	American Edition	St. Louis Edition	Weimar Edition
17, 239-262	51, 331-354	12, 1962-1984	49, 588-615
18, 196-205	51, 35-43	12, 1302-1313	1, 267-273
18, 205-211	51, 44-49	12, 1314-1321	1, 273-277
18, 359-372	51, 231-243	12, 2072-2085	36, 237-254
18, 372-384	51, 243-255	12, 2086-2099	36, 255-270
19, 72-88	51, 313-329	7, 696-711	49, 124-135
19, 296-328	51, 257-287	9, 882-913	36, 352-375
20, 1-45	46, 207-258	10, 416-459	30^{II}, 517-588
20, 45-56	51, 355-367	10, 588-599	49, 797-805
20, 57-87	45, 11-49	10, 598-628	10^{II}, 275-304
20, 87-89 53, 156-157	45, 3-9	10, 628-629	10^{II}, 265-266
20, 89-122 22, 199-226	45, 231-310	10, 914-937 10, 824-855	15, 293-313 15, 321-322 6, 36-60
20, 179-193	35, 3-22	10, 1232-1245	2, 714-723
20, 193-290	44, 15-114	10, 1298-1389	6, 202-276
20, 290-294 var 3, 442-446	42, 83-93	14, 1414-1421	2, 175-179

Erlangen Edition	American Edition	St. Louis Edition	Weimar Edition
20, 301-308	44, 231-242	10, 1692-1701	7, 795-802
21, 17-19	53, 119-121	10, 14-17	30^{I}, 383-387
21, 156-227 45, 203-207	42, 15-81	7, 752-821	2, 80-130
21, 253-274 var 3, 453-473	42, 95-115	10, 1984-2001	2, 685-697
21, 274-360	44, 115-217	10, 266-351	6, 404-469
22, 3-32 65, 266-268	43, 3-45	3, 1352-1361	10^{II}, 375-428
22, 32-38	43, 47-55	10, 2002-2007	10^{II}, 322-326
22, 43-59	45, 51-74	10, 360-373	8, 676-687
22, 59-105	45, 75-129	10, 374-417	11, 245-280
22, 105-112	45, 159-176	10, 954-961	12, 11-15
22, 112-130 53, 196-197	45, 176-194	10, 960-977	12, 18-30
22, 140-151	39, 301-314	10, 1538-1549	11, 408-416
22, 151-156	53, 7-14	10, 220-225	12, 35-37
22, 157-166	53, 95-103	10, 2136-2143	12, 42-48
22, 158-159	53, 142	10, 2140	12, 43
22, 161	53, 144	10, 2142	12, 44
22, 168-199	45, 339-378	10, 458-485	15, 27-53
22, 199-226 20, 89-122	45, 231-310	10, 914-937 10, 824-855	15, 293-313 15, 321-322 6, 36-60

Erlangen Edition	American Edition	St. Louis Edition	Weimar Edition
22, 226-244	53, 51-90	10, 226-257	19, 72-113
22, 244-290 53, 391-392	46, 87-137	10, 488-531	19, 623-662
22, 290-294	53, 106-109	10, 2144-2147	19, 537-541
22, 291	53, 142-143	10, 2144	19, 539
22, 291-292	53, 143-144	10, 2144-2145	12, 43-44
22, 294-316 53, 408	43, 139-165	10, 1960-1961	23, 402-431
22, 317-341 53, 408	43, 113-138	10, 2008-2029	23, 339-379
23, 1-70	40, 263-320	10, 1628-1687	26, 195-240
23, 91-154	46, 259-320	10, 754-809	30^{III}, 205-248
23, 154-162	43, 167-177	10, 1712-1719	30^{II}, 700-710
23, 162-207	38, 91-137	10, 2170-2209	30^{II}, 595-626
23, 207-213	53, 110-115	10, 720-725	30^{III}, 74-80
23, 213	53, 144-145	10, 725	30^{III}, 80
23, 214-238	43, 187-211	10, 1394-1415	38, 358-375
23, 251-281	34, 197-229	10, 992-1019	50, 262-283
23, 338-343	43, 243-250	10, 730-735	53, 205-208
24, 52-150	32, 3-99	15, 1476-1565	7, 309-457
24, 150-164	31, 379-395	15, 1619-1631	7, 161-182
24, 202-209	44, 219-229	19, 808-815	7, 290-298
24, 257-286	46, 3-43	16, 45-71	8, 291-334
24, 287-294	46, 45-55	16, 71-77	18, 357-361
24, 294-319	46, 57-85	16, 77-99	18, 384-401
24, 329-379	34, 3-61	16, 946-992	30^{II}, 268-356
25, 1-50	47, 3-55	16, 1624-1665	30^{III}, 276-320
25, 51-88	34, 63-104	16, 1666-1700	30^{III}, 331-388

Erlangen Edition	American Edition	St. Louis Edition	Weimar Edition
25, 146-175	34, 231-267	16, 1971-1994	50, 288-308
25, 219-388	41, 3-178	16, 2144-2303	50, 509-653
26, 1-75	41, 179-256	17, 1313-1381	51, 469-572
26, 108-228	41, 257-376	17, 1019-1132	54, 206-299
26, 229-254 39, 221-223	43, 251-288	17, 1396-1419	54, 389-411
26, 254-294	40, 225-262	17, 2187-2225	26, 144-174
26, 313-337	32, 261-286	21, 687-709	18, 224-240
27, 25-50	35, 45-73	19, 426-449	2, 742-758
27, 50-70	39, 3-22	19, 884-901	6, 63-75
27, 85-139	39, 49-104	18, 1002-1053	6, 285-324
27, 139-173	35, 75-111	19, 1036-1067	6, 353-378
27, 173-199	31, 327-377	19, 986-1011	7, 1-38 7, 42-73
27, 200-205	39, 105-115	18, 1250-1255	7, 262-265
27, 205-220	39, 117-135	18, 1256-1271	7, 271-283
27, 221-308	39, 137-224	18, 1270-1353	7, 621-688
27, 308-318	39, 225-238	18, 1352-1363	8, 247-254
28, 27-141	36, 127-230	19, 1068-1177	8, 482-563
28, 141-201	39, 239-299	19, 668-727	10^{II}, 105-158
28, 205-215	51, 70-75	20, 8-17	10^{III}, 1-13
28, 216-221	51, 75-78	20, 17-22	10^{III}, 13-20
28, 221-228	51, 79-83	20, 22-28	10^{III}, 21-30
28, 228-235	51, 84-88	20, 28-34	10^{III}, 30-40

Erlangen Edition	American Edition	St. Louis Edition	Weimar Edition
28, 235-239	51, 88-91	20, 34-38	10^{III}, 40-47
28, 239-244	51, 92-95	20, 39-43	10^{III}, 48-54
28, 244-247	51, 95-96	20, 43-45	10^{III}, 55-58
28, 247-251	51, 97-100	20, 46-51	10^{III}, 58-64
28, 285-318	36, 231-267	20, 62-93	10^{II}, 11-41
28, 318-343	35, 125-153	19, 598-621	10^{II}, 72-92
28, 388-421	36, 269-305	19, 1308-1337	11, 431-456
29, 16-33 53, 162	45, 131-158	19, 1730-1745	12, 232-244
29, 45-74	45, 195-229	20, 1792-1821	11, 314-336
29, 102-113	43, 81-96	19, 1674-1685	15, 86-94
29, 113-133	36, 307-328	19, 1198-1215	18, 22-36
29, 134-297	40, 73-223	20, 132-287	18, 62-125 18, 134-214
29, 318-327	46, 139-154	19, 1689-1693	19, 287-293
29, 328-359	36, 329-361	20, 734-763	19, 482-523
30, 14-150	37, 3-150	20, 762-893	23, 64-283
30, 151-373	37-151-372	20, 894-1105	26, 261-509
31, 31-80	46, 155-205	20, 2108-2155	30^{II}, 107-148
31, 126-184	40, 321-377	19, 902-957	30^{II}, 465-507 30^{III}, 584-588
31, 213-226	40, 379-394	20, 1664-1677	30^{III}, 518-527
31, 307-377	38, 139-214	19, 1220-1285	38, 195-256
31, 377-391	38, 215-233	19, 1286-1299	38, 262-272
31, 416-449	47, 57-98	20, 1828-1861	50, 312-337
32, 1-14	47, 99-119	20, 1610-1623	50, 468-477
32, 74-99	43, 213-241	20, 2194-2217	51, 585-625
32, 99-274	47, 121-306	20, 1860-2029	53, 417-552

Erlangen Edition	American Edition	St. Louis Edition	Weimar Edition
32, 396-425	38, 279-319	20, 1764-1791	54, 141-167
32, 425-430	34, 361-366	21, 3374-3377	54, 192-194
33, 3-21	35, 155-174	3, 2-17	16, 363-393"U"
37, 1-104	15, 265-352	3, 1880-1973	54, 28-100
37, 250-266	35, 203-223	4, 124-137	38, 9-17
		4, 198-199	38, 69
37, 340-442	14, 137-205	4, 1654-1743	18, 479-530
38, 369-453	14, 207-277	5, 1-75	19, 552-615
39, 4-61	12, 1-136	5, 74-237	40^{II}, 193-312
			45, 205-250
39, 61-105	12, 145-194	5, 254-307	51, 267-295
39, 106-122			17^{I}, 228-243
39, 178-220	13, 1-37	5, 656-695	8, 4-35
39, 221-223	43, 251-288	17, 1396-1419	54, 389-411
26, 229-254			
39, 224-265	13, 39-72	5, 696-731	31^{I}, 189-218
39, 265-364	13, 143-224	5, 800-887	51, 200-264
40, 38-192	13, 225-348	5, 922-1055	41, 79-239
40, 192-240	13, 349-387	5, 1056-1097	31^{I}, 393-426
40, 240-280	13, 389-420	5, 1098-1131	19, 297-336
40, 280-328	14, 1-39	5, 1132-1173	31^{I}, 223-257
41, 7-91	14, 41-106	5, 1174-1251	31^{I}, 65-182
41, 115-128	43, 97-112	5, 1272-1283	15, 69-78
53, 233			
41, 128-250	45, 311-337	5, 1284-1303	15, 360-378
53, 281			
41, 151-185	14, 107-135	5, 1302-1333	31^{I}, 430-456
41, 237-258	35, 294-313	6, 896-917	DB 11^{II}, 3-49
41, 294-324	35, 313-316	6, 940-943	DB 11^{II}, 125-131
41, 324-414	19, 33-104	14, 836-911	19, 185-251
42, 1-108	19, 149-237	14, 1416-1507	19, 349-435
42, 108-362	20, 153-347	14, 1768-1975	23, 485-664
43, 1-368	21, 1-294	7, 346-677	32, 299-544

Erlangen Edition	American Edition	St. Louis Edition	Weimar Edition
45, 203-207 21, 156-227	42, 15-81	7, 752-821	2, 80-130
45, 211-290 45, 215	21, 295-358 53, 176-179	7, 1372-1445 7, 1376	7, 538-604 7, 546
45, 294-422 46, 1-378 47, 1-226	22, 1-530	7, 1538-2147	46, 538-789 47, 1-231
47, 226-394	23, 1-197	7, 2192-2417	33, 1-314
48, 1-409	23, 198-422	8, 1-255	33, 314-675
49, 1-392 50, 1-154	24, 1-422	8, 264-745	45, 465-733 46, 1-111
51, 1-69	28, 1-56	8, 1026-1085	12, 92-142
NFex 51, 70-275	28, 57-213	8, 1088-1273	36, 481-696
51, 324-494	30, 1-145	9, 958-1111	12, 259-399
52, 212-272	30, 147-199	9, 1342-1397	14, 14-74
52, 272-287	30, 201-215	9, 1742-1755	14, 75-91
53, 1-2	48, 49-52	21, 77-79	Br 1, 119-120
53, 5-7	48, 96-100	15, 696-698	Br 1, 289-291
53, 9-10	48, 120-121	21, 165	Br 1, 386-387
53, 28-29	48, 127-129	15, 757-758	Br 1, 535-536
53, 29-30	48, 139-141	21, 216-217	Br 1, 598-599
var 4, 84-135 53, 31-34	42, 117-166	10, 1820-1917	6, 104-134
53, 52-53	48, 181-183	21, 303-304	Br 2, 204-206
53, 53-54	48, 184-185	21, 308-309	Br 2, 217-218
53, 56-58	48, 194-197	15, 1887-1890	Br 2, 253-255
53, 64-65	48, 200-203	15, 1935-1937	Br 2, 305
53, 65-71	48, 203-209	15, 1893-1899	Br 2, 307-310
53, 74-77	48, 244-247	19, 814-817	8, 138-140
53, 86-92	48, 329-336	19, 1500-1507	8, 573-576
53, 86-92 var 6, 234-376	44, 243-400	19, 1507-1665	8, 577-669
53, 95-99	48, 339-350	19, 548-553	Br 2, 405-408

Erlangen Edition	American Edition	St. Louis Edition	Weimar Edition
53, 103-104	48, 386-388	15, 1984-1985	Br 2, 448-449
53, 104-109	48, 388-393	15, 1989-1993	Br 2, 453-457
53, 109-112	48, 393-399	15, 1998-2001	Br 2, 459-462
53, 119-129	43, 57-70	15, 1662-1672	10^{II}, 53-60
53, 137	49, 8-9	21, 421	Br 2, 556
53, 156-157 20, 87-89	45, 3-9	10, 628-629	10^{II}, 265-266
53, 159-161	49, 25-28	21, 471-472	Br 3, 13-14
53, 162 29, 16-33	45, 131-158	19, 1730-1745	12, 232-244
53, 163-167	49, 35-42	15, 2187-2191	Br 3, 75-77
53, 194-195	49, 45-47	21, 534-535	Br 3, 124-125
53, 196-197 22, 112-130	45, 176-194	10, 960-977	12, 18-30
53, 197-201	43, 71-79	10, 1758-1761	Br 3, 138-140
53, 219-220	49, 50-55	10, 912-913	Br 3, 176-177
53, 230 22, 32-38	43, 47-55	10, 2002-2007	10^{II}, 322-326
53, 233 41, 115-128	43, 97-112	5, 1272-1283	15, 69-78
53, 235-236	49, 74-76	21, 601-602	Br 3, 258-259
53, 236-244	45, 379-393	10, 712-721	15, 163-169
53, 255-268	40, 45-49	16, 4-17	15, 210-221
53, 268-269	49, 83-85	21, 647-648	Br 3, 342-343
53, 270-277	40, 61-71 49, 94-96	15, 2047-2053	15, 391-397
53, 281 41, 128-150	45, 311-337	5, 1284-1303	15, 360-378

Erlangen Edition	American Edition	St. Louis Edition	Weimar Edition
53, 283-284	49, 96-99	21, 715-716	Br 3, 432-433
53, 285	53, 104-105	10, 2256-2257	Br 3, 462-463
53, 291-294	49, 106-112	16, 126-129	Br 3, 480-482
53, 315-321	53, 41-50	10, 258-263	18, 417-421
53, 329-332	49, 130-137	21, 798-801	Br 3, 594-596
53, 336-338	49, 137-139	21, 812-813	Br 3, 628-629
53, 380-381	49, 151-153	21, 868-869	Br 4, 87
53, 391-392 22, 244-290	46, 87-137	10, 488-531	19, 623-662
53, 399-400	49, 161-164	21, 929-930	Br 4, 180-181
53, 408 22, 317-341	43, 113-138	10, 2008-2029	23, 339-379
54, 5-6	49, 195-196	21, 1153	Br 4, 465
54, 30-34	49, 204-210	10, 2256-2261	Br 4, 533-536
54, 34-35	49, 210-211	21, 1197-1198	Br 4, 545-546
54, 69	49, 218-219	21, 1294-1295	Br 5, 61
54, 72-74	49, 221-228	21, 1303-1306	Br 5, 75-77
54, 83-85	49, 228-231	17, 1935-1937	Br 5, 101-102
54, 107-108	49, 234-239	21, 1366-1367	Br 5, 154
54, 110-112	49, 244-250	10, 552-555	Br 5, 181-183
54, 116-117 64, 294-296	42, 179-186	10, 1732-1736	7, 784-791
54, 130-133	49, 267-271	10, 1794-1799	Br 5, 239-241
54, 138-142	49, 272-280	10, 544-549	Br 5, 258-261
54, 145-146	49, 295-299	16, 657-658	Br 5, 319-320
54, 146-150	49, 305-311	16, 690-694	Br 5, 324-327
54, 151-154	49, 299-304	17, 1960-1963	Br 5, 328-332
54, 156-157	49, 321-324	21, 1491-1492	Br 5, 377-378
54, 168-169	49, 356-359	21, 1513-1514	Br 5, 444-445
54, 169-172	49, 359-365	16, 814	Br 5, 453-455 Br 12, 117-119
54, 183-186	49, 394-399	16, 1764-1767	Br 5, 530-532
54, 186	49, 399-400	16, 1084	Br 5, 544-545

99   Letter to Mrs. Martin Luther: Coburg, August 15, 1530

99   Letter to Elector John: Coburg, August 26, 1530

99   Letter to Mrs. Martin Luther: Coburg, September 24, 1530

99   Letter to Lazarus Spengler: Wittenberg, February 15, 1531

99   Letter to Mrs. Margaret Luther: Wittenberg, May 20, 1531

99   Letter to Elector John: Wittenberg, about February 12, 1532

99   Letter to Mrs. Martin Luther: Torgau, February 27, 1532

99   Letter to Thomas Zink: Wittenberg, April 22, 1532

99   Letter to Elector John: Wittenberg, June 29, 1532

99   Letter to the Regents and Councilors of the
       Margraviate of Brandenburg-Ansbach and to
       the Council of the City of Nuernberg:
       Wittenberg, August 1, 1532

99   Letter to Duke Joachim of Brandenburg: Wittenberg,
       August 3, 1532

99   Letter to John Loeser: Wittenberg, January 29, 1533

99   Letter to the Council of the City of Nuernberg:
       Wittenberg, April 18, 1533

99   Letter to Mrs. Martin Luther: Dessau, July 29, 1534

99   Letter to Elector John Frederick: Wittenberg, August 20, 1535

99   Letter to Elector John Frederick: Wittenberg, September 12, 153-

99   Letter to Elector John Frederick: Wittenberg, January 11, 1536

99   Letter to Caspar Mueller: Wittenberg, January 19, 1536

99   Letter to Elector John Frederick: Wittenberg, March 28, 1536

99   Letter to Francis Burchart: Wittenberg, April 20, 1536

99   Letter to Mrs. Martin Luther: Tambach, February 27, 1537

99   Letter to Elector John Frederick: Wittenberg, July 8, 1539

99   Letter to Elector John Frederick: Wittenberg, October 23, 1539

99   Letter to Elector John Frederick: Wittenberg, October 23, 1539

99   Letter to Mrs. Martin Luther: Weimar, July 2, 1540

99   Letter to Mrs. Martin Luther: Eisenach, July 16, 1540

99   Letter to Mrs. Martin Luther: Eisenach, July 26, 1540

99   Letter to Mrs. Martin Luther: Wittenberg, September 18, 1541

99   Letter to Elector John: Wittenberg, September 6, 1525

Erlangen Edition	American Edition	St. Louis Edition	Weimar Edition
54, 187-188	49, 400-403	21, 1541-1542	Br 5, 545-546
54, 188-192	49, 403-412	16, 1414-1417	Br 5, 572-574
54, 194	49, 424-425	21, 1571-1572	Br 5, 633-634
54, 213-214	50, 9-12	10, 570-572	Br 6, 35-37
54, 232-236	50, 17-21	10, 1798-1803	Br 6, 103-106
54, 269-271	50, 41-47	16, 1810-1812	Br 6, 259-26
54, 275-276	50, 47-50	21, 1731-1732	Br 6, 270-271
54, 293-295	50, 50-53	10, 2046-2047	Br 6, 300-302
54, 312-314	50, 56-60	16, 1812-1814	Br 6, 324-327
54, 316-320	50, 61-67	21, 1761-1765	Br 6, 338-342
54, 320-322	50, 68-71	21, 1765-1767	Br 6, 343-345
55, 4-5	50, 73-74	21, 1802-1803	Br 6, 425-426
55, 8-10	50, 75-78	21, 1811-1813	Br 6, 453-455
54, 61	50, 79-81	21, 1920	Br 7, 91
54, 104	50, 81-85	16, 1888-1889	Br 7, 237-238
55, 105-107	50, 100-102	17, 283-284	Br 7, 266-267
55, 117-118	50, 117-122	21, 2031-2033	Br 7, 341-343
55, 119-121	50, 124-130	21, 2037-2039	Br 7, 348-350
55, 128-130	50, 132-135	21, 2051-2052	Br 7, 381-384
55, 133-134	50, 138-141	17, 282-283	Br 7, 400-404
55, 174-175	50, 165-169	21, 2156-2157	Br 8, 50-51
55, 234-235	50, 185-187	21, 2352-2353	Br 8, 488-491
55, 243-247	50, 192-194	17, 265-269	Br 8, 572-575
55, 248-249	50, 204-206	17, 269-270	Br 8, 577-578
55, 225-227	50, 207-212	21, 2485-2486	Br 9, 167-168
55, 287-288	50, 218-220	21, 2490	Br 9, 174-175
55, 288-289	50, 221-223	21, 2501-2502	Br 9, 204-205
55, 332-333	50, 223-225	21, 2650	Br 9, 518-519
56, viii-x	49, 125-130	21, 775-776	Br 3, 569-570

717   Luther's Will, 1542

99   Letter to King Christian of Denmark: Wittenberg, April 14, 1545

99   Letter to Duke Albrecht of Prussia: Wittenberg, May 2, 1545

99   Letter to Elector John Frederick: Wittenberg, May 7, 1545

99   Letter to Mrs. Martin Luther: Zeitz, July 28, 1545

99   Letter to Count Albrecht of Mansfeld: Wittenberg,
      December 6, 1545

99   Letter to Mrs. Martin Luther: Halle, January 25, 1546

99   Letter to Mrs. Martin Luther: Eisleben, February 1, 1546

99   Letter to Mrs. Martin Luther: Eisleben, February 6, 1546

99   Letter to Mrs. Martin Luther: Eisleben, February 7, 1546

99   Letter to Mrs. Martin Luther: Eisleben, February 7, 1546

99   Letter to Mrs. Martin Luther: Eisleben, February 14, 1546

99   Letter to Mrs. Martin Luther: Coburg, September 8, 1530

246   A Preface for All Good Hymnals, 1538

246   Preface to the Wittenberg Hymnal, 1524

246   Preface to the Weiss Hymnal, 1528

246   Preface to the Burial Hymns, 1542

246   Preface to the Babst Hymnal, 1545

415, 232   Dear Christians, Let Us Now Rejoice, 1523

415, 232   Ah, God, from Heaven Look Down, 1523

415, 232   Although the Fools Say with Their Mouth, 1523

415, 232   From Trouble Deep I Cry to Thee, 1523

415, 232   Jesus Christ, Our God and Savior, 1524

415, 232   Let God Be Blest, 1524

415, 232   O Thou Dear Lord God

415, 232   We Give Thanks to Thee, Almighty God

Erlangen Edition	American Edition	St. Louis Edition	Weimar Edition
56, 2-5	34, 289-297	21, 2695-2698	9, 572-574
56, 130-131	50, 250-252	21, 3077-3078	Br 11, 69-70
56, 133-134	50, 252-255	21, 3084-3085	Br 11, 83-84
56, 134-135	50, 255-261	21, 3088-3089	Br 11, 88
56, 139-140	50, 273-281	21, 3125-3126	Br 11, 148-150
56, 146-147	50, 281-284	21, 3161-3162	Br 11, 225-226
56, 148-149	50, 284-287	21, 3186	Br 11, 268-269
56, 149-150	50, 290-292	21, 3191-3192	Br 11, 275-276
56, 150-151	50, 299-300	21, 3194	Br 11, 283-284
56, 151-153	50, 301-304	21, 3194-3196	Br 11, 286-287
56, 153-154	50, 305-308	21, 3198-3199	Br 11, 290-291
56, 154-155	50, 310-313	21, 3203-3204	Br 11, 299-300
56, 181-183	49, 415-419	21, 1564-1565	Br 5, 608-609
56, 295-296	53, 319-320	10, 1432-1434	35, 483-484
56, 296-297	53, 315-316	10, 1422-1425	35, 474-475
56, 298-299	53, 317-318	10, 1424-1425	35, 475-476
56, 299-306	53, 325-331	10, 1424-1431	35, 478-483
56, 306-308	53, 332-334	10, 1430-1433	35, 476-477
56, 309-310	53, 217-220	10, 1436-1438	35, 422-425 35, 493-495
56, 311-312	53, 225-228	10, 1438-1439	35, 415-417 35, 488-490
56, 312-313	53, 229-231	10, 1439-1440	35, 441-443 35, 505
56, 313-315	53, 221-224	10, 1440-1441	35, 419-420 35, 492-493
56, 315-317	53, 249-251	10, 1443-1444	35, 435-437 35, 500-501
56, 317-318	53, 252-254	10, 1444-1445	35, 452-453 35, 514-515
56, 318	53, 137	10, 1445	35, 556
56, 318	53, 137-138	10, 1445	19, 102

415, 232   Would That the Lord Would Grant Us Grace, 1523

415, 232   Jesus Christ, Our Savior True, 1524

415, 232   Almighty God, Who by the Death of Thy Son
415, 232   Almighty Lord God, Grant to Us Who Believe
415, 232   Death Held Our Lord in Prison, 1524

415, 232   These Are the Holy Ten Commands, 1524

415, 232   Man, Wouldst Thou Live All Blissfully, 1524

415, 232   Come, the Heathen's Healing Light, 1523

415, 232   Dear Lord God, Awaken Us
415, 232   Jesus We Now Must Laud and Sing, 1523?

415, 232   All Praise to Thee, O Jesus Christ, 1523?

415, 232   Come, God Creator Holy Ghost, 1524

415, 232   Come, Holy Spirit Lord and God, 1524

415, 232   In Peace and Joy I Now Depart, 1524

415, 232   Almighty Eternal God, We Heartily Pray Thee
415, 232   Merciful Everlasting God, Who Didst Not Spare
        Thine Own Son
415, 232   Almighty Father, Eternal God, Who Didst Allow
415, 232   In One True God We All Believe, 1524

415, 232   God the Father with Us Be, 1524

415, 232   Almighty Eternal God, Who Hast Taught Us
415, 232   Happy Who in God's Fear Doth Stay, 1524

Erlangen Edition	American Edition	St. Louis Edition	Weimar Edition
56, 318-319	53, 232-234	10, 1441-1442	35, 418-419 35, 490-492
56, 319-320	53, 258-259	10, 1446-1447	35, 445 35, 507-508
56, 320	53, 134	10, 1447	35, 553-554
56, 320	53, 134-135	10, 1447	35, 554
56, 321-322	53, 255-257	10, 1447-1448	35, 443-445 35, 506-507
56, 322-324	53, 277-279	10, 1452-1453	35, 426-428 35, 495-497
56, 324-325	53, 280-281	10, 1457	35, 428-429 35, 497
56, 325-326	53, 235-236	10, 1449	35, 430-431 35, 497-498
56, 326	53, 131	10, 1449	35, 552
56, 327-328	53, 237-239	10, 1450-1451	35, 431-433 35, 498-499
56, 328-329	53, 240-241	10, 1442-1443	35, 434-435 35, 499
56, 329-330	53, 260-262	10, 1452	35, 446-447 35, 508-509
56, 330-331	53, 265-267	10, 1451	35, 448-449 35, 510-512
56, 331-332	53, 247-248	10, 1455	35, 438-439 35, 503-504
56, 332	53, 132	10, 1456	35, 553
56, 332	53, 132-133	10, 1456	35, 553
56, 332	53, 133	10, 1456	35, 553
56, 333	53, 271-273	10, 1454	35, 451-452 35, 513-514
56, 334-335	53, 268-270	10, 1454-1455	35, 450 35, 512-513
56, 335	53, 136	10, 1455	35, 554
56, 335-336	53, 242-244	10, 1442	35, 437-438 35, 501-502

415, 232   Were God Not with Us at This Time, 1524

415, 232   Now Let Us Pray to the Holy Ghost, 1524

415, 232   Lord God, Dear Father Who Through Thy Holy
            Spirit

415, 232   In the Midst of Life We Are, 1524

415, 232   A New Song Here Shall Be Begun, 1523

415, 232   Isaiah 'Twas the Prophet, 1526

415, 232   Our God He Is a Castle Strong, 1527/1528

415, 232   Lord God, Heavenly Father, Who Createst Holy Desire

415, 232   Grant Peace in Mercy, Lord, We Pray, 1528/1529

415, 232   The Te Deum, 1529?

415, 232   Lord God, Thy Praise We Sing, 1531

415, 232   Almighty God, Who Art the Protector

415, 232   Lord God, Heavenly Father, from Whom
            Without Ceasing We Receive

415, 232   From Heaven on High I Come to You, 1534-1535

415, 232   To Me She's Dear, the Worthy Maid, 1535-1545

415, 232   Our Father in the Heaven Who Art, 1539

415, 232   Lord God Almighty, Who Dost Not Disdain

415, 232   Lord God, Heavenly Father, Thou Knowest

415, 232   Herod, Why Dreadest Thou a Foe, 1541

415, 232   Lord, Keep Us Steadfast in Thy Word, 1541/1542

Erlangen Edition	American Edition	St. Louis Edition	Weimar Edition
56, 336-337	53, 245-246	10, 1457-1458	35, 440-441 35, 504-505
56, 337-338	53, 263-264	10, 1458	35, 447-448 35, 510
56, 338	53, 135	10, 1459	35, 554
56, 338-339	53, 274-276	10, 1445-1446	35, 453-454 35, 515-516
56, 340-343	53, 211-216	10, 1434-1436	35, 411-415 35, 487-488
56, 343	53, 282, 82-83	10, 1459-1462	35, 455 35, 516-518
56, 343-344	53, 283-385	10, 1460-1462	35, 455-457 35, 518-520
56, 345	53, 138	10, 1462	35, 233
56, 345	53, 286-287	10, 1462	35, 458 35, 521
56, 345-347	53, 171-175	10, 1458-1461	35, 458-459 35, 521-524
56, 345-347	53, 288, 171-175	10, 1458-1461	35, 458 35, 521-524
56, 347	53, 136-137	10, 1461	19, 86
56, 347	53, 138-139	10, 1460	35, 249
56, 348-349	53, 289-291	10, 1462-1464	35, 459-461 35, 524-525
56, 350-351	53, 292-294	10, 1464	35, 462-463 35, 525-527
56, 351-353	53, 295-298	10, 1465-1466	35, 463-467 35, 527-528
56, 352-353	53, 139-140	10, 1479	35, 555
56, 353	53, 140, 169	10, 1480-1481	30^{III}, 36
56, 353-354	53, 302-303	10, 1467	35, 470-471 35, 528
56, 354	53, 304-305	10, 1469	35, 467-468 35, 528

Erlangen Edition	American Edition	St. Louis Edition	Weimar Edition
56, 355-356	53, 299-301	10, 1467-1468	35, 468-470
			35, 490-491
			35, 528
56, 357-358	53, 131-132	10, 1470	35, 264
56, 357-358	53, 306-307	10, 1469	35, 471-473
			35, 528
56, 358	53, 308-309	10, 1470	35, 473
			35, 529
56, 360-366	53, 153-170	10, 1474-1481	30^{III}, 29-42
56, 362	53, 140, 169	10, 1480-1481	30^{III}, 35
56, 362	53, 141, 170	10, 1478-1479	30^{III}, 36
56, 368	53, 184-188		35, 287-296
	53, 292-294		
	54, 3-114		TR 1, 1-656
	54, 115-121		TR 1, 657-684
	54, 123-165		TR 2, 1232-1889
	54, 167-200		TR 2, 1950-3416
	54, 201-249		TR 3, 3465-3659
	54, 251-364		TR 3, 3683-4719
	54, 365-409		TR 4, 4858 to 5, 5341
	54, 411-464		TR 5, 5379-5603
	54, 465-476		TR 5, 5659-5675
57, 1-107	22, 1-65		
57, 108-220	22, 64-137		
57, 220-280	22, 138-181		
57, 280-362	22, 182-239		
57, 362-385	22, 238-257		
57, 385-391	22, 256-259		
58, 1-152	22, 260-353		
58, 153-162	22, 354-355		

Erlangen Edition	American Edition	St. Louis Edition	Weimar Edition
58, 162-213		22, 356-383	
58, 214-239		22, 382-391	
58, 239-268		22, 392-415	
58, 269-338		22, 414-445	
58, 338-413		22, 416-489	
58, 413-445		22, 488-509	
59, 1-34		22, 510-535	
59, 34-44		22, 534-539	
59, 44-74		22, 540-555	
59, 74-87		22, 554-563	
59, 87-130		22, 562-595	
59, 131-155		22, 594-609	
59, 155-180		22, 610-627	
59, 181-285		22, 628-697	
58, 285-288		22, 696-701	
59, 289-348		22, 700-781	
60, 1-75			
60, 75-80		22, 780-785	
60, 80-176		22, 784-841	
60, 176-311		22, 840-935	
60, 312-327		22, 936-947	
60, 327-331		22, 946-949	
60, 331-356		22, 950-969	
60, 356-372		22, 970-983	
60, 372-382		22, 982-989	
60, 382-390		22, 990-997	
60, 390-395		22, 996-999	

Erlangen Edition	American Edition	St. Louis Edition	Weimar Edition
60, 395-404		22, 998-1007	
60, 404-405		22, 1006-1007	
61, 1-125		22, 1008-1095	
61, 125-132		22, 1094-1099	
61, 132-149		22, 1098-1113	
61, 150-152		22, 1112-1115	
61, 152-159		22, 1114-1119	
61, 159-164		22, 1118-1121	
61, 164-304		22, 1122-1215	
61, 305-327		22, 1214-1231	
61, 327-397		22, 1230-1283	
61, 397-403		22, 1284-1289	
61, 404-417		22, 1288-1299	
61, 417-447		22, 1298-1319	
62, 1-14		22, 1318-1327	
62, 15-18		22, 1328-1331	
62, 18-28		22, 1330-1339	
62, 28-35		22, 1338-1345	
62, 36-40		22, 1344-1349	
62, 41-71		22, 1348-1371	
62, 71-87		22, 1370-1381	
62, 88-97		22, 1382-1389	
62, 97-113		22, 1388-1401	
62, 113-124		22, 1400-1409	
62, 125-139		22, 1408-1417	
62, 139-159		22, 1418-1433	
62, 160-169		22, 1432-1437	
62, 169-180		22, 1438-1447	
62, 180-189		22, 1446-1453	
62, 189-209		22, 1454-1467	

Erlangen Edition	American Edition	St. Louis Edition	Weimar Edition
62, 209-214		22, 1468-1471	
62, 214-284		22, 1472-1521	
62, 285-307		22, 1522-1537	
62, 307-311		22, 1536-1541	
62, 311-317		22, 1540-1543	
62, 317-328		22, 1544-1553	
62, 329-334		22, 1554-1557	
62, 334-339		22, 1558-1561	
62, 339-352		22, 1560-1571	
62, 352-379		22, 1570-1591	
62, 379-405		22, 1590-1611	
62, 405-435		22, 1612-1633	
62, 435-443		22, 1634-1639	
62, 443-451		22, 1640-1667	
62, 451-452		22, 1646-1647	
62, 453-460		22, 1648-1653	
62, 461-474		22, 1654-1663	
63, 7-25	35, 233-251	14, 2-17	DB 8, 10-32
63, 25-27	35, 251-253	14, 18-19	DB 10^{I}, 5-6
63, 27-32	35, 253-257	14, 20-25	DB 10^{I}, 99-105
63, 35-38	35, 258-261	14, 26-29	DB 10^{II}, 7-10
63, 38-40	35, 261-263	14, 28-31	DB 10^{II}, 2-4
63, 40-41	35, 263-264	14, 30-33	DB 10^{II}, 104-106
63, 42-52	35, 265-273	14, 32-41	DB 11^{I}, 3-15
63, 52-59	35, 273-278	6, 4-9	DB 11^{I}, 17-25
63, 59-62	35, 279-282	14, 40-43	DB 11^{I}, 191-195
63, 62-64	35, 282-283	14, 44-45	DB 11^{I}, 393
63, 64-74	35, 284-293	14, 45-53	DB 11^{I}, 395-409
63, 74-75	35, 317-318	14, 54-55	DB 11^{II}, 183
63, 75-77	35, 318-319	14, 54-57	DB 11^{II}, 213-215
63, 77-78	35, 320-321	14, 56-59	DB 11^{II}, 227-229
63, 79-80	35, 321-322	14, 58-59	DB 11^{II}, 251-253

83   Preface to the Prophet Jonah

83   Preface to the Prophet Micah

83   Preface to the Prophet Nahum

83   Preface to the Prophet Habakkuk

83   Preface to the Prophet Zephaniah

83   Preface to the Prophet Haggai

83   Preface to the Prophet Zechariah

83   Preface to the Prophet Malachi

83   Preface to the Book of Judith

83   Preface to the Wisdom of Solomon

83   Preface to the Book of Tobit

83   Preface to the Book of Jesus Sirach

83   Preface to the Book of Baruch

83   Preface to the First Book of Maccabees

83   Preface to the Second Book of Maccabees

83   Preface to Parts of Esther and Daniel

83   Preface to the New Testament

83   Preface to the Acts of the Apostles

83   Preface to the Epistle of St. Paul to the Romans

83   Preface to the First Epistle of St. Paul to the Corinthians

83   Preface to the Second Epistle to the Corinthians

83   Preface to the Epistle of St. Paul to the Galatians

83   Preface to the Epistle of St. Paul to the Ephesians

83   Preface to the Epistle of St. Paul to the Philippians

83   Preface to the Epistle of St. Paul to the Colossians

83   Preface to the First Epistle of St. Paul to the Thessalonians

83   Preface to the Second Epistle of St. Paul to the Thessalonians

83   Preface to the First Epistle of St. Paul to Timothy

83   Preface to the Second Epistle of St. Paul to Timothy

83   Preface to the Epistle of St. Paul to Titus

83   Preface to the Epistle of St. Paul to Philemon

83   Preface to the First Epistle of St. Peter

Erlangen Edition	American Edition	St. Louis Edition	Weimar Edition
63, 80-81	35, 323-324	14, 60-61	DB 11^{II}, 259-261
63, 82	35, 324-325	14, 60-63	DB 11^{II}, 271
63, 83	35, 326	14, 62-63	DB 11^{II}, 289
63, 84-85	35, 327-328	14, 1421-1423	DB 11^{II}, 299-301
63, 85-86	35, 328-329	14, 64-65	DB 11^{II}, 311
63, 86-87	35, 329-330	14, 64-67	DB 11^{II}, 321
63, 88-89	35, 330-331	14, 66-67	DB 11^{II}, 329-331
63, 89-90	35, 332-333	14, 68-69	DB 11^{II}, 363-365
63, 91-93	35, 337-339	14, 68-71	DB 12, 5-7
63, 93-98	35, 340-344	14, 72-77	DB 12, 49-55
63, 98-100	35, 345-347	14, 76-77	DB 12, 109-111
63, 100-102	35, 347-349	14, 78-81	DB 12, 145-149
63, 103-104	35, 349-350	14, 80-81	DB 12, 291
63, 104-106	35, 350-352	14, 80-83	DB 12, 315-317
63, 106-107	35, 352-353	14, 82-85	DB 12, 417-419
63, 107-108	35, 353-354	14, 84-85	DB 12, 493
63, 108-115	35, 357-362	14, 84-91	DB 6, 2-10
63, 116-119	35, 363-365	14, 92-95	DB 6, 415-417
63, 119-138	35, 365-380	14, 94-109	DB 7, 2-27
63, 138-141	35, 380-383	14, 110-113	DB 7, 82-87
63, 142-143	35, 383-384	14, 114-115	DB 7, 138-139
63, 143-144	35, 384	14, 114-115	DB 7, 172-173
63, 144	35, 385	14, 116-117	DB 7, 190-191
63, 145	35, 385	14, 116-117	DB 7, 210-211
63, 145-146	35, 386	14, 116-117	DB 7, 224-225
63, 146-147	35, 386-387	14, 118-119	DB 7, 238-239
63, 147-148	35, 387-388	14, 118-119	DB 7, 250-251
63, 148-149	35, 388	14, 120-121	DB 7, 258-259
63, 149	35, 389	14, 120-121	DB 7, 272-273
63, 150	35, 389-390	14, 122-123	DB 7, 284-285
63, 150-151	35, 390	14, 122-123	DB 7, 292-293
63, 151-152	35, 390-391	14, 122-125	DB 7, 298-299

Erlangen Edition	American Edition	St. Louis Edition	Weimar Edition
63, 152-153	35, 391-392	14, 124-125	DB 7, 314-315
63, 153-154	35, 393	14, 126-127	DB 7, 326-327
63, 154-155	35, 394-395	14, 126-129	DB 7, 344-345
63, 156-158	35, 395-398	14, 128-131	DB 7, 384-387
63, 158-169	35, 399-411	14, 130-139	DB 7, 406-421
63, 169-170	35, 398-399	14, 140-141	DB 7, 404
63, 238-240	31, 71-76	14, 182-185	1, 378-379
63, 353-355	34, 269-278	14, 376-381	50, 383-385
63, 401-406 1, 67-72	34, 279-288	14, 432-437	50, 657-661
64, 290-293	53, 122-126	10, 1602-1605	38, 423-431
64, 292	53, 145-146	10, 1604-1605	38, 429
64, 294-296 54, 116-117	42, 179-186	10, 1732-1736	7, 784-791
64, 298-300	43, 179-186	10, 1776-1779	32, 547-548
65, 88-91	38, 3-89	17, 1939-1943	30^{III}, 110-171
65, 102-123	35, 175-202	19, 968-985	30^{II}, 632-646
65, 266-268 22, 3-32	43, 3-45	3, 1352-1361	10^{II}, 375-428
ex 1, 1-2, 116	1, 1-359	1, 1-437	42, 1-263
ex 2, 116-3, 276	2, 1-399	1, 436-921	42, 264-549
ex 3, 277-5, 67	3, 1-365	1, 920-1369	42, 550-673 43, 1-137
ex 5, 67-6, 243	4, 1-409	1, 1368-1765 2, 1-123	43, 137-430
ex 6, 243-7, 354	5, 1-386	2, 122-609	43, 430-695
ex 8, 1-9, 162	6, 1-407	2, 608-1159	44, 1-304
ex 9, 162-10, 313	7, 1-377	2, 1158-1655	44, 304-581
ex 10, 313-11, 325	8, 1-333	2, 1654-2091	44, 581-825
ex 13, 1-351	9, 1-311	3, 1370-1639	14, 489-744
ex 14, 1-89	14, 279-349	4, 220-301	5, 19-74
ex 18, 8-127	12, 1-136	5, 74-237	40^{II}, 193-212
ex 39, 4-61			45, 205-250
ex 18, 130-260	12, 197-410	5, 340-619	40^{II}, 472-610

Erlangen Edition	American Edition	St. Louis Edition	Weimar Edition
ex 19, 10-154			40^{II}, 315-470
ex 18, 264-334	13, 73-141	5, 732-799	40^{III}, 484-594
ex 21, 1-248	15, 1-187	5, 1372-1579	20, 7-203
ex 21, 267-368	15, 189-264	5, 1580-1659	31^{II}, 586-769
ex 22, 9-406	16, 1-349	6, 8-471	31^{II}, 1-260
ex 22, 406-23, 296	17, 1-416	6, 470-851	31^{II}, 261-585
ex 24, 1-88	18, 1-76	6, 946-1029	13, 1-66
ex 25, 55-125	18, 77-123	6, 1414-1479	13, 88-122
ex 25, 377-481	18, 125-190	6, 1684-1773	13, 158-206
ex 25, 507-527	18, 191-204	14, 808-823	13, 215-223
ex 26, 43-76	19, 1-31	14, 912-943	13, 241-258
ex 26, 149-233	18, 205-277	14, 978-983 14, 1178-1257	13, 299-343
ex 27, 61-110	18, 279-315	14, 1332-1373	13, 371-394
ex 27, 169-220	19, 105-148	14, 1506-1533	12, 424-448
ex 27, 283-350	18, 317-364	14, 1604-1657	13, 480-509
ex 27, 391-416	18, 365-387	14, 1708-1733	13, 532-544
ex 28, 5-200	20, 1-152	14, 1976-2159	13, 546-669
ex 28, 287-323	18, 389-419	14, 2158-2195	13, 675-703
gal 1, 1-12	27, 145-149	9, 8-17	40^{I}, 33-39
gal 1, 13-2, 286	26, 1-461	9, 16-601	40^{I}, 40-688
gal 2, 286-3, 120	27, 1-144	9, 600-771	40^{II}, 1-184
gal 3, 121-485	27, 151-410	8, 1352-1661	2, 445-618
var 1, 15-24	34, 323-338	14, 438-449	34, 179-187
var 1, 101-104	51, 14-17	10, 1284-1289	1, 63-65
var 1, 156-161	51, 17-23	12, 1794-1801	1, 111-115
var 1, 171-176	51, 26-31	12, 1762-1769	1, 138-141
var 1, 200-202	51, 23-26	12, 1814-1817	1, 128-130
var 1, 285-293	31, 17-33	18, 70-81	1, 233-238
var 1, 313-321	31, 3-16	18, 18-27	1, 224-228

Erlangen Edition	American Edition	St. Louis Edition	Weimar Edition
var 1, 387-404	31, 35-70	18, 36-71	1, 353-374
var 2, 136-293	31, 77-252	18, 100-269	1, 529-628
var 2, 329-339	31, 293-306	10, 1262-1277	2, 145-152
var 2, 367-392	31, 253-292	15, 612-616	2, 6-26
		15, 568-569	
		15, 571-587	
		15, 617-625	
		15, 539-547	
var 3, 12-17	31, 307-325	18, 718-721	2, 158-161
		15, 1162-1170	Br 1, 420-424
var 3, 217-224	51, 53-60	11, 2306-2313	2, 244-249
15, 396-403			
var 3, 394-410	35, 23-43	10, 2112-2127	2, 727-737
var 3, 410-419	42, 3-14	11, 574-583	2, 136-142
11, 144-152			
var 3, 442-446	42, 83-93	14, 1414-1421	2, 175-179
20, 290-294			
var 3, 446-452	44, 3-14	10, 630-637	2, 166-171
16, 158-165			
var 3, 453-473	42, 95-115	10, 1984-2001	2, 685-697
21, 253-274			
var 4, 84-135	42, 117-166	10, 1820-1917	6, 104-134
53, 31-34			
var 4, 152-171	39, 23-47	19, 786-807	6, 157-169
var 4, 378-389	34, 105-132	19, 1436-1450	39^{I}, 44-62
var 4, 389-394	34, 145-196	19, 1450-1455	39^{I}, 82-126
var 4, 413-416	34, 133-144	19, 1462-1467	39^{I}, 175-180
var 4, 452-455	34, 299-321	19, 1468-1473	39^{II}, 187-203
var 4, 458-461	38, 235-277	10, 1168-1173	39^{II}, 3-30
var 4, 480-492	34, 339-360	19, 1808-1817	54, 415-443
var 5, 16-118	36, 3-126	19, 4-129	6, 497-573
var 5, 397-521	32, 133-260	18, 1056-1201	8, 43-128

Erlangen Edition	American Edition	St. Louis Edition	Weimar Edition
var 6, 5-23	32, 101-131	15, 1916-1935	7, 814-857
var 6, 234-376 53, 86-92	44, 243-400	19, 1507-1665	8, 577-669
var 6, 492-535	40, 3-44	10, 1554-1603	12, 169-196
var 7, 1-20	53, 15-40	10, 2232-2255	12, 205-220
var 7, 116-368	33, 3-295	18, 1668-1969	18, 600-787
E_2 16, 420-429	51, 104-110		10^{III}, 341-346
E_2 16, 429-436	51, 111-117		10^{III}, 347-352

ALPHABETICAL INDEX
to the Contents of
Luther's Works

Defense and Explanation of All Articles, 1521
(32, 3-99)

Articles, Marburg

Marburg Colloquy and the Marburg Articles,
1529 (38, 3-89)

Articles, Twelve

Admonition to Peace, a Reply to the Twelve
Articles of the Peasants in Swabia, 1525 (46,
3-43)

Augsburg

Exhortation to All Clergy Assembled at Augsburg, 1530 (34, 3-61)
Proceedings at Augsburg, 1518 (31, 253-292)

Augustinians

L Augustinians at Erfurt: Wittenberg, Sep 22,
1512 (48, 5-7)
L The Augustinians in Wittenberg: Wartburg,
Nov 1521 (48, 324-325; 36, 133-135)

Babst

Preface to the Babst Hymnal, 1545 (53, 332-
334)

Babylonian Captivity

Babylonian Captivity of the Church, 1520 (36,
3-126)

Ban

S Sermon on the Ban, 1520 (39, 3-22)

Baptism

Concerning Baptism, 1528 (40, 225-262)
Holy Sacrament of Baptism, 1519 (35, 23-43)
Order of Baptism, 1523 (54, 95-103)
Order of Baptism, Newly Revised, 1526 (53,
106-109)
S Sermon on Baptism, 1528 (51, 182-188)
S Sermon on Mt 3:13-17 at the Baptism of
Bernhard von Anhalt, preached in Dessau,
Apr 2, 1540 (51, 313-329)

Barnes, Robert

L Barnes, Robert: Wittenberg, Sep 3, 1531
(50, 27-40)

Baruch

Preface to the Book of Baruch, 1534 (35, 349-
350)

Bernhard von Anhalt

S Sermon on Mt 3:13-17 at the Baptism of
Bernhard von Anhalt, preached in Dessau,
Apr 2, 1540 (51, 313-329)

BIBLE, NEW TESTAMENT

Preface to the New Testament, 1522 (35, 357-
362)

Acts

Preface to the Acts of the Apostles, 1533 (35,
363-365)

Colossians

Preface to the Epistle of St Paul to the Colossians, 1522 (35, 386)

1 Corinthians

Preface to the First Epistle of Paul to the
Corinthians, 1530 (35, 380-383)
1 Corinthians 7, 1523 (28, 1-56)
1 Corinthians 15, 1532-1533 (28, 57-213)

2 Corinthians

Preface to the Second Epistle to the Corinthians, 1522 (35, 383-384)
S Sermon on the Epistle for the Twelfth Sunday after Trinity, 2 Cor 3:4-6, preached on the
afternoon of Aug 27, 1531 (51, 221-227)

Ephesians

Preface to the Epistle of St Paul to the Ephesians, 1522 (35, 385)

Galatians

Preface to the Epistle of St Paul to the Gala-
tians, 1522 (35, 384)
Galatians 1-4, 1535 (26, 1-461)
Galatians 5-6, 1535 (27, 1-144)
Luther's Preface to Galatians, 1535 (27, 145-
149)
Galatians 1-6, 1519 (27, 151-410)

Hebrews

Hebrews, 1517-1518 (29, 107-241)
Preface to the Epistle to the Hebrews, 1522
(35, 394-395)
S Sermon preached at the Marriage of Sigis-
mund von Lindenau in Merseburg, He 13:4,
Aug 4, 1545 (51, 355-367)

James

Preface to the Epistles of St James and St
Jude, 1522 (35, 395-398)

John

Preface to the Three Epistles of St John, 1522
(35, 393)
John 1-4, 1537-1540 (22, 1-530)
John 6, 1530 (23, 1-197)
John 7 and 8, 1530-1532 (23, 198-422)

John 14-16, 1537-1538 (24, 1-422)

S Gospel for the Main Christmas Service, Jn 1:1-14, 1522 (52, 41-88)

John

Disputation Concerning the Passage "The Word Was Made Flesh" 1539 (38, 235-277)

S Sermon on the Man Born Blind, Jn 9:1-38, preached on the Wednesday after Laetare, Mar 17, 1518 (51, 35-43)

S Sermon on the Raising of Lazarus, Jn 11:1-45, preached on the Friday after Laetare, Mar 19, 1518 (51, 44-49)

S Sermon preached in Castle at Pleissenburg on the Occasion of the Inauguration of the Reformation in Leipzig. Jn 14:23-31, May 24, 1539 (51, 301-312)

S Sermon preached at Erfurt on the Journey to Worms, Jn 20:19-20, Apr 7, 1521 (51, 60-66)

1 John

1 John, 1527 (30, 217-327)

Jude

Preface to the Epistles of St James and St. Jude, 1522 (35, 395-398)

Jude, 1523 (30, 201-215)

Luke

Magnificat, 1521 (21, 295-358)

Gospel for Christmas Eve, Lk 2:1-14, 1522 (52, 7-31)

S Sermon on the Afternoon of Christmas Day, Lk 2:1-14, Dec 25, 1530 (51, 209-218)

Gospel for the Early Christmas Service, Lk 2:15-20, 1522 (52, 32-40)

Gospel for New Year's Day, Lk 2:21, 1522 (52, 149-158)

Gospel for the Sunday after Christmas, Lk 2:33-40, 1522 (52, 102-148)

S Sermon at the Dedication of the Castle Church in Torgau, Lk 14:1-11, Oct 5, 1544 (51, 331-354)

S Sermon on the Tenth Sunday after Trinity, Lk 18:9-14, Jul 27, 1516 (51, 14-17)

Matthew

S Sermon on the Mount, Matthew 5,6, and 7, 1532 (21, 1-294)

Gospel for the Festival of the Epiphany, Mt 2:1-12, 1522 (52, 159-286)

S Sermon on Mt 3:13-17 at the Baptism of Bernhard von Anhalt, preached in Dessau Apr 2, 1540 (51, 313-329)

S Luther's First (?) Sermon, Mt 7:12, 1510 in Erfurt (51, 5-13)

S Sermon on the Fourth Sunday after the Epiphany, Mt 8:23-27, Feb 1, 1517 (51, 23-26)

S Sermon on St. Matthew's Day, Mt 11:25-30, Feb 24, 1517 (51, 26-31)

S Sermon on St Matthias' Day, Mt 11:25-30, Feb 5, 1525 (51, 119-132)

S Sermon on St. Matthew's Day, Mt 11:25-30, Feb 24, 1517 (51, 26-31)

S Sermon, Mt 22:37-39, the Morning of October 19, 1522 (51, 104-110)

S Sermon, Mt 22:37-39, the Afternoon of October 19, 1522 (51, 111-117)

Gospel for St Stephen's Day, Mt 23:34-39, 1522 (52, 89-101)

1 Peter

Preface to the First Epistle of St Peter, 1522 (35, 390-391)

1 Peter, 1523 (30, 1-145)

S Sermon on Soberness and Moderation Against Drunkenness, 1 Pe 4:7-11, May 18, 1539 (51, 289-299)

2 Peter

2 Peter, 1523 (30, 147-199)

Preface to the Second Epistle of St Peter, 1522 (35, 391-392)

Philemon

Preface to the Epistle of St Paul to Philemon, 1522 (35, 389-390)

Philemon, 1527 (29, 91-105)

Philippians

Preface to the Epistle of St Paul to the Philippians, 1522 (35, 385)

Revelation

Preface to the Revelation of St. John (2) 1530 (35, 399-411)

Preface to the Revelation of St. John (1) 1522 (35, 389-399)

Romans

Romans, 1515-1516 (25, 1-524)

Preface to the Epistle of St Paul to the Romans, 1522 (35, 365-380)

S Last Sermon in Wittenberg, Ro 12:3, Jan 17, 1546 (51, 369-380)

1 Thessalonians

Preface to the First Epistle of St Paul to the Thessalonians, 1522 (35, 386-387)

246

Church

On the Councils and the Church: 1539 (41, 3-178)

City Council, Leisnig

L Council of the City of Leisnig: Wittenberg, Jan 29, 1523 (49, 28-32)

City Council, Stettin

L Council of the City of Stettin: Wittenberg, Jan 11, 1523 (49, 25-28)

Clergy

Exhortation to all Clergy Assembled at Augsburg, 1530 (34, 3-61)

Collects (In Their Sequential and Chronological Order)

Collect: O Almighty God, Father of Our Lord Jesus Christ, Look Upon This Night, 1526 (53, 142)

Collect: O Almighty Eternal God, Father of Our Lord Jesus Christ, I Cry to Thee, 1526 (53, 142-143)

Collect: Almighty Eternal God, Who According to Thy Righteous Judgment, 1526 (53, 143-144)

Collect: Lord, Holy Father, Almighty Eternal God, 1526 (53, 144)

Collect: Almighty God, Who Art the Protector, 1526 (53, 136-137)

Collect: We Give Thanks to Thee, Almighty God, 1526 (53, 137-138)

Collect: Lord God, Heavenly Father, from Whom Without Ceasing We Receive, 1529 (53, 138-139)

Collect: Lord God Almighty, Who Dost Not Disdain, 1529 (53, 139-140)

Collect: Lord God, Heavenly Father, Who Hast No Pleasure, 1529 (53, 140 and 169)

Collect: Lord God, Heavenly Father, Thou Knowest, 1529 (53, 140 and 169)

Collect: Almighty Everlasting God, Who Through Thy Holy Spirit, 1529 (53, 141 and 170)

Collect: O God, Who Hast Created Man and Woman, 1529 (53, 144-145)

Collect: Dear Lord God, Awaken Us, 1533 (53, 131)

Collect: Help, Dear Lord God, that We May Become and Remain Partakers, 1533 (53, 131-132)

Collect: Almighty Eternal God, We Heartily Pray Thee, 1533 (53, 132)

Collect: Merciful Everlasting God, Who Didst Not Spare Thine Own Son, 1533 (53, 132-133)

Collect: Almighty Father, Eternal God, Who Didst Allow, 1533 (53, 133)

Collect: Almighty God, Who by the Death of Thy Son, 1533 (53, 134)

Collect: Lord God, Dear Father, Who Through Thy Holy Spirit, 1533 (53, 135)

Collect: Almighty Eternal God, Who Has Taught Us, 1533 (53, 136)

Collect: O Thou Dear Lord God, 1533 (53, 137)

Collect: Lord God, Heavenly Father, Who Createst Holy Desire, 1533 (53, 138)

Collect: Merciful God, Heavenly Father, Thou Hast Said to Us, 1535 (53, 145-146)

Collect: Almighty Lord God, Grant to Us Who Believe, 1543 (53, 134-135)

Colloquy, Marburg

Marburg Colloquy and the Marburg Articles, 1529 (38, 3-89)

Comfort

Comfort for Women Who Have Had a Miscarriage, 1542 (43, 243-250)

Comfort When Facing Grave Temptations, 1521 (42, 179-186)

Four Psalms of Comfort: Psalm 37, Psalm 62, Psalm 94, Psalm 109, 1526 (14, 207-277)

Sayings in Which Luther Found Comfort, 1530 (43, 167-177)

Commandment

Hymn: These Are the Holy Ten Commands, 1524 (53, 277-279)

S Sermon: First Commandment, 1528 (51, 137-141)

S Sermon: Fourth Commandment, 1528 (51, 145-150)

S Sermon: Fourth, Fifth, and Sixth Commandment, 1528 (51, 150-155)

S Sermon: Second and Third Commandment, 1528 (51, 141-145)

S Sermon: Seventh, Eighth, Ninth, and Tenth Commandment, 1528 (51, 155-161)

Common Chest

Fraternal Agreement on the Common Chest of the Entire Assembly at Leisnig, 1523 (45, 176-194)

Ordinance of Common Chest, — Preface, 1523, (45, 159-176)

248

Debate

Leipzig Debate, 1519 (31, 307-325)

Dedication

Dedication to Count Mansfeld, 1521 (52, 3-6)

Defense

Defense and Explanation of All Articles, 1521 (32, 3-99)

Defense on the Translation of the Psalms, 1531 (35, 203-223)

Denmark

L King Christian of Denmark: Wittenberg, Apr 14, 1545 (50, 250-252)

Diet

Luther at the Diet of Worms, 1521 (32, 101-131)

Dietrich, Veit

Table Talks Recorded by Veit Dietrich, 1531-1533 (54, 3-114)

Disputation

Disputation Against Scholastic Theology, 1517 (31, 3-16)

Disputation Concerning Justification, 1536 (34, 145-196)

Disputation Concerning Man, 1536 (34, 133-134)

Disputation Concerning the Passage "The Word Was Made Flesh" 1539 (38, 235-277)

Heidelberg Disputation, 1518 (31, 35-70)

Doctrines of Men

Avoiding the Doctrines of Men and a Reply to the Texts Cited in Defense of the Doctrines of Men, 1522 (35, 125-153)

Dressel, Michael

L Dressel, Michael: Wittenberg Sep 25, 1516 (48, 20-23)

Drunkenness

S Sermon on Soberness and Moderation Against Drunkenness, 1 Pe 4:7-11, May 18, 1539 (51, 289-299)

Duke Albrecht

L Duke Albrecht of Prussia: Wittenberg, May 2, 1545 (50, 252-255)

Edict

Commentary on the Alleged Imperial Edict, 1531 (34, 63-104)

Elector Frederick

L Elector Frederick: Wittenberg, about Nov 6, 1517 (48, 49-52)

L Elector Frederick: Altenburg, Jan 5 or 6, 1519 (48, 96-100)

L Elector Frederick: Wittenberg, between Jan 13 and 19, 1519 (48, 103-106)

L Elector Frederick: Wittenberg, about May 15, 1519 (48, 120-121)

L Elector Frederick: Wittenberg, Oct 15, 1519 (48, 127-129)

L Elector Frederick: Wittenberg, Jan 25, 1521 (48, 194-197)

L Elector Frederick: Wartburg, about Feb 22, 1522 (48, 386-388)

L Elector Frederick: Borna, Mar 5, 1522 (48, 388-393)

L Elector Frederick: Wittenberg, Mar 7 or 8, 1522 (48, 393-399)

L Elector Frederick: Wittenberg, May 29, 1523 (49, 35-42)

L Elector Frederick: Leisnig, Aug 11, 1523 (49, 45-47)

L Elector Frederick: Wittenberg, mid Nov 1523 (49, 57-59)

L Elector Frederick: Wittenberg, Mar 23, 1524 (49, 74-76)

Elector John

L Elector John: Wittenberg, Sep 6, 1525 (49, 125-130)

L Elector John: Wittenberg, Oct 31, 1525 (49, 130-137)

L Elector John: Wittenberg, Nov 30, 1525 (49, 137-139)

L Elector John: Wittenberg, Sep 16, 1527 (49, 169-171)

L Elector John: Weimar, May 1 or 2, 1528 (49, 189-195)

L Elector John: Wittenberg, Sep 3, 1528 (49, 210-211)

L Elector John: Wittenberg, May 22, 1529 (49, 221-228)

L Elector John: Wittenberg, Nov 18, 1529 (49, 244-250)

L Elector John: Wittenberg, Dec 24, 1529 (49, 254-260)

L Elector John: Wittenberg, Mar 6, 1530 (49, 272-280)

L Elector John: Coburg, May 15, 1530 (49, 295-299)

Sacrament of the Body and Blood of Christ Against the Fanatics, 1526 (36, 329-361)

That These Words of Christ "This Is My Body" Still Stand Firm Against the Fanatics, 1527 (37, 3-150)

Fox, Edward

L Fox, Edward: Wittenberg, May 12, 1538 (50, 177-180)

Freedom

Freedom of a Christian, 1520 (31, 327-377)

Fuchs, Thomas

L Fuchs, Thomas: Wittenberg, Dec 23, 1519 (48, 139-141)

George of Anhalt

L George of Anhalt: Eisleben, Jan 29, 1546 (50, 288-289)

L George of Anhalt: Eisleben, Feb 10, 1546 (50, 309-310)

Gerbel, Nicholas

L Gerbel, Nicholas: Wartburg, Nov 1, 1521 (48, 317-322)

L Gerbel, Nicholas: Wittenberg, May 6, 1524 (49, 81-83)

L Gerbel, Nicholas: Wittenberg, Jul 28, 1528 (49, 199-202)

German Language

Preface to the Complete Edition of a German Theology, 1518 (31, 71-76)

German Nation

To the Christian Nobility of the German Nation, 1520 (44, 115-217)

German People

Dr Martin Luther's Warning to His Dear German People, 1531 (47, 3-55)

German Theology

Preface to the Complete Edition of a German Theology, 1518 (31, 71-76)

Glaser, Martin

L Glaser, Martin: Wittenberg, May 30, 1519 (48, 124-126)

Gloria in Excelsis

Gloria in Excelsis, 1537 (53, 184-188 and 292-294)

Gospel

Brief Instruction on What to Look For and Expect in the Gospels, 1521 (35, 113-124)

Gospel for Christmas Eve, Lk 2:1-14, 1522 (52, 7-31)

Gospel for the Early Christmas Service, Lk 2:15-20, 1522 (52, 32-40)

Gospel for St Stephen's Day, Mt 23:34-39, 1522 (52, 89-101)

Gospel for the Sunday After Christmas, Lk 2:33-40, 1522 (52, 102-148)

Gospel for New Year's Day, Lk 2:21, 1522 (52, 149-158)

Gospel for the Festival of the Epiphany, Mt 2:1-12, 1522 (52, 159-286)

Gospel for the Main Christmas Service, Jn 1:1-14, 1522 (52, 41-88)

Halle

L Letter of Consolation to the Christians at Halle, 1527 (43, 139-165)

Hanswurst

Against Hanswurst, 1541 (41, 179-256)

Hausmann, Nicholas

L Hausmann, Nicholas: Wittenberg, Mar 17, 1522 (48, 399-402)

L Hausmann, Nicholas: Wittenberg, end of Oct, 1523 (49, 55-56)

L Hausmann, Nicholas: Wittenberg, Nov 17, 1524 (49, 87-91)

L Hausmann, Nicholas: Wittenberg, Jan 10, 1527 (49, 159-161)

L Hausmann, Nicholas: Wittenberg, Mar 29, 1527 (49, 161-164)

L Hausmann, Nicholas: Wittenberg, Jul 13, 1527 (49, 167-169)

L Hausmann, Nicholas: Wittenberg, Aug 5, 1528 (49, 202-203)

L Hausmann, Nicholas: Wittenberg, beg of Feb, 1530 (49, 264-267)

L Hausmann, Nicholas: Coburg, Apr 18, 1530 (49, 280-287)

L Hausmann, Nicholas: Coburg, Jul 6, 1530 (49, 348-352)

L Hausmann, Nicholas: Coburg, Sep 23, 1530 (49, 419-424)

L Hausmann, Nicholas: Wittenberg, Jan 17, 1536 (50, 122-124)

L Hausmann, Nicholas: Wittenberg, Torgau, Sep 20, 1536 (50, 148-151)

L Hausmann, Nicholas: Wittenberg, Feb 23, 1538 (50, 174-176)

Heidelberg

Heidelberg Disputation, 1518 (31, 35-70)

Herod

Hymn: Herod, Why Dreadest Thou a Foe, 1541 (53, 302-303)

Hess, John

L Hess, John: Wittenberg, about Jun 13, 1528 (49, 196-199)

Hessus, Eobanus

L Hessus, Eobanus: Wittenberg, Mar 29, 1523 (49, 32-35)

Heydenreich, Caspar

Table Talks recorded by Caspar Heydenreich, 1542-1543 (54, 411-464)

Hymn

Hymn: All Glory, Laud, And Praise Be Given, 1537 (53, 184-188 and 294)

Hymn: All Praise To Thee, O Jesus Christ, 1523 (53, 240-241)

Hymn: A New Song Here Shall Be Begun, 1523 (53, 211-216)

Hymn: Although The Fools Say With Their Mouth, 1523 (53, 229-231)

Hymn: Come, God Creator Holy Ghost, 1524 (53, 260-262)

Hymn: Come, Holy Spirit God And Lord, 1524 (53, 265-267)

Hymn: Come, The Heathen's Healing Light, 1523 (53, 235-236)

Hymn: Dear Christians, Let Us Now Rejoice, 1523 (53, 217-220)

Hymn: Death Held Our Lord In Prison, 1524 (53, 255-257)

Hymn: From Heaven On High I Come To You, 1534-1535 (53, 289-291)

Hymn: From Heaven The Angel Troop Came Near, 1534 (53, 306-307)

Hymn: From Trouble Deep I Cry To Thee, 1523 (53, 221-224)

Hymn: God The Father With Us Be, 1524 (53, 268-270)

Hymn: Grant Peace In Mercy, Lord, We Pray, 1528 (53, 286-287)

Hymn: Happy Who In God's Fear Doth Stay, 1524 (53, 242-244)

Hymn: Herod, Why Dreadest Thou A Foe, 1541 (53, 302-303)

Hymn: In One True God We All Believe, 1524 (53, 271-273)

Hymn: In Peace And Joy I Now Depart, 1524 (53, 247-248)

Hymn: In The Midst Of Life We Are, 1524 (53, 274-276)

Hymn: Isaiah 'Twas The Prophet, 1526 (53, 282-283)

Hymn: Jesus Christ, Our God And Savior, 1524 (53, 249-251)

Hymn: Jesus Christ, Our Savior True, 1524 (53, 258-259)

Hymn: Jesus We Now Must Laud And Sing, 1523 (53, 237-239)

Hymn: Let God Be Blest, 1524 (53, 252-254)

Hymn: Lord God, Thy Praise We Sing, 1531 (53, 288 and 171-175)

Hymn: Lord, Keep Us Steadfast In Thy Word, 1541-1542 (53, 304-305)

Hymn: Man, Wouldst Thou Live All Blissfully, 1524 (53, 280-281)

Hymn: Now Let Us Pray To The Holy Ghost, 1524 (53, 263-264)

Hymn: Oh, God, From Heaven Look Down, 1523 (53, 225-228)

Hymn: Our Father In The Heaven Who Art, 1539 (53, 295-298)

Hymn: Our God He Is A Castle Strong, 1527-1528 (53, 283-285)

Hymn: These Are The Holy Ten Commands, 1524 (53, 277-279)

Hymn: Thou Who Art Three In Unity, 1534 (53, 308-309)

Hymn: To Jordan When Our Lord Had Gone, 1541 (53, 299-301)

Hymn: To Me She's Dear, The Worthy Maid, 1535-1545 (53, 292-294)

Hymn: Were God Not With Us At This Time, 1524 (53, 245-246)

Hymn: Would That The Lord Would Grant Us Grace, 1523 (53, 232-234)

Preface to the Burial Hymns, 1542 (53, 325-331)

Hymnal

Preface for All Good Hymnals, 1538 (53, 319-320)

Preface to the Babst Hymnal, 1545 (53, 332-334)

Preface to Weiss Hymnal, 1528 (53, 317-318)

Preface to the Wittenberg Hymnal, 1524 (53, 315-316)

Images

Against the Heavenly Prophets in the Matter of Images and Sacraments, 1525 (40, 73-223)

Order of Marriage for Common Pastors, 1529 (53, 110-115)

Te Deum, 1529 (53, 171-175)

Livonians

Christian Exhortation to the Livonians Concerning Public Worship and Concord, 1525 (53, 41-50)

Loescher, Thomas

L Loescher, Thomas: Wittenberg, Aug 26, 1529 (49, 232-234)

Loeser, John

L Loeser, John: Wittenberg, Jan 29, 1533 (50, 73-74)

Lord's Prayer

Exposition of the Lord's Prayer for Simple Laymen, 1519 (42, 15-81)

S Sermon: On Prayer and the First Three Petitions, 1528 (51, 169-176)

S Sermon: Fourth, Fifth, Sixth, and Seventh Petitions, 1528 (51, 176-182)

Lord's Supper

Abomination of the Secret Mass, 1525 (36, 307-328)

Admonition Concerning the Sacrament of the Body and Blood of Our Lord, 1530 (38, 91-137)

Adoration of the Sacrament, 1523 (36, 269-305)

The Blessed Sacrament of the Holy and True Body of Christ and the Brotherhoods, 1519 (35, 45-73)

Brief Confession Concerning the Holy Sacrament, 1544 (38, 279-319)

Confession Concerning Christ's Supper, 1528 (37, 151-372)

Exhortation to the Communicants, 1525 (53, 104-105)

Letter of Dr Martin Luther Concerning His Book on the Private Mass, 1534 (38, 215-233)

Misuse of the Mass, 1521 (36, 127-230)

Order of Mass and Communion for the Church At Wittenberg, 1523 (53, 15-40)

Private Mass and the Consecration of Priests, 1533 (38, 139-214)

Receiving Both Kinds in the Sacrament, 1522 (36, 231-267)

Sacrament of the Body and Blood of Christ Against the Fanatics, 1526 (36, 329-361)

S Sermon on the Worthy Reception of the Sacrament, 1521 (42, 167-177)

S Sermon: The Lord's Supper, 1528 (51, 188-193)

That These Words of Christ "This is My Body" Still Stand Firm Against the Fanatics, 1527 (37, 3-150)

A Treatise on the New Testament, That Is the Holy Mass, 1520 (35, 75-111)

Louvain

Against the Thirty-five Articles of the Louvain Theologians, 1545 (34, 339-360)

Luebeck

L Some Pastors of the City of Luebeck: Wittenberg, Jan 12, 1530 (49, 261-263)

Luther's Death

Italian Lie Concerning Dr Martin Luther's Death, 1545 (34, 361-366)

Luther's German Writings

Preface to the Wittenberg Edition of Luther's German Writings, 1539 (34, 279-288)

Luther's Latin Writings

Preface to the Complete Edition of Luther's Latin Writings, 1545 (34, 323-338)

Luther, Hans

L Luther, Hans: Wartburg, Nov 21, 1521 (48, 329-336)

L Luther, Hans: Wittenberg, Feb 15, 1530 (49, 267-271)

L Luther, Hans: Wittenberg, Jan 27, 1537 (50, 151-153)

Luther, John

L Luther, John: Coburg, about Jun 19, 1530 (49, 321-324)

L Luther, John: Wittenberg, Dec 27, 1542 (50, 240-241)

Luther, Mrs Martin

L Luther, Mrs Martin: Marburg, Oct 4, 1529 (49, 234-239)

L Luther, Mrs Martin: Coburg, Jun 5, 1530 (49, 311-316)

L Luther, Mrs Martin: Coburg, Aug 14, 1530 (49, 399-400)

L Luther, Mrs Martin: Coburg, Aug 14, 1530 (49, 400-403)

L Luther, Mrs Martin: Coburg, Sep 8, 1530 (49, 415-419)

L Luther, Mrs Martin: Coburg, Sep 24, 1530 (49, 424-425)

Meditation

Meditation on Christ's Passion, 1519 (42, 3-14)

Melanchthon, Philip

L Melanchthon, Philip: Wartburg, about May 8, 1521 (48, 210-213)

L Melanchthon, Philip: Wartburg, May 12, 1521 (48, 215-217)

L Melanchthon, Philip: Wartburg, May 26, 1521 (48, 228-244)

L Melanchthon, Philip: Wartburg, Jul 13, 1521 (48, 256-263)

L Melanchthon, Philip: Wartburg, Aug 1, 1521 (48, 277-282)

L Melanchthon, Philip: Wartburg, Aug 3, 1521 (48, 283-289)

L Melanchthon Philip: Wartburg, Sep 9, 1521 (48, 296-304)

L Melanchthon, Philip: Wartburg, Jan 13, 1522 (48, 364-372)

L Melanchthon, Philip: Coburg, Apr 24, 1530 (49, 287-291)

L Melanchthon, Philip: Coburg, Jun 5, 1530 (49, 316-319)

L Melanchthon, Philip: Coburg, Jun 7, 1530 (49, 320-321)

L Melanchthon, Philip: Coburg, Jun 29, 1530 (49, 324-333)

L Melanchthon, Philip: Coburg, Jul 3, 1530 (49, 342-347)

L Jonas, Justus, George Spalatin, Philip Melanchthon, John Agricola: Coburg, Jul 15, 1530 (49, 372-377)

L Melanchthon, Philip: Coburg, Jul 21, 1530 (49, 378-393)

L Melanchthon, Philip: Wittenberg, Aug 29, 1535 (50, 85-92)

L Melanchthon, Philip: Wittenberg, beg of Dec, 1535 (50, 113-117)

L Melanchthon, Philip: Eisleben, Feb 1, 1546 (50, 292-295)

L Melanchthon, Philip: Eisleben, Feb 3, 1546 (50, 295-297)

L Melanchthon, Philip: Eisleben, Feb 6, 1546 (50, 297-299)

L Melanchthon, Philip: Eisleben, Feb 14, 1546 (50, 313-318)

Ministers

Ordination of Ministers of the Word, 1539 (53, 122-126)

Ministry

Concerning the Ministry, 1523 (40, 3-44)

Keys, 1530 (40, 321-377)

Miscarriage

Comfort for Women Who Have Had a Miscarriage, 1542 (43, 243-250)

Mittenberg

L Christian Letter of Consolation to the People of Mittenberg, 1524 (43, 97-112)

Moses

How Christians Should Regard Moses, 1525 (35, 155-174)

Motet

Motet: I Shall Not Die But Live, 1545 (53, 335-341)

Mueller, Caspar

L Mueller, Caspar: Wittenberg, Jan 19, 1536 (50, 124-130)

Murner

Answer to the HyperChristian, Hyperspiritual and Hyperlearned Book by Goat Emser in Leipzig — Including Some Thoughts Regarding His Companion, the Fool Murner, 1521 (39, 137-224)

Nobility

To the Christian Nobility of the German Nation, 1520 (44, 115-217)

Nuernberg

L Council of the City of Nuernberg: Wittenberg, Apr 18, 1533 (50, 75-78)

Nun

How God Rescued an Honorable Nun, 1524 (43, 81-96)

Oecolampadius, John

L Oecolampadius, John: Wittenberg, Jun 20, 1523 (49, 42-45)

Order of Service

German Mass and Order of Service, 1526 (53, 51-90)

Ordinance

Ordinance of Common Chest — Preface, 1523 (45, 159-176)

258

Preface to Galeatius Capella's History, 1538 (34, 269-278)

Preface to George Rhau's Symphoniae Lucundae, 1538 (53, 321-324)

Preface to Parts of Esther and Daniel, 1533 (35, 353-354)

Preface To Solomon's "The Preacher," 1524 (35, 263-264)

Preface to the Acts of the Apostles, 1533 (35, 363-365)

Preface to the Babst Hymnal, 1545 (53, 332-334)

Preface to the Book of Baruch, 1534 (35, 349-350)

Preface to the Book of Jesus Sirach, 1533 (35, 347-349)

Preface to the Book of Job, 1524 (35, 251-253)

Preface to the Book of Tobit, 1534 (35, 345-347)

Preface to the Books of Judith, 1534 (35, 337-339)

Preface to the Books of Solomon, 1534 (35, 258-261)

Preface to the Burial Hymns, 1542 (53, 325-331)

Preface to the Complete Edition of a German Theology, 1518 (31, 71-76)

Preface to the Complete Edition of Luther's Latin Writings, 1545 (34, 323-338)

Preface to the Epistle of St Paul to the Colossians, 1522 (35, 386)

Preface to the Epistle of St Paul to the Galatians, 1522 (35, 384)

Preface to the Epistle of St Paul to the Ephesians, 1522 (35, 385)

Preface to the Epistle of St Paul to the Philippians, 1522 (35, 385)

Preface to the Epistle of St Paul to Philemon, 1522 (35, 389-390)

Preface to the Epistle of St Paul to the Romans, 1522 (35, 365-380)

Preface to the Epistle of St Paul to Titus, 1522 (35, 389-390)

Preface to the Epistles of St James and St Jude, 1522 (35, 395-398)

Preface to the First Book of Maccabees, 1533 (35, 350-352)

Preface to the First Epistle of St Paul to the Corinthians, 1530 (35, 380-383)

Preface to the First Epistle of St Paul to the Thessalonians, 1522 (35, 386-387)

Preface to the First Epistle of St Paul to Timothy, 1522 (35, 388)

Preface to the First Epistle of St Peter, 1522 (35, 390-391)

Preface to the New Testament, 1522 (35, 357-362)

Preface to the Prophet Amos, 1532 (35, 320-321)

Preface to the Prophet Daniel, 1530 (35, 294-316)

Preface to the Prophet Ezekiel, 1532 (35, 282-283)

Preface to the Prophet Habakkuk, 1526 (35, 327-328)

Preface to the Prophet Haggai, 1532 (35, 329-330)

Preface to the Prophet Hosea, 1532 (35, 317-318)

Preface to the Prophet Isaiah, 1528 (35, 273-278)

Preface to the Prophet Jeremiah, 1532 (35, 274-282)

Preface to the Prophet Joel, 1532 (35, 318-319)

Preface to the Prophet Jonah, 1532 (35, 323-324)

Preface to the Prophet Malachi, 1532 (35, 332--333)

Preface to the Prophet Micah, 1532 (35, 324-325)

Preface to the Prophet Nahum, 1532 (35, 326)

Preface to the Prophet Obadiah, 1532 (35, 321-322)

Preface to the Prophets, 1532 (35, 265-273)

Preface to the Prophet Zechariah, 1532 (35, 330-331)

Preface to the Prophet Zephaniah, 1532 (35, 328-329)

Preface to the Proverbs of Solomon, 1524 (35, 261-263)

Preface to the Psalter, 1528 (35, 253-257)

Preface to the Revelation of St John (1), 1522 (35, 389-399)

Preface to the Revelation of St John (2), 1530 (35, 399-411)

Preface to the Second Book of Maccabees, 1533 (35, 352-353)

Preface to the Second Epistle of St Paul to the Thessalonians, 1522 (35, 387-388)

Preface to the Second Epistle of St Paul to Timothy, 1522 (35, 389)

S Sermon on the Afternoon of Christmas Day, Lk 2:1-14, Dec 25, 1530 (51, 209-218)

S Sermon on the Epistle for the Twelfth Sunday After Trinity, 2 Cor 3:4-6, preached on the afternoon of Aug 27, 1531 (51, 221-227)

S Sermon at the Funeral of the Elector, Duke John of Saxony, 1 Th 4:13-14, Aug 18, 1532 (51, 231-243)

S Second Sermon at the Funeral of the Elector, Duke John of Saxony, 1 Th 4:13-18, Aug 22, 1532 (51, 243-255)

S Sermon on the Sum of Christian Life, 1 Tm 1:5-7, Preached at Woerlitz, Nov 24, 1532 (51, 257-287)

S Sermon on the Mount, Matthew 5,6, and 7, 1532 (21, 1-294)

S Sermon on Soberness and Moderation Against Drunkenness, 1 Pe 4:7-11, May 18, 1539 (51, 289-299)

S Sermon Preached in Castle at Pleissenburg on the Occasion of the Inauguration of the Reformation in Leipzig, Jn 14:23-31, May 24, 1539 (51, 301-312)

S Sermon on Mt 3:13-17 at the Baptism of Bernhard von Anhalt, preached in Dessau, Apr 2, 1540 (51, 313-329)

S Sermon at the Dedication of the Castle Church in Torgau, Lk 14:1-11, Oct 5, 1544 (51, 331-354)

S Sermon Preached at the Marriage of Sigismund von Lindenau in Merseburg, He 13:4, Aug 4, 1545 (51, 355-367)

S Last Sermon in Wittenberg, Ro 12:3, Jan 17, 1546 (51, 369-380)

S Last Sermon, preached in Eisleben, Feb 15, 1546 (51, 381-392)

Sermon on the Mount

S Sermon on the Mount, Matthew 5, 6, and 7, 1532 (21, 1-294)

Sermons

S Eight Sermons at Wittenberg, Mar 9 to Mar 16, 1522 (51, 70-100)

Shrive

How One Should Teach Common Folk to Shrive Themselves, 1531 (53, 119-121)

Sickingen, Francis von

L Sickingen, Francis von: Wartburg, Jun 1, 1521 (48, 244-247)

Sigismund von Lindenau

S Sermon Preached at the Marriage of Sigismund von Lindenau in Merseburg, He 13:4, Aug 4, 1545 (51, 355-367)

Soberness

Sermon on Soberness and Moderation Against Drunkenness, 1 Pe 4:7-11, May 18, 1539 (51, 289-299)

Soldiers

Whether Soldiers Too Can Be Saved, 1526 (46, 87-137)

Solomon

Preface to the Books of Solomon, 1534 (35, 258-261)

Preface to the Wisdom of Solomon, 1529 (35, 340-344)

Spalatin, George

L Spalatin, George: Wittenberg, Aug 5, 1514 (48, 8-11)

L Spalatin, George: Wittenberg, Apr 8, 1516 (48, 11-14)

L Spalatin, George: Wittenberg, Aug 24, 1516 (48, 17-18)

L Spalatin, George: Wittenberg, Sep 9, 1516 (48, 18-19)

L Spalatin, George: Wittenberg, Oct 19, 1516 (48, 23-26)

L Spalatin, George: Wittenberg, Dec 14, 1516 (48, 32-36)

L Spalatin, George: Wittenberg, the end of August, 1517 (48, 42-43)

L Spalatin, George: Wittenberg, Jan 18, 1518 (48, 52-55)

L Spalatin, George: Wittenberg, Feb 22, 1518 (48, 56-59)

L Spalatin, George: Wittenberg, May 18, 1518 (48, 60-63)

L Spalatin, George: Wittenberg, Aug 8, 1518 (48, 70-73)

L Spalatin, George: Wittenberg, Aug 28, 1518 (48, 73-76)

L Spalatin, George: Wittenberg, Aug 31, 1518 (48, 76-80)

L Spalatin, George: Wittenberg, Sep 2, 1518 (48, 80-83)

L Spalatin, George: Wittenberg, Oct 14, 1518 (48, 83-87)

L Spalatin, George: Wittenberg, Oct 31, 1518 (48, 90-93)

L Spalatin, George: Wittenberg, Nov 25, 1518 (48, 93-94)

L Spalatin, George: Wittenberg, Dec 9, 1518 (48, 95-96)

L Spalatin, George: Wittenberg, Feb 7, 1519 (48, 106-107)

L Spalatin, George: Wittenberg, Mar 13, 1519 (48, 111-116)

L Spalatin, George: Wittenberg, May 22, 1519 (48, 122-124)

L Spalatin, George: Wittenberg, Jul 20, 1519 (48, 126)

L Spalatin, George: Liebenswerda, Oct 9, or Wittenberg, Oct 10, 1519 (48, 126-127)

L Spalatin, George: Wittenberg, Nov 1, 1519 (48, 130-131)

L Spalatin, George: Wittenberg, Nov 7, 1519 (48, 132-133)

L Spalatin, George: Wittenberg, Nov 29, 1519 (48, 133-134)

L Spalatin, George: Wittenberg, Dec 31, 1519 (48, 141-143)

L Spalatin, George: Wittenberg, Jan 14, 1520 (48, 143-148)

L Spalatin, George: Wittenberg, about Feb 14, 1520 (48, 151-153)

L Spalatin, George: Wittenberg, Mar 19, 1520 (48, 154-155)

L Spalatin, George: Wittenberg, Apr 13, 1520 (48, 156-159)

L Spalatin, George: Wittenberg, Apr 16, 1520 (48, 159-161)

L Spalatin, George: Wittenberg, May 1, 1520 (48, 161-162)

L Spalatin, George: Wittenberg, May 31, 1520 (48, 163-165)

L Spalatin, George: Wittenberg, Jun 25, 1520 (48, 165-167)

L Spalatin, George: Wittenberg, Jul 14, 1520 (48, 167-169)

L Spalatin, George: Wittenberg, Aug 23, 1520 (48, 171-173)

L Spalatin, George: Wittenberg, Aug 24, 1520 (48, 173-174)

L Spalatin, George: Lichtenberg, Oct 12, 1520 (48, 179-181)

L Spalatin, George: Wittenberg, Dec 10, 1520 (48, 186-187)

L Spalatin, George: Wittenberg, Dec 29, 1520 (48, 188-191)

L Spalatin, George: Frankfurt Am Main, Apr 14, 1521 (48, 197-198)

L Spalatin, George: Wartburg, May 14, 1521 (48, 222-228)

L Spalatin, George: Wartburg, Jun 10, 1521 (48, 253-256)

L Spalatin, George: Wartburg, Jul 15, 1521 (48, 268-270)

L Spalatin, George: Wartburg, soon after Jul 15, 1521 (48, 270-271)

L Spalatin, George: Wartburg, soon after Jul 15, 1521 (48, 272-273)

L Spalatin, George: Wartburg, Jul 31, 1521 (48, 274-276)

L Spalatin, George: Wartburg, Aug 6, 1521 (48, 289-291)

L Spalatin, George: Wartburg, Aug 15, 1521 (48, 291-296)

L Spalatin, George: Wartburg, Sep 9, 1521 (48, 305-310)

L Spalatin, George: Wartburg, Sep 17, 1521 (48, 312-315)

L Spalatin, George: Wartburg, Oct 7, 1521 (48, 315-317)

L Spalatin, George: Wartburg, Nov 1, 1521 (48, 323-324)

L Spalatin, George: Wartburg, Nov 11, 1521 (48, 325-328)

L Spalatin, George: Wartburg, Nov 22, 1521 (48, 337-338)

L Spalatin, George: Wartburg, about Dec 5, 1521 (48, 350-352)

L Spalatin, George: Wartburg, about Dec 12, 1521 (48, 353-355)

L Spalatin, George: Wartburg, Jan 17, 1522 (48, 380-381)

L Spalatin, George: Wartburg, Jan 22, 1522 (48, 382-386)

L Spalatin, George: Wittenberg, Mar 30, 1522 (49, 3-4)

L Spalatin, George: Wittenberg, May 20, 1522 (49, 5)

L Spalatin, George: Wittenberg, Jun 17, 1522 (49, 8-9)

L Spalatin, George: Wittenberg, about Sep 20, 1522 (49, 13-15)

L Spalatin, George: Wittenberg, about Dec 12, 1522 (49, 17-20)

L Spalatin, George: Wittenberg, end of 1523 (49, 68-70)

L Spalatin, George: Wittenberg, Jan 14, 1524 (49, 70-72)

L Spalatin, George: Wittenberg, Mar 14, 1524 (49, 72-74)

L Spalatin, George: Wittenberg, Nov 30, 1524 (49, 91-94)

L Spalatin, George: Wittenberg, Apr 16, 1525 (49, 102-105)

L Spalatin, George: Wittenberg, Jun 21, 1525 (49, 115-116)

L Spalatin, George: Wittenberg, Mar 27, 1526 (49, 143-147)

L Spalatin, George: Coburg, Apr 24, 1530 (49, 292-295)

L Spalatin, George: Coburg, Jun 30, 1530 (49, 333-337)

L Jonas, Justus, George Spalatin, Philip Melanchthon, John Agricola: Coburg, Jul 15, 1530 (49, 372-377)

L Spalatin, George: Coburg, Aug 26, 1530 (49, 412-414)

L Spalatin, George: Wittenberg, Sep 6, 1535 (50, 97-100)

L Spalatin, George: Wittenberg, Jun 10, 1536 (50, 141-143)

L Spalatin, George: Wittenberg, Mar 21, 1537 (50, 169-170)

Spengler, Lazarus

L Spengler, Lazarus: Wittenberg, Nov 17, 1520 (48, 184-185)

L Spengler, Lazarus: Wittenberg, Feb 4, 1525 (49, 96-99)

L Spengler, Lazarus: Wittenberg, Aug 15, 1528 (49, 204-210)

L Spengler, Lazarus: Coburg, Jul 8, 1530 (49, 356-359)

L Spengler, Lazarus: Wittenberg, Feb 15, 1531 (50, 9-12)

Staupitz, John von

L Staupitz, John von: Wittenberg, May 30, 1518 (48, 64-70)

L Staupitz, John von: Wittenberg, Feb 20, 1519 (48, 108-111)

L Staupitz, John von: Wittenberg, Jan 14, 1521 (48, 191-194)

L Staupitz, John von: Wittenberg, Jun 27, 1522 (49, 10-13)

L Staupitz, John von: Wittenberg, Sep 17, 1523 (49, 48-50)

Stein, Wolfgang

L Stein, Wolfgang: Wittenberg, beg of Sep, 1524 (49, 83-85)

Stettin

L Council of the City of Stettin: Wittenberg, Jan 11, 1523 (49, 25-28)

Stifel, Michael

L Stifel, Michael: Wittenberg, Dec 31, 1525 (49, 139-141)

L Stifel, Michael: Wittenberg, Aug 11, 1526 (49, 153-156)

L Stifel, Michael: Wittenberg, Jun or Jul, 1531 (50, 26-27)

Strassburg

L Christians in Strassburg: Wittenberg, about Dec 15, 1524 (49, 94-96 and 40, 65-71)

L Letter to the Christians in Strassburg in Opposition to the Fanatic Spirit, 1524 (40, 61-71)

Suffering

L Letter of Consolation to All Who Suffer, 1522 (43, 57-70)

S Sermon on the Cross and Suffering, Preached at Coburg the Saturday Before Easter, Based on the Passion History, Apr 16, 1530 (51, 193-208)

That a Christian Should Bear his Cross with Patience, 1530 (43, 179-186)

Symbols

Three Symbols or Creeds of the Christian Faith, 1538 (34, 197-229)

Symphoniae Lucundae

Preface to George Rhau's Symphoniae Lucundae, 1538 (53, 321-324)

Table Talks

Table Talks recorded by Veit Dietrich, 1531-1533 (54, 3-114)

Table Talks recorded by John Schlaginhaufen, 1531-1532 (54, 123-165)

Table Talks recorded by George Roerer, 1531-1535 (54, 115-121)

Table Talks collected by Conrad Cordatus, 1532-1533 (54, 167-200)

Table Talks recorded by Anthony Lauterbach and Jerome Wedler, 1536-1537 (54, 201-249)

Table Talks recorded by Anthony Lauterbach, 1538-1539 (54, 251-364)

Table Talks recorded by John Mathesius, 1540 (54, 365-409)

Table Talks recorded by Caspar Heydenreich, 1542-1543 (54, 411-464)

CHRONOLOGICAL INDEX
to the Contents of
Luther's Works

Heidelberg Disputation, 1518 (31, 35-70)

S Sermon on the Raising of Lazarus, Jn 11:1-45, Preached on the Friday after Laetare, Mar 19, 1518 (51, 44-49)

S Sermon on the Man Born Blind, Jn 9:1-38, Preached on the Wednesday after Laetare, March 17, 1518 (51, 35-43)

Explanations of the Ninety-Five Theses, 1518 (31, 77-252)

L Spalatin, George: Wittenberg, May 18, 1518 (48, 60-63)

L Spalatin, George: Wittenberg, Aug 8, 1518 (48, 70-73)

L Spalatin, George: Wittenberg, Aug 28, 1518 (48, 73-76)

L Spalatin, George: Wittenberg, Aug 31, 1518 (48, 76-80)

L Spalatin, George: Wittenberg, Sep 2, 1518 (48, 80-83)

L Spalatin, George: Wittenberg, Oct 14, 1518 (48, 83-87)

L Spalatin, George: Wittenberg, Oct 31, 1518 (48, 90-93)

L Spalatin, George: Wittenberg, Nov 25, 1518 (48, 93-94)

L Spalatin, George: Wittenberg, Dec 9, 1518 (48, 95-96)

1519

Two Kinds of Righteousness, 1519 (31, 293-306)

On Rogationtide Prayer and Procession, 1519 (42, 83-93)

Leipzig Debate, 1519 (31, 307-325)

L Elector Frederick: Altenburg, Jan 5 or 6, 1519 (48, 96-100)

L Pope Leo X: Altenburg, Jan 5 or 6, 1519 (48, 100-102)

L Elector Frederick: Wittenberg, between Jan 13 and 19, 1519 (48, 103-106)

L Spalatin, George: Wittenberg, Feb 7, 1519 (48, 106-107)

L Spalatin, George: Wittenberg, Mar 13, 1519 (48, 111-116)

L Staupitz, John von: Wittenberg, Feb 20, 1519 (48, 108-111)

L Erasmus of Rotterdam: Wittenberg, Mar 28, 1519 (48, 116-119)

L Elector Frederick: Wittenberg, about May 15, 1519 (48, 120-121)

L Spalatin, George: Wittenberg, May 22, 1519 (48, 122-124)

L Spalatin, George: Wittenberg, Jul 20, 1519 (48, 126)

L Spalatin, George: Liebenswerda, Oct 9, or Wittenberg, Oct 10, 1519 (48, 126-127)

L Elector Frederick: Wittenberg, Oct 15, 1519 (48, 127-129)

L Spalatin, George: Wittenberg, Nov 1, 1519 (48, 130, 131)

L Spalatin, George: Wittenberg, Nov 7, 1519 (48, 132-133)

L Spalatin, George: Wittenberg, Nov 29, 1519 (48, 133-134)

L Spalatin, George: Wittenberg, Dec 31, 1519 (48, 141-143)

The Holy Sacrament of Baptism, 1519 (35, 23-43)

The Blessed Sacrament of the Holy and True Body of Christ and the Brotherhoods 1519 (35, 45-73)

L Fuchs, Thomas: Wittenberg, Dec 23, 1519 (48, 139-141)

L Glaser, Martin: Wittenberg, May 30, 1519 (48, 124-126)

L Lang, John: Wittenberg, Dec 18, 1519 (48, 135-139)

Exposition of the Lord's Prayer for Simple Laymen, 1519 (42, 15-81)

S Sermon on the Estate of Marriage, 1519 (44, 3-14)

Meditation on Christ's Passion, 1519 (42, 3-14)

Sacrament of Penance, 1519 (35, 3-22)

S Sermon on Preparing to Die, 1519 (42, 95-115)

Psalms 1 and 2, 1519-1521 (14, 279-349)

Galatians 1-6, 1519 (27, 151-410)

1520

On the Papacy in Rome, Against the Most Celebrated Romanist in Leipzig, 1520 (39, 49-104)

Freedom of a Christian, 1520 (31, 327-377)

To the Christian Nobility of the German Nation, 1520 (44, 115-217)

L Spalatin, George: Wittenberg, Jan 14, 1520 (48, 143-148)

L Spalatin, George: Wittenberg, About Feb 14, 1520 (48, 151-153)

L Spalatin, George: Wittenberg, Mar 19, 1520 (48, 154-155)

L Spalatin, George: Wittenberg, Apr 13, 1520, (48, 156-159)

L Spalatin, George: Wittenberg, Apr 16, 1520 (48, 159-161)

L Spalatin, George: Wittenberg, May 1, 1520 (48, 161-162)

L Spalatin, George: Wittenberg, May 31, 1520 (48, 163-165)

L Spalatin, George: Wittenberg, Jun 25, 1520 (48, 165-167)

L Spalatin, George: Wittenberg, Jul 14, 1520 (48, 167-169)

L Spalatin, George: Wittenberg, Aug 23, 1520 (48, 171-173)

L Spalatin, George: Wittenberg, Aug 24, 1520 (48, 173-174)

L Emperor Charles V: Wittenberg, Aug 30, 1520 (48, 175-179)

L Spalatin, George: Lichtenberg, Oct 12, 1520 (48, 179-181)

L Duke John Frederick: Wittenberg, Oct 30, 1520 (48, 181-183)

L Spalatin, George: Wittenberg, Dec 10, 1520 (48, 186-187)

L Spalatin, George: Wittenberg, Dec 29, 1520 (48, 188-191)

Babylonian Captivity of the Church, 1520 (36, 3-126)

S Sermon on the Ban, 1520 (39, 3-22)

Discussion on How Confession Should Be Made, 1520 (39, 23-47)

Fourteen Consolations, 1520 (42, 117-166)

Treatise on Good Works, 1520 (44, 15-114)

L Lang, John: Wittenberg, Jan 26, 1520 (48, 148-151)

L Link, Wenceslas: Wittenberg, Aug 19, 1520 (48, 169-171)

A Treatise on the New Testament, That Is the Holy Mass, 1520 (35, 75-111)

Why the Books of the Pope and His Disciples Were Burned by Dr. Martin Luther, 1520 (31, 379-395)

L Spengler, Lazarus: Wittenberg, Nov 17, 1520 (48, 184-185)

1521

To the Goat in Leipzig, 1521 (39, 105-115)

Concerning the answer of the goat in Leipzig, 1521 (39, 117-135)

Against Latomus, 1521 (32, 133-260)

S Sermon Preached at Erfurt on the Journey to Worms, Jn 20:19-20, Apr 7, 1521 (51, 60-66)

L Staupitz, John Von: Wittenberg, Jan 14, 1521 (48, 191-194)

L Elector Frederick: Wittenberg, Jan 25, 1521 (48, 194-197)

L Spalatin, George: Frankfurt am Main, Apr 14, 1521 (48, 197-198)

L Melanchthon, Philip: Wartburg, about May 8, 1521 (48, 210-213)

L Melanchthon, Philip: Wartburg, May 12, 1521 (48, 215-217)

L Amsdorf, Nicholas von: Wartburg, May 12, 1521 (48, 218-220)

L Agricola, John: Wartburg, May 12, 1521 (48, 220-222)

L Spalatin, George: Wartburg, May 14, 1521 (48, 222-228)

L Melanchthon, Philip: Wartburg, May 26, 1521 (48, 228-244)

L Spalatin, George: Wartburg, Jun 10, 1521 (48, 253-256)

L Melanchthon, Philp: Wartburg, Jul 13, 1521 (48, 256-263)

L Amsdorf, Nicholas von: Wartburg, Jul 15, 1521 (48, 264-268)

L Spalatin, George: Wartburg, Jul 15, 1521 (48, 268-270)

L Spalatin, George: Wartburg, soon after Jul 15, 1521 (48, 270-271)

L Spalatin, George: Wartburg, soon after Jul 15, 1521 (48, 272-273)

L Spalatin, George: Wartburg, Jul 31, 1521 (48, 274-276)

L Melanchthon, Philip: Wartburg, Aug 1, 1521 (48, 277-282)

L Melanchthon, Philip: Wartburg, Aug 3, 1521 (48, 283-289)

L Spalatin, George: Wartburg, Aug 6, 1521 (48, 289-291)

L Spalatin, George: Wartburg, Aug 15, 1521 (48, 291-296)

L Melanchthon, Philip: Wartburg, Sep 9 1521 (48, 296-304)

L Spalatin, George: Wartburg Sept 9, 1521 (48, 305-310)

L Amsdorf, Nicholas von: Wartburg, Sep 9, 1521 (48, 310-312)

L Spalatin, George: Wartburg, Sep 17, 1521 (48, 312-315)

L Spalatin, George: Wartburg, Oct 7, 1521 (48, 315-317)

L Spalatin, George: Wartburg, Nov 1, 1521 (48, 323-324)

L The Augustinians in Wittenberg: Wartburg, Nov, 1521 (48, 324-325; 36, 133-135)

Collect: We Give Thanks To Thee, Almighty God, 1526 (53, 137-138)

L Spalatin, George: Wittenberg, Mar 27, 1526 (49, 143-147)

L Agricola, John: Wittenberg, May 11, 1526 (49, 150-151)

Sacrament of the Body and Blood of Christ against the Fanatics, 1526 (36, 329-361)

Preface to the Prophet Habakkuk, 1526 (35, 327-328)

German Mass and Order of Service, 1526 (53, 51-90)

Answer to Several Questions on Monastic Vows, 1526 (46, 139-154)

L Ruehel, John: Wittenberg, Jun 8, 1526 (49, 151-153)

L Schwenkfeld, Caspar von: Wittenberg, Apr 14, 1526 (49, 148-150)

L Stifel, Michael: Wittenberg, Aug 11, 1526 (49, 153-156)

L Zwilling, Gabriel: Wittenberg, Jan 2, 1526 (49, 142)

Psalm 112, 1526 (13, 389-420)

Four Psalms of Comfort: Psalm 37, Psalm 62, Psalm 94, Psalm 109, 1526 (14, 207-277)

Ecclesiastes, 1526 (15, 1-187)

Jonah (from the German text) (1), 1526 (19, 33-104)

Habakkuk (from the German text) (1), 1526 (19, 149-237)

Zechariah (from the Latin text), 1526 (20, 1-152)

1527

L Letter of Consolation to the Christians at Halle, 1527 (43, 139-165)

Hymn: Our God He Is A Castle Strong, 1527-1528 (53, 283-285)

L Elector John: Wittenberg, Sep 16, 1527 (49, 169-171)

L Brenz, John: Torgau, Nov 28, 1527 (49, 177-180)

That These Words of Christ "This is my body" Still Stand Firm Against the Fanatics, 1527 (37, 3-150)

L Hausmann, Nicholas: Wittenberg, Mar 29, 1527 (49, 161-164)

L Hausmann, Nicholas: Wittenberg, Jul 13, 1527 (49, 167-169)

L Hausmann, Nicholas: Wittenberg, Jan 10, 1527 (49, 159-161)

L Jonas, Justus: Wittenberg, Nov 10, 1527 (49, 171-177)

L Jonas, Justus: Wittenberg, Dec 10, 1527 (49, 180-185)

L Jonas, Justus: Wittenberg, Dec 30, 1527 (49, 185-186)

L Link, Wenceslas: Wittenberg, Jan 1, 1527 (49, 157-159)

L Link, Wenceslas: Wittenberg, May 4, 1527 (49, 164-165)

L Link, Wenceslas: Wittenberg, Jul 5, 1527 (49, 166-167)

Whether One May Flee from a Deadly Plague, 1527 (43, 113-138)

Isaiah 1-39, 1527-1529 (16, 1-439)

Isaiah 40-66, 1527-1529 (17, 1-416)

Titus, 1527 (29, 1-90)

Philemon, 1527 (29, 91-105)

1 John, 1527 (30, 217-327)

Zechariah (from the German text) 1527 (20, 153-347)

1528

Concerning Baptism, 1528 (40, 225-262)

Preface to Weiss Hymnal, 1528 (53, 317-318)

Preface to the Psalter, 1528 (35, 253-257)

Preface to the Prophet Isaiah, 1528 (35, 273-278)

S Sermon: on Baptism, 1528 (51, 182-188)

Hymn: Grant Peace in Mercy, Lord, We Pray, 1528 (53, 286-287)

L Amsdorf, Nicholas von: Wittenberg, Apr 16, 1528 (49, 187-188)

L Elector John: Weimar, May 1 or 2, 1528 (49, 189-195)

L Duke John Frederick: Wittenberg, May 18, 1528 (49, 195-196)

L Elector John: Wittenberg, Sep 3, 1528 (49, 210-211)

L Agricola, John: Wittenberg, Sep 11, 1528 (49, 212-213)

L Amsdorf, Nicholas von: Wittenberg, Nov 1, 1528 (49, 213-214)

Confession Concerning Christ's Supper, 1528 (37, 151-372)

S Sermon: Seventh, Eighth, Ninth, and Tenth Commandment, 1528 (51, 155-161)

S Sermon: First Commandment, 1528 (51, 137-141)

S Sermon: Second and Third Commandment, 1528 (51, 141-145)

L Luther, Mrs Martin: Coburg, Jun 5, 1530 (49, 311-316)

L Melanchthon, Philip: Coburg, Jun 5, 1530 (49, 316-319)

L Luther, John: Coburg, about Jun 19, 1530 (49, 321-324)

L Spalatin, George: Coburg, Jun 30, 1530 (49, 333-337)

L Melanchthon, Philip: Coburg, Jun 7, 1530 (49, 320-321)

L Melanchthon, Philip: Coburg, Jun 29, 1530 (49, 324-333)

L Agricola, John: Coburg, Jun 30, 1530 (49, 338-342)

L Melanchthon, Philip: Coburg, Jul 3, 1530 (49, 342-347)

L Cordatus, Conrad: Coburg, Jul 6, 1530 (49, 353-356)

L Elector John: Coburg, Jul 9, 1530 (49, 359-365)

L Melanchthon, Philip: Coburg, Jul 21, 1530 (49, 378-393)

L Brueck, Gregory: Coburg, Aug 5, 1530 (49, 394-399)

L Luther, Mrs Martin: Coburg, Aug 14, 1530 (49, 399-400)

L Luther, Mrs Martin: Coburg, Aug 14, 1530 (49, 400-403)

L Elector John: Coburg, Aug 26, 1530 (49, 403-412)

L Spalatin, George: Coburg, Aug 26, 1530 (49, 412-414)

L Luther, Mrs Martin: Coburg, Sep 8, 1530 (49, 415-419)

L Luther, Mrs Martin: Coburg, Sep 24, 1530 (49, 424-425)

L Senfl, Louis: Coburg, Oct 4, 1530 (49, 426-429)

L The Electoral Saxon Government: Torgau, about Oct 27, 1530 (49, 429-433)

L Landgrave Philip of Hesse: Torgau, Oct 28, 1530 (49, 433-437)

Admonition Concerning the Sacrament of the Body and Blood of Our Lord, 1530 (38, 91-137)

That a Christian Should Bear His Cross with Patience, 1530 (43, 179-186)

S Sermon on the Cross and Suffering, preached at Coburg the Saturday before Easter, based on the Passion History, Apr 16, 1530 (51, 193-208)

L Hausmann, Nicholas: Wittenberg, beg of Feb, 1530 (49, 264-267)

L Hausmann, Nicholas: Coburg, Apr 18, 1530 (49, 280-287)

L Hausmann, Nicholas: Coburg, Jul 6, 1530 (49, 348-352)

L Hausmann, Nicholas: Coburg, Sept 23, 1530 (49, 419-424)

L Jonas, Justus, George Spalatin, Philip Melanchthon, John Agricola: Coburg, July 15, 1530 (49, 372-377)

L Jonas, Justus, Coburg, Jul 9, 1530 (49, 366-372)

Keys, 1530 (40, 321-377)

On Translating, an Open Letter, 1530 (35, 175-202)

S Sermon on Keeping Children in School, 1530 (46, 207-258)

L Spengler, Lazarus: Coburg, Jul 8, 1530 (49, 356-359)

Psalm 82, 1530 (13, 39-72)

Psalm 111, 1530 (13, 349-387)

Psalm 117, 1530 (14, 1-39)

Psalm 118, 1530 (14, 41-106)

Song of Solomon, 1530-1531 (15, 189-264)

John 6, 1530 (23, 1-197)

John 7 and 8, 1530-1532 (23, 198-422)

1531

Dr Martin Luther's Warning to His Dear German People, 1531 (47, 3-55)

Defense on the Translation of the Psalms, 1531 (35, 203-223)

Commentary on the Alleged Imperial Edict, 1531 (34, 63-104)

Table Talks recorded by Veit Dietrich, 1531-1533 (54, 3-114)

Table Talks recorded by John Schlaginhaufen, 1531-1532 (54, 123-165)

Table talks recorded by George Roerer, (54, 1531-1535)

How One Should Teach Common Folk to Shrive Themselves, 1531 (53, 119-121)

Sermon on the Epistle for the Twelfth Sunday after Trinity, 2 Cor 3:4-6, preached on the afternoon of Aug 27, 1531 (51, 221-227)

Hymn: Lord God, Thy Praise We Sing, 1531 (53, 288 and 171-175)

L Elector John: Wittenberg, about Jan 16, 1531 (50, 3-6)

L Bucer, Martin: Wittenberg, Jan 22, 1531 (50, 6-9)

L Luther, Mrs Margaret: Wittenberg, May 20, 1531 (50, 17-21)

L Brueck, Gregory: Wittenberg, end of May, 1531 (50, 22-23)

L Elector John: Wittenberg Jun 16, 1531 (50, 23-26)

L Barnes, Robert: Wittenberg, Sep 3, 1531 (50, 27-40)

L Link, Wenceslas: Wittenberg, May 12, 1531 (50, 13-17)

L Spengler, Lazarus: Wittenberg, Feb 15, 1531 (50, 9-12)

L Stifel, Michael: Wittenberg, Jun or Jul, 1531 (50, 26-27).

Psalm 19, 1531 (12, 139-144)

1532

Infiltrating and Clandestine Preachers, 1532 (40, 379-394)

Table Talks collected by Conrad Cordatus, 1532-1533 (54, 167-200)

Preface to the Prophets, 1532 (35, 265-273)

Preface to the Prophet Jeremiah, 1532 (35, 274-282)

Preface to the Prophet Ezekiel, 1532 (35, 282-283)

Preface to the Prophet Hosea, 1532 (35, 317-318)

Preface to the Prophet Joel, 1532 (35, 318-319)

Preface to the Prophet Amos, 1532 (35, 320-321)

Preface to the Prophet Obadiah, 1532 (35, 321-322)

Preface to the Prophet Jonah, 1532 (35, 323-324)

Preface to the Prophet Micah, 1532 (35, 324-325)

Preface to the Prophet Nahum, 1532 (35, 326)

Preface to the Prophet Zephaniah, 1532 (35, 328-329)

Preface to the Prophet Haggai, 1532 (35, 329-330)

Preface to the Prophet Zechariah, 1532 (35, 330-331)

Preface to the Prophet Malachi, 1532 (35, 332-333)

S Sermon at the funeral of the Elector, Duke John of Saxony, 1 Th 4:13-14, Aug 18, 1532 (51, 231-243)

S Second sermon at the funeral of the Elector, Duke John of Saxony, 1 Th 4:13-18, Aug 22, 1532 (51, 243-255)

S Sermon on the Sum of Christian Life, 1 Tm 1:5-7, preached at Woerlitz, Nov 24, 1532 (51, 257-287)

L Elector John: Wittenberg, about Feb 12, 1532 (50, 41-47)

L Luther, Mrs Martin: Torgau, Feb 27, 1532 (50, 47-50)

L Zink, Thomas: Wittenberg, Apr 22, 1532 (50, 50-53)

L Amsdorf, Nicholas: Wittenberg, Jun 13, 1532 (50, 53-56)

L Elector John: Wittenberg, Jun 29, 1532 (50, 56-60)

L Regents and Councilors of the Margraviate of Brandenburg-Ansbach and to the Council of the City of Nuernberg: Wittenberg, Aug 1, 1532 (50, 61-67)

L Duke Joachim of Brandenburg: Wittenberg, Aug 3, 1532 (50, 68-71)

L Amsdorf, Nicholas von: Wittenberg, Nov 2, 1532

Psalm 2, 1532 (12, 1-136)

Psalm 45, 1532 (12, 197-410)

Psalm 147, 1532 (14, 107-135)

Sermon on the Mount, Matthew 5, 6, and 7, 1532 (21, 1-294)

1 Corinthians 15, 1532-1533 (28, 57-213)

1533

Magnificat, 1533 (53, 176-179)

Communio, 1533 (53, 181-183)

Preface to the Book of Jesus Sirach, 1533 (35, 347-349)

Preface to the First Book of Maccabees, 1533 (35, 350-352)

Preface to the Second Book of Maccabees, 1533 (35, 352-353)

Preface to parts of Esther and Daniel, 1533 (35, 353-354)

Preface to the Acts of the Apostles, 1533 (35, 363-365)

Collect: Dear Lord God, Awaken Us, 1533 (53, 131)

Collect: Help, Dear Lord God, That We May Become and Remain Partakers, 1533 (53, 131-132)

Collect: Almighty Eternal God, We Heartily Pray Thee, 1533 (53, 132)

278

L Hausmann, Nicholas: Wittenberg, Torgau, Sep 20, 1536 (50, 148-151)

Psalm 23, 1536 (12, 145-194)

1537

Gloria in Excelsis, 1537 (53, 184-188 and 292-294)

Hymn: All Glory, Laud, And Praise Be Given, 1537 (53, 184-188 and 294)

L Luther, Hans: Wittenberg, Jan 27, 1537 (50, 151-153)

L Jonas, Justus: Altenburg, Feb 1, 1537 (50, 153-157)

L Elector John Frederick: Smalcald, about Feb 9, 1537 (50, 157-165)

L Luther, Mrs Martin: Tambach, Feb 27, 1537 (50, 165-169)

L Spalatin, George: Wittenberg, Mar 21, 1537 (50, 169-170)

L Capito, Wolfgang: Wittenberg, Jul 9, 1537 (50, 171-174)

Psalm 8, 1537 (12, 1-136)

John 1-4, 1537-1540 (22, 1-530)

John 14-16, 1537-1538 (24, 1-422)

1538

Three Symbols or Creeds of the Christian faith, 1538 (34, 197-199)

Counsel of a Committee of Several Cardinals with Luther's Preface, 1538 (34, 231-267)

Against the Sabbatarians — Letter to a Good Friend, 1538 (47, 57-98)

Preface to George Rhau's Symphoniae Lucundae, 1538 (53, 321-324)

Preface to Galeatius Capella's history, 1538 (34, 269-278)

Preface for All Good Hymnals, 1538 (53, 319-320)

Table Talks recorded by Anthony Lauterbach, 1538-1539 (54, 251-364)

L Hausmann, Nicholas: Wittenberg, Feb 23, 1538 (50, 174-176)

L Fox, Edward: Wittenberg, May 12, 1538 (50, 177-180)

L Propst, James: Wittenberg, Sep 15, 1538 (50, 181-184)

Genesis 15-20, 1538-1539 (3, 1-365)

Psalm 51, 1538 (12, 197-410)

1539

Against the Antinomians: 1539 (47, 99-119)

On the Councils and the Church: 1539 (41, 3-178)

Disputation Concerning the Passage "The Word was made flesh" 1539 (38, 235-277)

Ordination of Ministers of the Word, 1539 (53, 122-126)

S Sermon on Soberness and Moderation against Drunkenness, 1 Pt 4:7-11, May 18, 1539 (51, 289-299)

S Sermon Preached in Castle at Pleissenburg on the Occasion of the Inauguration of the Reformation in Leipzig, Jn 14:23-31, May 24, 1539 (51, 301-312)

Hymn: Our Father in the Heaven Who Art, 1539 (53, 295-298)

L Elector John Frederick: Wittenberg, Jul 8, 1539 (50, 185-187)

L Bucer, Martin: Wittenberg, Oct 14, 1539 (187-191)

L Elector John Frederick: Wittenberg, Oct 23, 1539 (50, 192-194)

L Elector John Frederick: Wittenberg, Oct 23, 1539 (50, 204-206)

Preface to the Wittenberg Edition of Luther's German Writings, 1539 (34, 279-288)

Genesis 21-25, 1539-1540 (4, 1-409)

1540

Table Talks recorded by John Mathesius, 1540 (54, 365-409)

S Sermon on Mt 3:13-17 at the Baptism of Bernhard von Anhalt, preached in Dessau. Apr 2, 1540 (51, 313-329)

L Luther, Mrs Martin: Weimar, Jul 2, 1540 (50, 207-212)

L Luther, Mrs Martin: Eisenach, Jul 10, 1540 (50, 212-217)

L Luther, Mrs Martin: Eisenach, Jul 16, 1540 (50, 218-220)

L Luther, Mrs Martin: Eisenach, Jul 26, 1540 (50, 221-223)

1541

Against Hanswurst, 1541 (41, 179-256)

New Preface to the Prophet Ezekiel, 1541 (35, 284-293)

Hymn: To Jordan When Our Lord Had Gone, 1541 (53, 299-301)

Hymn: Herod, Why Dreadest Thou A Foe, 1541 (53, 302-303)

Hymn: Lord, Keep Us Steadfast In Thy Word, 1541-1542 (53, 304-305)

L Luther, Mrs Martin: Wittenberg, Sep 18, 1541 (50, 223-225)

L Melanchthon, Philip: Eisleben, Feb 6, 1546
(50, 297-299)

L Luther, Mrs Martin: Eisleben, Feb 6, 1546
(50, 299-300)

L Luther, Mrs Martin: Eisleben, Feb 7, 1546
(50, 301-304)

L Luther, Mrs Martin: Eisleben, Feb 10, 1546
(50, 305-308)

L George of Anhalt: Eisleben, Feb 10, 1546
(50, 309-310)

L Luther, Mrs Martin: Eisleben, Feb 14, 1546
(50, 310-313)

L Melanchthon, Philip: Eisleben, Feb 14, 1546
(50, 313-318)